African American Studies: 50 Years at the University of Florida

Edited by Jacob U'Mofe Gordon and Paul Ortiz

Published by the LibraryPress@UF

Editorial Liaisons: Chelsea Johnston and Laurie Taylor

Design: Tracy MacKay-Ratliff

https://ufl.pb.unizin.org/africanamericanstudies

Publication Information

Names: Gordon, Jacob U'Mofe, editor. | Ortiz, Paul, editor. | George A. Smathers Libraries, publisher.

Title: African American studies: 50 years at the University of Florida / edited by Jacob U'Mofe Gordon and Paul Ortiz.

Description: Gainesville, FL : Library Press @ UF, 2021 | Summary: African American Studies: 50 Years at the University of Florida provides an overview of the history of African American Studies at the University of Florida. Chapters are based on papers presented at the 50th Anniversary Commemoration of the African American Studies Program at the University of Florida. In addition to providing a comprehensive history of African American Studies at the University of Florida, the book also documents the research of Black faculty at UF; examines how students, faculty, and staff involved with African American Studies practice community engagement and service; contains testimonies from community elders; and includes reflections by and about prominent UF alumni such as Judge Stephan Mickle and Dr. David Horne.

Identifiers: ISBN 9781944455156

Subjects: LCSH: University of Florida. African-American Studies Program. | African Americans–Study and teaching (Higher). | African American scholars. | Community and college–Florida–Gainesville. | Education, Higher–Social aspects–United States.

Classification: LCC E184.7.A314 2021

Copyright

African American Studies: 50 Years at the University of Florida by Jacob U'Mofe Gordon and Paul Ortiz is licensed under a Creative Commons Attribution-NonCommercial 4.0 International License, except where otherwise noted.

Copyright © 2021 Jacob U'Mofe Gordon and Paul Ortiz. Authors retain copyright to individual chapters.

Table of Contents

Foreword by David A. Canton..vii

Acknowledgements...xii

About the Contributors...xiv

About the Editors..xv

A Note on Image Quality..xvii

Chapter 1: The Development of African American Studies at the University of Florida by Patricia Hilliard-Nunn..........................1

Chapter 2: Black Students' Struggles for Justice at the University of Florida by David L. Horne..15

Chapter 3: Oral History, Democracy, and the Power of Memory by Paul Ortiz..33

Chapter 4: The State of African American Studies Collections at the University of Florida by Stephanie Birch..................................57

Chapter 5: Publications by African American Studies Faculty at the University of Florida by Sharon D. Wright Austin..................82

Chapter 6: University of Florida and Black Community Engagement..105

    Section 1: Faculty Research and Service – Missions of a Public University by Barbara McDade Gordon..............105

    Section 2: Educational Outreach – The Upward Bound Program at UF by Gwenuel W. Mingo............................129

    Section 3: Religious Connections – The Pentecostal Initiative at UF by Sherry Sherrod DuPree......................145

Chapter 7: Reflections on African American Studies Program at the University of Florida by Harry B. Shaw............................158

Chapter 8: The Life and Times of Stephan P. Mickle - First UF African American Graduate and the College of Law Connection by Jacob U'Mofe Gordon..179

Chapter 9: Summary and Conclusions by Jacob U'Mofe Gordon and Paul Ortiz..209

Appendix: List of Publications by African American Studies Program Faculty at the University of Florida............................219

Foreword by David A. Canton

In April 1967, Martin Luther King gave his famous anti-Vietnam War speech at the Riverside Church in New York where his radicalism took center stage. One year later, James Earl Ray assassinated King at the Lorraine Motel in Memphis, TN, three years after Congress passed the 1965 Voting Rights Act. By the late sixties, the beloved Dr. King was one of most hated individuals in the nation. He castigated the nation's embrace of the three evils—capitalism, militarism, and poverty—and advocated a guaranteed income and affirmative action (King, 1967). King's radicalism annoyed President Johnson and white liberals, and caught on among young Black student activists such as Ruby Doris Smith Robinson, John Lewis, Ann Moody, and Kwame Toure, members of Student Non-Violent Coordinating Committee (SNCC) who promoted a radical agenda from the organization's inception in 1960. At the 1964 Democratic Convention in Atlantic City, NJ, SNCC members supported the Mississippi Freedom Democratic Party (MFDP) who challenged the white racist Democratic Party in Mississippi, supported Palestinian liberation, and opened Freedom Schools in the south that taught African and African American history (Carson, 1981). After King's assassination, over one hundred rebellions occurred across the nation; this is the genesis of the discipline of African American Studies.

In addition to SNCC activists, Black and progressive college students protested and demanded universities to hire Black faculty and teach more courses about African Americans. Black student activists and their allies protested the Eurocentric curriculum in higher education that viewed Western Civilization as "universal" and for all other civilizations to emulate. In 1968, most American college graduates could not name the capitals of ten African nations and had not read one book by an African American scholar. However, in 1968, the majority of African American students attended Historically Black Colleges and Universities and engaged in what historian Jelani Favors refers to as the "second curriculum," where they studied the Black intellectual tradition and took African history courses (Favors, 2019, p. 7).

Between 2018-2020, hundreds of Afro/American/Black, African American, Africana, African/African American Studies, Programs, Institutes, and Departments held Golden Anniversary celebrations. These celebrations highlighted the origin stories of the discipline, progress, challenges, and the intellectual impact of African American Studies in universities and local communities alike. African American Studies is a discipline that teaches the same skills—critical reading, writing, and thinking—as other disciplines. Black Studies is not a hobby designed to appease angry Black students or hire a few Black faculty members. During the late sixties, Black students and faculty understood that in order for African American Studies to succeed, it must become a department which addresses institutional racism within the academy. Black faculty and students recognized departments provide tenure, track, appointments, and power. African American Studies is a discipline born of struggle and over the last 50 years the discipline has developed a number of schools of thought: African Centered (Carr, 1998); Afrocentric (Asante, 1994); African American (DuBois, 1903); Black Feminist (Hill Collins, 1990); Africana Womanism (Weems, 1993; Watkins, 1998); Black Radical Tradition (Robinson, 1982); and areas of concentration such as Hip Hop Studies (Rose, 1994); Black Queer Studies (Johnson, 2016); Black Male Studies (Curry, 2017); Critical Race and Digital Studies (Noble, 2018); Black Girlhood Studies (Webster, 2020); African American Studies textbooks and readers (Karenga, 1982), (Anderson, 1993), (Hayes, 1992), (Asante, 1996), (Norment, 2001); and Africana Studies research methods (McDougal, 2014).

Historians have examined Black student protests at predominantly white and Historically Black Colleges and Universities, and this scholarship has created a master narrative in the history of African American Studies (Rojas, 2010), (Rogers, 2012), (Biondi, 2014), (Bradley, 2014), (Favors, 2019). Consequently, most students are familiar with the 1968 Black Studies Department origin story at San Francisco State University, the Black student boycotts and demonstrations at Ivy Leagues and other predominantly white universities, the creation of the first Ph.D. Program in African American Studies at Temple University, and the "legitimacy" of African American Studies due to the rise of "Black public intellectuals," (Black faculty in African American Studies programs at Ivy League schools who have access to major white-owned media outlets such as *The New York Times*, *The Washington Post*, National Public Radio, *The New Republic*, CNN, and MSNBC. African American scholars such as Henry Louis Gates (Harvard), Cornell West (Harvard), Michael Eric Dyson (Vanderbilt University, taught at University of Pennsylvania), Melissa Harris-Perry (Wake Forest, taught at Princeton), Eddie Glaude (Princeton), Marc Lamont Hill (Temple University, taught at Columbia University), Trisha Rose (Brown), Imani Perry (Princeton), Keeanga-Yamahtta Taylor (Princeton), and Jelani Cobb (Columbia) have access to "whitestream" media. The African American Studies master narrative is necessary and informative, but there is a need for a local study on the development of African American Studies programs and departments.

This book is the first to document the history of African American Studies at an institution, the University of Florida. The history of African American Studies at the University of Florida is similar to many others. During the late sixties, Black students formed a Black Student Union and demanded that the University of Florida admit more Black students and hire Black faculty. As David Horne notes, the Black Students Union at UF was a part of the "Black Campus Movement" and in 1970 African American Studies began at the University of Florida (Horne, 2021). The book chronicles the long history of African American Studies, documents the research of Black faculty at UF, examines African American Studies Program community engagement, and includes testimonies from community elders who, as Dr. Paul Ortiz states, used "testimonial culture" (Ortiz, 2021) to teach younger African Americans about the students' central role in history of the African American Studies Program at UF and in Gainesville. This book also includes reflections by and about prominent UF alumni, such as Judge Stephan Mickle and Dr. David Horne.

As the new Director of African American Studies at the University of Florida, it was my honor and privilege to write the foreword for this monograph. This local study of the history of African American Studies at the University of Florida will serve as a model for other African American Studies departments.

References

Anderson, T. (1993). *Introduction to African American Studies: Cultural Concepts and Theory.* Dubuque, IA: Kendall/Hunt.

Asante, M.K. and Abarry, A.S. (Eds.). (1996). *African Intellectual Heritage: A Book of Sources.* Philadelphia, PA: Temple University Press.

Asante, M.K. (1990). *Kemet, Afrocentricity and Knowledge.* Trenton, NJ: Africa World Press.

Biondi, M. (2014). *The Black Revolution on Campus.* Berkeley, CA: University of California Press.

Bradley, S. (2018). *Upending the Ivory Tower: Civil Rights, Black Power, and the Ivy Leagues.* New York, NY: New York University Press. https://doi.org/10.1111/hisn.13219

Carr, G.K. (1998). "The African-Centered Philosophy of History: An Exploratory Essay on the Genealogy of Foundationalist Historical Thought and African Nationalist Identity Construction" in J.H. Carruthers and L. C. Harris (Eds.), *African World History Project: The Preliminary Challenge* (285-320). Los Angeles, CA: Association for the Study of Classical African Civilization.

Carson, C. (1981). *In Struggle: SNCC and the Black Awakening of the 1960s.* Cambridge, MA: Harvard University Press. https://doi.org/10.1086/ahr/86.5.1175

Curry, T.J. (2017). *The Man-Not: Race, Class, Genre, and the Dilemmas of Black Manhood.* Philadelphia, PA: Temple University Press.

DuBois, W.E.B. (1903). *The Souls of Black Folks.* Chicago: A.C. McClurg.

Favors, J. (2019). *Shelter in a Time of Storm: How Black College Fostered Generations of Leadership and Activism.* Chapel Hill, NC: The University of North Carolina Press.

Hayes, F. III. (1992). *A Turbulent Voyage: Readings in African American Studies.* San Diego: CA. Collegiate Press.

Hill-Collins, P. (1990). *Black Feminist Thought: Knowledge, Consciousness, and the Politics of Empowerment.* New York: Routledge.

Horne, D. (2021). "The Black Students Struggle for Justice at the University of Florida" in *African American Studies: 50 Years at the University of Florida.* (J.U. Gordon and P. Ortiz, Eds.) (2021). Gainesville, FL: LibraryPress@UF.

Johnson, P.E. (Ed.) (2016). *No Tea, No Shade: New Writings in Black Queer Studies*. Durham, NC: Duke University Press.

Karenga, M. (1982). *Introduction to Black Studies*. Los Angeles, CA: The University of Sankore Press.

King, M.L., Jr. (1967). *Where Do We Go From Here: Chaos or Community*. New York, NY: Harper and Row.

McDougal, S. (2014). *Research Methods in Africana Studies*. New York, NY: Peter Lang Publishing.

Noble, S. (2018). *Algorithms of Oppression: How Search Engines Reinforce Racism*. New York, NY: New York University Press.

Norment, N., Jr. (2001). *The African American Studies Reader*. Durham, NC: Carolina Academic Press.

Ortiz, P. (2021). "Oral History, Democracy, and the Power of Memory" in J.U. Gordon and P. Ortiz (Eds.) *African American Studies: 50 Years at the University of Florida*. Gainesville, FL: LibraryPress@UF.

Robinson, C. (1983). *Black Marxism: The Making of the Black Radical Tradition*. London: Zed Press.

Rogers, I.H. (2012). *The Black Campus Movement: Black Students and the Radical Reconstitution of Higher Education, 1965-1972*. New York: Palgrave MacMillan.

Rojas, F. (2010). *From Black Power to Black Studies: How a Radical Social Movement Became an Academic Discipline*. Baltimore, MD: Johns Hopkins University Press.

Rose, T. (1994). *Black Noise: Rap Music and Black Culture in Contemporary America*. Middletown, CT: Wesleyan University Press.

Watkins, V. (1998). "Womanism and Black Feminism: Issues in the Manipulation of African Historiography" in J.H. Carruthers and L.C. Harris (Eds.), *African World History Project: The Preliminary Challenge* (245-284). Los Angeles, CA: Association for the Study of Classical African Civilization.

Webster, C. L. (2020). "The History of Black Girls and the Field of Black Girlhood Studies: At the Forefront of Academic Scholarship" in *The American Historian*.

Weems, C.H. (1993). *Africana Womanism: Reclaiming Ourselves*. Boston, MA: Bedford.

Acknowledgements

This book commemorates the 50th Anniversary of the establishment of the African American Studies Program (AASP) at the University of Florida in 1970, which was celebrated in a series of events on campus in February 2020. The publication provides a historical record of events that led to the establishment of the program. The celebration to commemorate the 50th Anniversary was organized by AASP faculty and staff and made possible by the support and contributions of the University of Florida Administration: President W. Kent Fuchs, Dean David Richardson of the College of Liberal Arts and Sciences (CLAS), Faculty and Affiliates in the African American Studies Program, and members of the Gainesville community. To all those involved in the Celebration of the 50th Anniversary of African American Studies at UF, we thank you.

We want to specifically acknowledge the members of the Working Committees charged with scheduling and programming events for the 50th Anniversary Celebration: Dr. Paul Ortiz, Professor of History and Director of the Samuel Proctor Oral History Program; the late Dr. Patricia Hilliard-Nunn, Senior Lecturer in African American Studies; and Dr. James Essegbey, Interim Director of African American Studies Program and Professor in the Department of Languages, Literatures, and Cultures. We are also thankful to the panelists and moderators at the Dr. Ronald Foreman, Jr. Symposium, which consisted of the Academic Panel: Dr. Patricia Hilliard-Nunn, Dr. Paul Ortiz, Dr. Manoucheka Celeste, Ms. Stephanie Birch, Dr. Harry B. Shaw, and Dr. Jacob U'Mofe Gordon (Moderator); Community Panel: Mrs. Sherry Sherrod DuPree, Ms. Kathy Benson Haskins, Ms. Vivian Filer, Mr. Otis Stover, and Dr. Patricia Hilliard-Nunn (Moderator); Alumni and Student Panel: Ms. Sharon Burney, Mr. Wallace Mazon, Mr. Chris Garcia-Wilde, and Dr. Vincent Adejumo (Moderator).

We are equally grateful to Ms. Stephanie Birch, African American Studies Librarian, the Dean of University Libraries, Judith G. Russell, and other administrators and staff at the George A. Smathers Libraries.

They identified and organized books and other research materials published by the African American Studies faculty at UF for the book exhibit in the Smathers Library to commemorate the 50th Anniversary of African American Studies Program at the University of Florida.

We appreciate the tireless efforts of Deborah Hendrix of the Samuel Proctor Oral History Program for video-recording the events, transcribing relevant materials, and organizing many of the photos included in this book. We are indebted to Ms. Tamarra Jenkins, Administrative Specialist I, Samuel Proctor Oral History Program, and Ms. Yesenia Jarrett, Administrative Specialist I, African American Studies Program, for coordinating the activities of the 50th Anniversary Celebrations. Their skillful coordination of activities and events was extremely helpful in carrying out the celebration, along with their many other contributions. I am grateful to Dr. Barbara McDade Gordon, Professor Emerita in Geography and African Studies, for her technical and editorial assistance throughout the preparation of the manuscript for this book.

Dr. Paul Ortiz wishes to thank Professor Jacob U'Mofe Gordon for being an exemplary mentor, friend, and colleague. I feel privileged beyond words to be able to work with Jake on this volume. Since my time as a professor at the University of Florida I have been constantly inspired by the students, staff, faculty, and alumni of the African American Studies Program. This generation's African American Studies students are carrying on the wonderful legacies of their ancestors in struggle. I can hardly wait to celebrate with the students during that not-so-distant moment in future when the program becomes a full-fledged department! My only regret is that our dear mutual friend, Dr. Patricia Hilliard-Nunn, did not live to see the completion of this volume. The editors and chapter authors of this book as well as the students, staff, and alumni of the African American Studies Program at the University of Florida pledge ourselves to continue Tricia's outstanding scholarship, community activism, and passion for learning and justice into the generations to come.

About the Contributors

Sharon Wright Austin, Ph.D., Professor of Political Science, and Director, African American Studies Program (2011-2019), University of Florida.
Stephanie Birch, M.A., MLS, Librarian, African American Studies, George A. Smathers Libraries, University of Florida.
David A. Canton, Ph.D., Associate Professor of History and Director, African American Studies Program, University of Florida.
Sherry Sherrod DuPree, Ed.S., AMLS, Library Science, CEO, DuPree Pentecostal Holiness Center, Gainesville, Florida.
Jacob U'Mofe Gordon, Ph.D., LL.D. (Hon); Professor Emeritus, Founding Chair, Department of African & African American Studies University of Kansas, and Former Kwame Nkrumah Endowed Chair, University of Ghana.
Patricia Hilliard-Nunn, Ph.D., Senior Lecturer, African American Studies Program, University of Florida, and Local Historian, Gainesville, Florida.
David L. Horne, Ph.D., Professor, Critical Thinking and African History, California State University Northridge, California. (UF Graduate, 1968).
Barbara McDade Gordon, Ph.D., Professor Emerita, Geography and African Studies, and Director, Upward Bound Program (2004-2012), University of Florida.
Gwenuel W. Mingo, Ph.D., Director, Upward Bound Program (1974-2003), University of Florida.
Paul Ortiz, Ph.D., Professor of History, Affiliate Faculty in African American Studies, and Director, Samuel Proctor Oral History Program, University of Florida.
Harry B. Shaw, Ph.D., Professor Emeritus, Department of English, and Associate Dean, College of Liberal Arts and Sciences, University of Florida.

About the Editors

Jacob U'Mofe Gordon, Ph.D.; LL.D. (Hon), Emeritus Professor of African and African American Studies, University of Kansas; Kwame Nkrumah Endowed Chair of African Studies, University of Ghana; and Senior Fulbright Scholar.

Dr. Gordon, a historian, was the Founding Chair of the Founding Chair of the Department of African Studies (now Department of African and African American Studies) at the University of Kansas in 1970. He is the author or co-author of over 30 books, book chapters, numerous articles in academic journals, and research reports. His published books include his most recent book, *The Selected Works of an African Scholar in the Diaspora: A Retrospective Analysis* (2021); *Africa and the African Diaspora in the Development of the Global North: The American Story* (2020); *Revisiting Kwame Nkrumah: Pathways for the Future* (2016); *African Traditional Leadership: Past, Present and the Future* (2014); *The African Presence in Black America* (2004); *African Studies for the 21st Century* (2004); *Black Leadership for Social Change* (2000); and *The African American Male in American Life and Thought* (2000). A recipient of many national and international Awards, Dr. Gordon is a Founding Life Member of the African Studies Association of Africa (ASAA) in 2013, in Accra, Ghana. He serves as Historian for the National Alumni Association of his alma mater, Bethune-Cookman University in Daytona Beach, Florida; and the Founding President of Alachua County African & African American Historical Society, Inc., in Gainesville, Florida.

Paul Ortiz, Ph.D., Professor of History, Affiliate Faculty in African American Studies, Faculty Advisory Council, Center for Latin American Studies, and Director, Samuel Proctor Oral History Program, University of Florida.

Dr. Ortiz is a third-generation military veteran and a first-generation university graduate. Between 2001 and 2008, he was a professor in the Department of Community Studies at the University of California, Santa Cruz. His book, *An African American and Latinx History of the*

United States, was identified by Bustle as one of "Ten Books About Race to Read Instead of Asking a Person of Color to Explain Things to You." In 2020, Fortune magazine listed the volume as one of the "10 books on American history that actually reflect the United States." Dr. Ortiz is also the author of *Emancipation Betrayed: The Hidden History of Black Organizing and White Violence in Florida* (2005). He co-edited and conducted oral history interviews for the award-winning book *Remembering Jim Crow: African Americans Tell About Life in the Segregated South* (2001; 2008). He recently co-edited *People Power: History, Organizing, and Larry Goodwyn's Democratic Vision in the Twenty-First Century*, which will be published by the University Press of Florida in 2021. Dr. Ortiz has published essays in *The American Historical Review, Latino Studies, The Oral History Review, Cultural Dynamics*, and many other academic journals. He has been interviewed by *Agencia De Noticias Del Estado Mexicano*, ARD German Radio and Television, *Newsweek, Telemundo, The Guardian*, BBC, *Hong Kong Daily Apple*, and a variety of other media sources on aspects of Latinx and African American history such as voter suppression, social movements, and immigration, among other topics. Dr. Ortiz was President of the Oral History Association in 2014-2015. He is currently President of the United Faculty of Florida-UF (FEA/NEA/AFT/AFL-CIO).

A Note on Image Quality

Images and photographs are included throughout this book, and are crucial to accurately illustrating the text. In many cases, higher quality images could not be obtained and lower quality images were the only available options.

Chapter 1: Development of African American Studies at the University of Florida (1969-2020) by Patricia Hilliard-Nunn

Figure 1.1: Dr. Patricia Hilliard-Nunn at AASP Desk. (The Fine Print Magazine.2.28.2014.)

This chapter was completed posthumously as a tribute to Dr. Patricia Hillard-Nunn (1963-2020)

Abstract: The growth of Black Studies, sometimes called Africana Studies and African American Studies, at colleges and universities in the United States was a national movement fueled by the students, faculty, administrators, and citizens in local communities. During the 1960s, the nation was polarized by struggles for voting rights, economic justice, and equality. Citizens protested against police violence, wars, employment discrimination, and other things via sit-ins, strikes, boycotts, marches, and other acts of resistance meant to transform the nation for the better. Desegregation efforts led to an increase in Black students at the University of Florida (UF). This included a nine-year legal battle by Virgil D. Hawkins to enter UF, George Starke being the first black person to enter UF, and W. George Allen, becoming the first black person to graduate from UF. Against the background of local, national, and international activism and struggle, UF's African America Studies Program was founded in 1969. This chapter critically examines the people, issues and processes that intersected to initiate and run the program. It outlines the trajectory of the challenges and successes that have underpinned the program during 50 years of existence.

The history of Black Studies, often referred to as Afro-American Studies, African American Studies, Africana Studies, African-centered Scholarship, is a product of several historical factors in American Life and Thought. The Black Studies Movement in the 1960s engaged Americans from diverse backgrounds: different age groups, race and color, gender, and educational levels. (Gordon and Rosser, 1974). The movement has been characterized by some scholars as a convergence of two movements: (1) the Anti-Vietnam War Movement and (2) the Black Power Movement (Joseph, 2003); (Small, 2009); and (Early, 2018). Notwithstanding the predictions of the death of Black Studies by some pessimists, Black Studies or African American Studies emerged as a multi-disciplinary academic field, primarily devoted to the study of the history, culture, and politics of peoples of African descent in the Americas. It should be noted here that the field has been defined in different ways, linking the field to the African Diaspora. The field includes scholars of African American, Caribbean Studies; African Studies; Afro-European Literature; history; politics; geography; religion; as well as those from disciplines such as sociology, psychology, anthropology, cultural studies, linguistics, archeology, economics, education, law, race relations, and other disciplines in the humanities and the social sciences (Rojas, 2010); (Rogers, 2012); (Biondi, 2014). And increasingly, the trend in African American Studies is the partnership with academic units in the STEM (Science, Technology, Engineering, and Mathematics) area (Gordon and Acheampong, 2016).

The birth, growth, and perseverance of African American Studies at the University of Florida (UF) resulted from a collective effort on the part of students, faculty, staff, administrators, and the community at large. For over 50 years, the program has exposed thousands of students to the themes, histories, and theories that encompass the many dynamic aspects of the Black experience. An Afro-American Studies Program, modeled after existing Area Studies Programs, was proposed by a Faculty Committee in the College of Arts and Sciences at UF in 1969 (Hinnant, 1969). It enrolled its first students during the fall of 1970 at the appointment of the first Director of the program, Dr. Ronald C. Foreman. In 1971, the program awarded its first certificate to qualified students. It began offering a minor area of concentration in 2006; a major degree in African American Studies was approved in 2013. The first B.A. degree was awarded in the Spring of 2014.

Founded in the spirit of the struggle that shaped early African American Studies programs and departments across the country, the program is indebted to the men and women who were among the first to enter UF and lay the foundation for those who would follow. The University of Florida opened in Gainesville, Florida in 1906. White women were permitted to enter the University of Florida in 1924. In 1949, Rose Boyd, Virgil D. Hawkins, William T. Lewis, Benjamin F. Finley, and Oliver R. Maxes sought entry to UF Professional and Graduate Schools but were ultimately rejected. From its founding in 1906 until 1958, UF either ignored or denied entry to Black people who applied for admission (McCarthy, 2003).

Although the others dropped out for various reasons, Hawkins waged a legal battle to gain entry to the College of Law. During his battle, the Supreme Court handed down its verdict in *Brown v. the Board of Education*, which legally ended the segregation of public schools in 1954. This decision ultimately led to the law in 1964 that ended segregation in all public facilities. The Supreme Court of the United States directed Florida courts to allow Hawkins to enter the law school. The Florida Supreme Court, however (including then Justice Stephen C. O'Connell who would later serve as president of UF), resisted the order. Hawkins continued to pursue his efforts to enter UF until 1958, when he agreed to give up his legal battle if UF desegregated its graduate and professional schools. That year, George Starke entered the law school and became the first Black student to enter UF. In 1959, Daphne Duval Williams would become the first Black woman to attend the university. W. George Allen entered the College of Law in 1960 and graduated in 1962; he was the first Black person to graduate. In 1963, seven Black undergraduates, including Stephan P. Mickle, entered UF. Mickle would be the first Black person to earn an undergraduate degree in 1965 and the second Black person to graduate from the law school in 1970.

The desegregation of UF took place during the Civil Rights Movement, a time when greater numbers of Black students were gaining access to predominantly white institutions (PWIs). Once on campus, Black students urged their institutions to infuse the African American experience in the curriculum and to increase the numbers of Black students, staff, and faculty. The April 1968 assassination of Dr. Martin Luther King, Jr. was one of many critical events that increased student activism and intensified their efforts to make the academic mission of their universities more inclusive. They were joined in their efforts by like-minded faculty, staff, and administrators who saw the importance of making the academy more egalitarian and responsive to student concerns. The first Black Studies Department in the nation was founded at San Francisco State University in the Fall of 1968. Working through the Afro American Students' Association in 1966, it would later be renamed the Black Student Union (BSU). Among other things, the Black students at UF organized to facilitate the establishment of Afro American Studies (later, African American Studies) at UF in 1970 and to make their vision of a well-rounded, quality education a reality.

It should be noted, however, that Afro American Studies, Black Studies, or African-centered Studies has its origin in movements that precede the movements for Black Studies in the 1960s. Popularly regarded as the "Father of Black History," Dr. Carter G. Woodson (1875-1950) established the Association for the Study of Negro Life and History, now the Association for the Study of African American Life and History (ASALH), in 1915. ASALH's official mission was and continues to be "to promote, research, preserve, interpret, and disseminate information about Black Life, History, and Culture to the global community." In 1926, Dr. Woodson launched the celebration of "Negro History Week," the precursor of Black History Month (Scott, 2011). The Association published three scholarly journals: *The Journal of African American History* (formerly *The Journal of Negro History*) founded in 1916; *The Black History Bulletin* (formerly *The Negro History Bulletin*) founded in 1937; and *Fire!!!: The Multimedia Journal of Black Studies*, launched in February 2011. Dr. Woodson wrote many historical works including his seminal work in 1933, *The Miseducation of the Negro*. Dr. Woodson was the second African American, after Dr. W.E. B. DuBois, to receive a doctorate (Ph.D.) from Harvard University.

The students who played a role in the development of African American Studies at UF included: Samuel Taylor (the President of the Black Student Union in 1970 who would become the first Black Student Government President in 1972), David E. Horne (a graduate student in African Studies and Instructor at Santa Fe College in African American History), and two other undergraduate students, Emerson Thompson and Larry Jordan.

Some of the UF administrators who were instrumental in establishing the African American Studies Program were: Dr. Manning J. Dauer, Chairman, Social Sciences Division; Dr. Harry H. Sisler, Dean, College of Arts and Sciences; and Dr. Harold Stahmer, Associate Dean, College of Arts and Sciences. The faculty who assisted in the earliest development of the program included: Dr. Hunt Davis, Jr. (History), Dr. Seldon Henry (History), Dr. Steve Conroy (Social Sciences), Dr. James Morrison (Political Science), and Dr. Augustus M. Burns (Social Sciences).

On August 15, 1971, the Black Student Union (BSU) convened and made the following demands (Sachs & McKinnon, 1971):

1. A commitment on the part of the University to recruit and admit 500 Black students out of the quota of 2,800 freshmen and a continuance of the critical year freshman program.
2. Establishment of a department of Minority Affairs under the direction of a full Vice President, and the immediate elevation of Mr. Roy Mitchell to this Vice Presidency.

3. Hire a Black administrator in Academic Affairs with the advice and recommendation of department of Minority Affairs to coordinate the recruitment of Black faculty.
4. The hiring of a Black assistant manager in personnel.
5. Intensification of recruitment and hiring of Black faculty so as to reflect the ratio of Black students admitted under the proposal in number 1.
6. The fair and equal treatments of our Black brothers and sisters, who are employed by the University.

Thus far, even though we have pleaded, begged, and worked diligently with the administration, our cries have been ignored. This University has consistently denied us these basic needs we deem necessary. We are the voice of the Black student, the Black worker, and the entire Black community. And to our full participation as students, employees, and citizens of this state, these needs must be met.

The day-long series of events on April 15, 1971 came to be known as Black Thursday (Figure 1.2); more than 60 Black students were arrested during the demonstrations.

Figure 1.2: Black Thursday. UF students prepare to enter Tigert Hall for encounter with President Stephen O'Connell. (The Alligator. 4.16.1971.)

Figure 1.3: Interim Director Essegbey speaks at Opening Symposium celebrating 50th Anniversary of AASP at UF, February 20, 2020. (Photo by J. U. Gordon)

Four important milestones were achieved during the 50th Anniversary of African American Studies at UF celebrations (Figures 1.3 and 1.4): (1) installation and dedication of a historical marker on the campus, acknowledging the significance of African American Studies Program to the mission of the University of Florida; (2) the commitment of the University to transition the program into a Ph.D.-granting academic department in the College of Liberal Arts and Sciences; (3) the renovation of new office space in Turlington Hall to accommodate African American Studies faculty and staff; and (4) the national search and appointment of a new Director, Dr. David A. Canton, and the hiring of four new tenure-track faculty members during the following academic year.

African American Studies at UF continues to evolve and grow. The number of students currently working towards earning degrees in AAS is almost one hundred. The program continues its mission of promoting academic excellence and service. Students, faculty, staff, affiliates, and administrators are honored to celebrate 50 years as we look forward to continued growth and development.

Figure 1.4: Unveiling of 50th Anniversary Marker on UF Campus. (Photo by B. M. Gordon)

Directors of the African American Studies Program, 1970 to the Present

- Ronald C. Foreman, 1970-2000. Ph.D. in Mass Communications, University of Illinois
- Darryl M. Scott, 2000-2003. Ph.D. in History, Stanford University
- Marilyn M. Thomas-Houston, Interim Director 2003-2004. Ph.D. in Cultural Anthropology, New York University
- Terry Mills, 2004-2006. Ph.D. in Sociology, University of Southern California
- Faye V. Harrison, 2006-2010. Ph.D. in Anthropology, Stanford University
- Stephanie Y. Evans, 2010-2011. Ph.D. in African American Studies, University of Massachusetts-Amherst
- Sharon Wright Austin, 2011-2019. Ph.D. in Political Science, The University of Tennessee, Knoxville
- James Essegbey, Interim Director 2019-2020. Ph.D. in Languages and Linguistics, Leiden University
- David A. Canton, 2020-Present. Ph.D. in History, Temple University

Current Core Faculty and Staff

- Vincent Adejumo, Senior Lecturer. Ph.D. in Political Science, University of Florida
- Manoucheka Celeste, Associate Professor. Ph.D. in Communications and Gender Studies, University of Washington
- Ashley Preston, Lecturer. Ph.D. in History, Howard University
- Rik Stevenson, Visiting Assistant Professor. Ph.D. in African American Studies, Michigan State University
- Yesenia Jarrett, Administrative Specialist I

Affiliate Faculty

- Stephanie Birch, Librarian in African American Studies, Smathers Libraries. M.L.S. in Library Science, University of Illinois-Urban Champaign; M.A. in History, University of Illinois-Springfield
- Clarence Gravlee, Associate Professor, Department of Anthropology. Ph.D. in Anthropology, University of Florida
- Paul Ortiz, Professor of History and Director, Samuel Proctor Oral History Program. Ph.D. in History, Duke University
- Leah Rosenberg, Associate Professor, Department of English. Ph.D. in Literature, Cornell University
- Samuel Stafford, Lecturer, Department of Political Science and Adjunct Professor, College of Law. J.D., Duke University
- Delia D. Steverson, Assistant Professor, Department of English. Ph.D. in Literature, University of Alabama

Advisory Committee

- Stephanie Birch, African American Studies Librarian, Smathers Libraries
- Steven Butler, Executive/Artistic Director, Actors Warehouse
- Kandice Simmons, President, Black Graduate Student Organization
- Eric Godet, President/CEO, Greater Gainesville Chamber of Commerce
- Jacob U'Mofe Gordon, Professor Emeritus, University of Kansas; President, Alachua County African and African American Historical Society, Inc.

- Robyn Hankerson, President, Association of Black Alumni
- Agnes Ngoma Leslie, Master Lecturer and Outreach Director, Center for African Studies
- Barbara McDade Gordon, Professor Emerita, Geography and African Studies
- Paul Ortiz, Professor of History and Director, Samuel Proctor Oral History Program
- Diamond Overstreet, Co-Founder, Duo Studios
- Jon Rehm, Curriculum Specialist Social Studies K-12, Alachua County School District
- E. Stanley Richardson, Alachua County Poet Laureate, Founder/Director of Art Speaks
- Eric Segal, Director of Education, The Harn Museum of Art
- Harry B. Shaw, Professor Emeritus, English
- Carl Simeon, Director, Black Affairs/Institute of Black Culture
- Lindsay Symphany, President, Black Student Union

African American Studies – Timeline

1906: UF opens in Gainesville, Florida and admits only while males.

1924: The State of Florida rules that white women can attend UF.

1949: Virgil Hawkins, Rose Boyd, Benjamin Finley, William Lewis, and Oliver Maxey apply to graduate and professional schools at UF. They are all rejected.

1954: *Brown vs. Board of Education*. U.S. Supreme Court orders public schools desegregated.

1957: The U.S. Supreme Court rules that Virgil Hawkins should be accepted at UF. The Florida Supreme Court, which included future UF president Justice Stephen C. O'Connell, ignored the decision.

1958: Virgil Hawkins agrees to end his legal battle to enter the College of Law after UF agrees to desegregate graduate and professional schools.

1958: George H. Starke is the first Black person to attend UF. He entered the College of Law.

1959: Daphne Duval Williams is the first Black woman to attend UF. She entered the College of Education.
1960: W. George Allen enters the UF College of Law.
1962: W. George Allen is the first Black person to graduate from UF.
1963: Seven Black undergraduate students enter UF.
1965: Stephan Mickle (who becomes Federal Judge Mickle) is the first Black undergraduate to graduate from UF.
1968: Visiting Professor Spencer Boyer is the first Black faculty member at UF Law School, teaching in the College of Law. He and his family are forced to leave Gainesville abruptly after receiving violent threats.
1968: Ron Coleman is the first Black scholarship athlete after earning a track and field scholarship.
1969: Roy Mitchell (now Dr. Roy I. Mitchell) becomes the first Black administrator at UF when he is hired as the Director of Minority Affairs.
1969: Leonard George and Willie B. Jackson are the first two Black football players at UF.
1969: Afro-American Studies Program is established. Dr. Selden Henry is the Advisor/Head.
1970: The Black Student Union (BSU) is formally recognized as a UF student organization.
1970: Dr. Thomas Miller Jenkins II, the former Dean of FAMU's Law School, is appointed to the UF College of Law faculty.
1970: Dr. Ronald C. Foreman begins as the first director of what was then labeled Afro American Studies. He, Dr. Carleton G. Davis (Food Resource Economics), and Dr. Elwyn Adams (Music) are the first three tenure-track Black faculty members at UF.
1971: After unsuccessful attempts to address concerns about the campus climate at UF, students hold a sit-in at Tigert Hall and present a list of 10 demands to the administration. That day, April 15, is known as "Black Thursday."

1971: In April, Roy I. Mitchell submits his letter of resignation (effective June 1) as head of Minority Affairs in the aftermath of Black Thursday. The resignation is accepted immediately.

1971: The first certificate in African American Studies is awarded.

1972: The Institute of Black Culture opens.

1972: Samuel Taylor is elected the first Black Student Government President.

1973: Cynthia Mays is elected as the first Black Miss Homecoming.

1974-75: James M. Webster, Jr. becomes the first Black Assistant Football Coach at UF.

1986: Pamela Bingham becomes the first Black woman elected as UF Student Government President.

1991: The Black Awareness Movement. Students take over the Student Government offices because of complaints about how Black History Month was funded.

1994: The first "Umoja Graduation Celebration" for Black Student at UF is held.

2001: Virgil D. Hawkins is awarded a UF law degree posthumously.

2006: The African American Studies Program begins offering a Minor.

2013: The African American Studies Bachelor of Arts degree is approved.

2014: The first three students majoring in African American Studies graduate.

2019: The African American Studies Program turns 50!

2020: Dr. James Essegbey is appointed as Interim AASP Director.

2020: African American Studies moves into new offices in 1012 Turlington Hall.

2020: Dr. David A. Canton is appointed as the Director of AASP.

Chapter 1 Study Questions

1. To what extent did the national movements for Black Studies on college/university campuses impact the development of African American Studies at the University of Florida?
2. Briefly discuss some of the major African American Studies milestones at the University of Florida.
3. What are some of the major contributions of African American Studies in higher education?

References

Asante, M.K. (2005). *Encyclopedia of Black Studies*. Thousand Oaks, CA: Sage Publications, Inc.

Bennett, L. Jr. (2005). "Carter G. Woodson, Father of Black History." United States Department of State archived from the original, retrieved September 10, 2020.

Biondi, M. (2014). *The Black Revolution on Campus*. Berkeley: University of California Press.

Early, G. (2018). African and African American Studies Frontrunners. *Washington Magazine*, digital.

Gordon, J.U. & Rosser, J.M. (1974). *The Black Studies Debate*. Lawrence: The University of Kansas.

Gordon, J.U. and Owoahene-Acheampong, S. (2016). *Trends in African Studies*. New York: Nova Science Publishers.

Hinnant, L. "Credit coming soon for UF Black Studies" (1969, August 1) *The Florida Alligator*, 1A.

Joseph, P. E. (2003). "Dashikis and Democracy: Black Studies, Student Activism, and the Black Power Movement." *The Journal of African American History*, 88(2), 182-203. https://doi.org/10.2307/3559065

McCarthy, K.M. (2003). African Americans at the University of Florida, *UF Sesquicentennial Committee*, Naples, FL.

Rogers, I.H. (2012). *The Black Campus Movement: Black Students and the Radical Reconstitution of Higher Education, 1965-1972*. New York: Palgrave Macmillan.

Rojas, F. (2010). *From Black Power to Black Studies: How a Radical Social Movement Became an Academic Discipline*. Baltimore: John Hopkins University Press.

Sachs, R. & McKinnon, K. "67 blacks jailed: Disturbance flares on campus" (1971, April 16) *The Florida Alligator*, 1A.

Scott, D.M. (2011). The History of Black History Month. Archived July 23, 2011, as the Wayback Machine on ASALH website.

Small, M.L. (2009). [Review of the book *From Black Power to Black Studies: How a Radical Social Movement Became an Academic Discipline*, by F. Rojas]. *Journal of Black Studies*, 39(6). 990-992. https://doi.org/10.1177/0021934708321242

White, D.E. (2010). From Desegregation to Integration: Race, Football, and "Dixie" at the University of Florida, *Florida Historical Quarterly*, 88(4), 469-496. Retrieved March 11, 2021, from http://www.jstor.org/stable/29765122

Video Productions

Samuel Proctor Oral History Program (SPOPH) (2018, April 3) *A Tale of Two Houses: A Dialogue on Black and Latinx History at UF*, Public Program featuring Dr. David L. Horne, [video]. https://www.youtube.com/watch?v=dXnXVgmhaDM&t=1834s

Samuel Proctor Oral History Program (2019) *From Segregation to Black Lives Matter: The Opening of the Joel Buchanan Archive of Oral History at the University of Florida*, Public Program, [video]. http://ufl.to/tu

African American Studies Ronald C. Foreman Symposium at the University of Florida (2020) *Looking Back and Moving Forward: African American Studies at the University of Florida Turns 50*. Public Program, [video]. http://ufl.to/tt

Chapter 2: Black Students' Struggles for Justice at the University of Florida by David L. Horne

Abstract: In this chapter Dr. David L. Horne, a 1968 graduate and one of the founding members of the Black Student Union (BSU) at the University of Florida, reflects on his experiences in the development of the BSU and African American Studies Program. In addition to his personal experiences as an undergraduate and graduate student at UF, Professor Horne documents Black life at UF including race relations and UF's response to several BSU demands for the establishment of an African American Studies academic department. Readers of this chapter are also encouraged to view the Samuel Proctor Oral History-produced documentary, *The Making of the Institute of Black Culture*: https://www.youtube.com/watch?v=hXxJaiIPGgw&t=40s

Dr. Horne notes that his historical account is augmented by conversations with Gainesville residents Walter Barnes, Charles Gaston, Otis Stover, Sandra Williams, and Joyce Kirkland.

I was told that I was born in a thunderstorm. Well, I wasn't really outside in it, I was in Brewster Hospital (for Colored People). But it was considered a good sign, as those things go. I came in as the elements were dark and raging, with the fight all around me. And though the household into which I was born was, as Poet Nikki Giovanni said, on poverty's edge, I was loved, and I was happy.

My father, Amon Horne, fell victim to the general despair of the day for Black men in 1940s Jacksonville, Florida. He was a big man with solid builder and chef skills, but he was disrespected and could not find steady work in the area. So, he, like many other Black men of that time, simply left, and my mother, Dora, had to handle all the family's heavy lifting.

She somehow kept us—my older brother Junior (Amon), my older sister Cookie (Edith), and me—decently clothed and fed. She also kept us in a

Baptist church and gave us a solid, long-lasting respect for education and due regard for adults. I played a lot and read a lot. Comic books helped propel my reading skills; I was reading *Ivanhoe* and other such works early in life. After finding out I could do almost all the schoolwork I was assigned fairly easily, I excelled in school and got used to being rewarded and praised for it.

I went to Susie E. Tolbert Elementary School, James Weldon Johnson Junior High, and New Stanton High School. At James Weldon, I played clarinet in the marching and concert band, and practiced being a debater. They taught all of us the "Negro National Anthem" ("Lift Every Voice and Sing"), which we sang in school every morning after reciting the Pledge of Allegiance.

In church and school, my community regularly taught that we were all either part of the "Talented Tenth" or we should want to be and should strive to be. Our teachers and church elders seemed to expect us all to do something worthwhile with our lives because none of us were born by accident. We had a purpose and we had to find it and pursue it. We were supposed to live a life of meaning, however long that was, and wherever we found ourselves living.

When I was in junior high school, my mother became a classroom teacher and joined the teachers' union. She started taking me with her to union meetings and strikes, and I remembered the fervor and intensity of the activists. I also remembered her telling me that many of the teachers refused to strike and protest. Then when there was a decent settlement—increased wages, better benefits, etc.—those who did not participate in the activism reaped all the benefits while the strikers got all the punishment. I never forgot that lesson.

My older brother, Junior, had a hard time in Jacksonville, so my mother sent him to live with my aunt and uncle in Cambridge, Massachusetts. After adjusting to the frigid temperatures there and the newness of Massachusetts, he eventually won a scholarship to Harvard University. I remember attending his graduation when I was a senior at James

Weldon, but it was cold there (even in the spring) and I wasn't impressed. Later, when he had gone on to Cambridge University in England and tried to convince me to leave Jacksonville and finish my high school years in Massachusetts (Phillips Andover Academy) or New Hampshire (Phillips Exeter Academy), I remembered Harvard and how cold it felt there. I was, and am, a warm body soul.

I did well academically all the way through school, and virtually lived on the honor roll. During my senior year in high school, three things galvanized me: the assassination of John Kennedy, the Civil Rights struggle going on in Jacksonville and other parts of the South, and a feeling that my time to choose my purpose was upon me.

John F. Kennedy Assassinated

The 35th President of the U.S. was tremendously popular with young people in the U.S. at the time, including Black students. Mr. Kennedy and his brother, Robert, were seen as youthful harbingers of a better American future. With the Kennedys in charge we all felt a little safer, and we felt the glow of a very possible and better tomorrow. His sudden death felt like a good friend of ours had died. Many of us discussed it in classes and on our walks home. It put a gloom on the rest of the school year, and this was only around Thanksgiving, in the fall (November 22, 1963). A malaise set in, even though no one at New Stanton High School actually knew or had talked to a Kennedy family member.

Taking the College Entrance Exam

The senior class had just finished taking the Florida State 12th Grade Exam, and some of us, including me, felt pretty confident we had done okay on it. I was especially buoyant because I thought mine would be a pretty high score. After all, a few months earlier, I had taken a tough standardized exam with a group of white students from across Duval County and had not felt crushed by the experience. It was for earning a scholarship to either Phillips Andover Academy or Phillips Exeter Academy, and had been arranged for me by my older brother as part of his plan to get me out of Jacksonville and the South. Besides the cultural difficulty of some of the questions, what I most vividly remember about that testing experience was the rather awkward exchange between a small group of the white students and me when we were on a lunch break. I heard them chatting about various test preparation classes and devices they had used to get ready for the exam. One member of the group decided to be polite and asked me what test preparation process I'd used. A bit taken aback in the moment by the question, I remember saying, "None." I hadn't taken any test prep. The incredulous look they all gave me stayed seared in my brain.

What I most remember about that episode was the realization that white students were actually taking test prep classes to get ready to pass hard exams. It was like learning that white girls pressed and hot combed their hair. It was a bit of a shock. We were led to believe that white students got the best part of regular schooling, so they were always smarter. Even though I felt I missed something by not having taken test prep classes, I also felt stimulated knowing that I was performing on just my raw ability; I actually knew many of the answers. Suffice it to say that, though I did hear that I hadn't embarrassed myself or my big brother by my exam scores, I did not receive any scholarship offers from either of the prep schools. Since I was not crazy about the idea of moving to chilly New England and becoming the token Black student in a sea of whiteness, I did not feel much rejection because of that result.

But the experience made me feel ready for the fabled Florida State Exam, in which I would have to compete with the smartest New Stanton High senior, a youth named Michael Wilson. He and I often had friendly competitions for the highest exam scores and end-of-semester grades. We also were perpetual locks for the honor roll each semester and were both in the Honor Society. Anyway, Michael did exceedingly well on that year's Florida State Exam, making the highest score among all students in the Negro high schools of Duval County (Douglas Edwards High, Mathew W. Gilbert High, and New Stanton). I made the second highest score in the county and at New Stanton, and was satisfied with that—although Michael did get special recognition and an award of distinction that I wished I had gotten.

Civil Rights in Jacksonville

In 1963-1964 (my senior year), the NAACP Youth Brigade started training some of us to participate in desegregation activities in downtown Jacksonville, particularly the integration of lunch counters and public service desks downtown. As I remember, it was J.C. Penney's and Woolworth stores that they were particularly interested in challenging. Some of New Stanton's more adventurous students participated in both the training and the demonstrations. My older sister, Cookie, did. I did not. I could not ever reconcile sitting still on a lunch counter stool while white citizens called me names, spat on me, punched me, and/or poured hot coffee on me. I was convinced I would ruin the sit-in experience for the NAACP. If, as my sister reported happened to her, someone spat on me and slapped me, I did not think I was capable of not jumping up and throwing punches back. Though I was no gang member, I did participate by standing on bridges and viaducts and throwing stones and bricks on white passengers in cars below. That kind of stuff I could do. The special kind of courage it took to do the sit-ins, I just did not have, and I did not beat myself up about it.

Enough New Stanton students participated in the activities and got chased from downtown to give New Stanton High a different kind of reputation than it generally had before in the Jacksonville community. New Stanton was the bourgeoisie school for wannabes. Except for our always formidable football program and our nationally famous marching band, New Stanton was not known for any kind of rock-'em-sock-'em. That reputation belonged to Matthew Gilbert.

Anyway, it was New Stanton students who mainly braved the ire of whites and policemen in downtown Jacksonville, and we all basked in that little light.

In fact, that new rep contributed to New Stanton's sudden national infamy in March of 1964. As described in *The New York Times* March 14th edition, with racial friction already roiling the city during that time, an incident started when a white milkman bringing supplies to the school cafeteria was razed by a group of students. The incident climaxed with a major clash between students, teachers, police, firemen, and journalists at the school. A journalist's car had been overturned and torched, and the police and firemen were pelted with bricks and bottles, forcing them to withdraw before they started beating and shooting the students. Eventually, teachers regained control of the situation and dismissed the riled-up students for the day. I watched most of the action from a big picture window in a school hallway as several students we called "hoodlums" on most days surrounded two white reporters and pummeled them as the burning car seemed on the brink of explosion. I gathered my girlfriend and everybody sensible quickly left the school for home, or headed to someone's house for a party.

That night in the neighborhood surrounding the school and in every other Black neighborhood nearby, we waited in the shadows for the usual autos full of young whites coming to punish us and remind us of our place in society. That night we were ready to turn the tables. Some young toughs had already stopped the city buses from driving through the neighborhoods bringing our parents' home. All the white drivers were chased off their routes and out of their vehicles. Confused or not, we all sought solace and satisfaction in "protecting" our own neighborhoods that one night. A change was in the wind.

Time to Choose: The Parting of the Waves

At the beginning of April, I was already late in applying for college entrance for September. We were to have over 300 graduates that year, and most of them would be going off to some college or university. That was New Stanton.

The vast majority were headed for Florida A&M, Bethune-Cookman, Florida Memorial, or the local Edward Waters College. I was not attracted to any of them because I knew that being close to too many high school friends meant too much partying and not enough real schoolwork. I opted for a scary try at the University of Florida, which only recently had been forced to integrate.

As a member of a "sophisticated gents" type of on-campus club called the Ambassadors, I had a lot of comradeship company once my choice was made public. Four other members of the Ambassadors applied to UF too, and all five of us were admitted. We became known as the New Stanton Five, and we carried the hopes and pride of a lot of people on our shoulders. We had to succeed.

School counselors set up a summer preparatory course just for us, our favorite math/science/English teachers kept patting us on our backs, our church pastors/deacons had several serious talks with us about how to conduct ourselves like we had had some decent home training, and the NAACP Youth Council kept trying to encourage us not to be intimidated.

So, in September, off we went.

Toes in the Water: UF

All our parents, some relatives, and a few well-wishers drove us to UF campus on the Saturday and Sunday before classes started. They were as antsy as we were to see the campus and feel the atmosphere. This was like a space adventure.

The freshmen dormitories were all in a block of congested buildings, and the Stanton Five were scattered in different directions. The dormitory assigner-in-chief apparently had social engineering on his or her mind, because we were all matched up with white roommates. My social experiment lasted all of five minutes. The student assigned to my room merely looked at me come in with my luggage and books, watched me dump everything on the lone empty bed in the room, and—without saying a word or offering a greeting—simply got up and walked out.

About a half-hour later someone else came into the room, gathered up all my would-be roommate's belongings, and left. I never saw the first roommate again, or if I did, I could not recognize him. On Sunday of that weekend, another young man came to the room, knocked, saw me, and walked away, dragging his belongings with him. Just before our first class started on Monday morning, Michael Sherfield, one of my New Stanton classmates, moved into the room. Apparently, the polka-dot part of the social engineering experiment was over. As I found out later, all the rest of the Stanton Five also got Black roommates, except Bernard Mackey, who gladly accepted his new white roommate and was accepted by him. Being very "high yella" (fair-skin), Bernard had already told us he intended to join a white fraternity on campus, maybe even get into the Blue Key Society, or whatever. He was open to change.

After Freshmen Orientation and getting our class assignments given to us (at this stage, choosing our own classes was not an option), we meandered around trying to get a feel for UF. I went to a presentation about future engineers and there found out that the average score on the Florida State Exam for students who entered the engineering program at UF was a good 80 points above my score. I was crushed. I had wanted to be a civil engineer since I was in junior high school and had done very well on the exam within the Black community, but was not even a blip on radar in the program being described. My first dream died the first day of orientation. Later, I found out that expertise in using slide rules was a standard qualification too, but though I had excelled in high school chemistry and physics, I had never been taught how to use a slide rule. And New Stanton, I always thought, was a modern, well-equipped school.

My roommate met and was befriended by a white student (I think Michael called him "Sarge") who had been a military brat, and thus had a broader travel and personnel experience than most of the rest of our freshmen class. Sarge sought Michael out to introduce himself and start a conversation. He seemed to be a good dude and later proved himself to be just that.

After the orientation, four of the Stanton Five got back together to explore the campus and the surrounding neighborhood. The dormitory complex was pretty boring, so—after finding out where the dining hall was—we went exploring off-campus.

Allies in the Gainesville Black Neighborhood

We accidently stumbled onto 5th Avenue and Mom's Kitchen. The regular denizens on the block teased us about being uppity Negroes and they knew we wouldn't be coming back down their way too often. Little did they (or we) know that this neighborhood would become our refuge and safety zone, even though it was pretty raunchy itself. I can safely say that the 5th Avenue neighborhood is what helped us keep our sanity at UF. And the down-home fried chicken, hamburgers-n-fries, and other soul food saved our palates.

That first evening on 5th Avenue, Michael also wandered off by himself, looking for the liquor store he knew had to be nearby. He introduced himself to the local winos and took a pint back to our room on campus, making me livid.

The First Classes

The protocol then was that most entering freshmen, unless they were in some special major or program, did not choose their class schedule for the first semester. My schedule, as I remember it, included Freshman English and Lab, Physical Sciences, Humanities, and Freshman Math (College Algebra). The classes that stood out were English, Physical Sciences, and Humanities.

For English, I had an excellent instructor (whose name I cannot recall) who actually treated me as if he fully expected me to perform well in his class and was not looking for me to flail or fail. He was a serious editor and whipped my writing into college-level phraseology. He even read my early attempts at writing short stories. In that class, I got a chance to feel as if I belonged.

As for the Physical Sciences class, the instructor approached where I sat during his opening address to the auditorium of students, and, looking directly in my face, announced that he fully expected over half of the class to flunk his course. Then, lowering his voice, he asked me why I was in his class. Though frightened at first, I got angry and decided I was not going to flunk this instructor's class. That chip on my shoulder got me through the class, too. I remember making a C for the semester, not a D or an F.

The Humanities class I remember was fun, with all kinds of films on Greek and Roman statuary, old buildings, English history, etc.—all European stuff. This was heady propaganda without a hint of modesty. The world was what Europeans had made it—other peoples and cultures did not count. But I was not intimidated.

By the Christmas Party at the end of the semester back in Jacksonville, when we all compared our progress, we had all gotten through that first semester above water. I had all C's, including one C+, Michael Sherfield had all B's, Walter had one B and the rest C's, Larry had all C's, and Bernard just said he passed everything. All our high school pals patted us on the back and shook our hands. So far, so good. We had at least shown we were capable and could do the work. I just breathed deeply, thankful that I had survived that first gauntlet. The Stanton Five had not embarrassed themselves, their high school, or their race.

The Social Milieu

We met two other new Black students also assigned to the freshmen dorms. One was from Lawtey, Florida, and he had decided to drive in on the days he had classes, but otherwise not stay on campus much. We called him "Big O" (I think his name was Arthur), not because of any resemblance to basketball legend Oscar Robertson, but because he asked us to do so. The other brother we called "Sig" because of his penchant for offering psychological comments on everything (I really do not remember Sig's given name). Every afternoon that it wasn't raining, we would play football catch in the field formed between the dorms. A week or two later, some of the white students joined us. After watching us from the dorm windows for a while, apparently they determined we were not a threat. We ended up playing flag football regularly in the afternoons and learned to ignore the occasional verbiage that slipped out (several whites scratching like monkeys when we made a good catch or trying to mouth off comments they half-remembered from *Amos 'n' Andy*).

There was an upper-division Black student who did not live in the dorms, but who regularly came to visit us. (Again, I do not remember his name.) He had a white girlfriend and one day decided to bring the young lady into the freshman dining hall for dinner. After we'd played football and were back in our dorm rooms that night, Michael's friend Sarge came banging on our door. He said there was a serious situation going on downstairs and we better get ready for trouble. A Black student had brought a white girl into the dining hall and a gang of rednecks were now searching for them to chastise her and punish him. There was a large crowd of white male students collected in one of the dorm rooms pumping themselves up to go after any Black male students they could find. Sarge asked whether there was any place we could go off campus until tempers had calmed. There wasn't. We then decided to go to the mob room and confront the students, with Sarge leading the way. The crowd was a lot larger than any of us expected, and we were soon sucked into it with no visible way of exiting. I thought of Jean-Paul Sartre's play, *No Exit*. Sarge went to find the ringleader to try and reason with him. Left floating in the middle of the gathering sea storm, we stood back-to-back, but nobody said anything to us, although several beer-drinkers in the crowd kept looking menacingly at Michael and me. I surveyed the dorm room windows for escape routes. After what seemed like a very long time, Sarge came back and told us it was time to go, and he literally pushed us outside the packed room. Away from the crowd, he said he'd yelled the ringleader into some common sense, threatening to have him expelled from school, and that we should be okay now. There'd be no lynching this night.

Towards the second half of the first semester, Michael had gone on a drinking binge. By this time, he was well known among the winos on the 5th Avenue block. Since he would often buy a round of drinks for most of them, he was now a "regular home boy." And when he had no money, they'd spot him some drinks. He would sometimes be gone for days somewhere drinking (God knows where he'd be sleeping), and I'd have to go find him. So, the winos pretty much recognized me too. One particular Friday evening, he'd disappeared again, and I got a call in the dormitory that he'd been rushed to the hospital. It seems he was walking groggily down 5th Avenue and got into a little yelling conversation with another denizen of the streets. The fellow broke an empty wine bottle on the sidewalk, grabbed a sharp piece of the glass, and cut Michael's forearm down to the base of his hand, barely missing the main artery. Michael was too drunk, apparently, to notice or care that he was bleeding profusely and started walking on his way again. Then he collapsed. Phileron Wright, a college student at FAMU home for the weekend and one of the allies we'd made in the neighborhood, just happened to be driving down 5th Avenue and saw Michael in grave trouble. He jumped out of his Volkswagen Bug, piled Michael into it and headed for the hospital, about 20 minutes away. When I got the phone call in the dorm, the staff was pumping Michael's stomach and trying to keep him from leaving the hospital. He was out of commission for two weeks, got himself back together, and passed all his class quizzes and exams; he ended up doing quite well academically.

Got to Get Out of This Dormitory

By the beginning of the second semester, psychologically, I was having real difficulty. Walking onto campus going to classes, I would have this tremendous urge to physically attack the first white male I saw along the path—the bigger, the better. That went on for several weeks. Then I called together a meeting of the Stanton Five minus Bernard Mackey and told them it was time to move out of the dorms. I was going to go shopping for an off-campus apartment or house and wanted to know who was with me. I was going regardless.

I found a house large enough for all of us close to campus, used all my monthly allowance to secure it, and simply moved out of the dorm. Gradually, they all moved too, though Walter—as we found out later—was already planning on transferring to Tennessee State University to be with his girlfriend.

Another Black student (I think his name was Ronnie) with a large pet Afghan hound, moved in with us to handle Walter's portion of the rent.

He was a bit of a bohemian and attracted a lot of white friends of his to the house. He liked throwing parties. I remember staying permanently irked at him because of that dog, which he liked to keep in the house, and his habit of inviting white students who liked to "go ghetto" at our house. They would get sauced on beer, then go up on the roof and pee down into the yard. Several of them considered themselves Civil Rights radicals and tried to chastise us for being at UF and instead of in Mississippi, where the real action was taking place. One of those conversations ended the frequent parties, as I yelled at one very boozy radical that he didn't have the credentials to criticize us for not being Black enough to go join the Freedom Riders and bridge marchers. We had valid reasons for staying the course we had chosen. If any of them felt that strongly about the Civil Rights struggle, then they should be in an auto caravan going farther South instead of at a party guzzling beer. Speaking for all the Black folk in the room, I strongly invited any of them who were willing to go in our stead to get going. "Go and stand for the cause or shut the hell up!" Feeling insulted, they thankfully stopped coming over.

Landlord: Can't Have Negroes on His Property

By the end of that second semester, the property owner came by one afternoon inebriated and told us we all had to vacate his place—that he couldn't have Negroes on his property. That was when we moved farther into the East Side, in the 600 block of 7th Avenue, Mrs. Stafford's. There, some of us hit our stride. But Larry Mathews suffered a bad motorcycle accident and eventually had to drop out of school, while Michael Sherfield dropped "out of phase" by scratching one semester, thereby getting behind his entering class. Uncle Sam came looking for him. He fought it off for as long as he could, then capitulated and made a deal to accept induction if he were allowed to graduate college and enter officer candidate's school.

Formation of the Afro American Students Association and BSU

During the first semester of my junior year (1966), we formed the first Afro American Students Association and registered as a campus organization. We had about 10 members, including Ms. Thomasina Harris. Within the first month, we changed the name to the Black Student Union (Figure 2.1) in league with what other students were doing on other campuses across the country. I was elected the Minister of Information in charge of news and correspondence, a position I kept for over five years. Larry Jordan was also a founding member, but except for me, none of the Stanton Five joined. Kitty Oliver and Emerson Thompson, both from Jacksonville, also joined later.

The Basic Agenda of the BSU at UF (accessed from notes)

Figure 2.1: BSU Seal, established in 1968. (UF Library Archives)

- Establish and maintain informational relationships with Black student groups in other cities and states.
- Invite quality Black speakers to the UF campus.
- Advocate for the hiring of Black faculty at UF.
- Advocate and petition for a Black Cultural Center on campus.
- Advocate for more inclusion of Black students in campus life.

Note: The BSU at UF was not, nor was it ever intended to be, a mass-population group. It was intended from the outset—and always remained—an organizing entity. We decided on projects and things to accomplish, identified what had to be done to accomplish those goals, then identified who and what we needed to accomplish the task at hand, and assigned roles to everybody. The 1971 student sit-in in (UF President) O'Connell's office is a case in point. (Kip Smith was president of the BSU then.) Some students were to rally outside and others were to pressure O'Connell in his office. If the police showed up, BSU members and affiliates were supposed to leave O'Connell's office immediately. However, the police or someone locked the office doors in order for the arrests to be made. Similarly, if trouble started outside, we were to disband and not get suckered into someone else's fight. So, when someone unknown to us threw a brick at one of the Tigert Hall office windows, those of us outside disbanded and left the plaza. I was arrested the next day after giving a speech on the Tigert Hall steps as part of the continuing student demonstrations, not as part of the O'Connell office sit-in.

Graduate School, Teaching at Santa Fe College

By my senior year I had married my Jacksonville sweetheart, and we moved into what used to be called the Flavet Village on the outskirts of the campus near the track and field facilities.

I graduated in 1968 with a major in psychology and attended the Black Power Conference in Gary, Indiana before entering graduate school in the new African Studies Center at UF the following fall.

By 1969, I was teaching two courses in African American History at Santa Fe Community College—then located not far from UF—and still working early mornings and late afternoons at the College Inn, right across the street from the main campus.

After several letters to the Dean's Office and to the President requesting the hiring of Black faculty and the recruitment of more Black students as part of Florida's obligation to its citizens, the BSU had a series of meetings with officials from the Dean's Office. (The chair of the Social Sciences Division then was Dr. Manning Dauer, who seemed quite interested in our pursuits.) Eventually, a serious effort was undertaken to hire Black faculty and a public lecture, as part of such a process, was scheduled for Dr. Ronald Foreman. He was excellent, and the BSU sent its recommendation in to hire him before another institution did. Around 1969-1970, there was also a huge public protest against the College Inn on University Avenue for not serving Black students. Everything had to be take-out. They couldn't sit in the eatery. All the kitchen help (including me) were Black. The main cook, James, said he would not get involved in all that and urged me to keep doing my work and stay out of it if I could. I needed the job, so I complied. Plus, James and his wife, Novella, were really nice people and had been at the Inn for a long time. By 1971, I was still slowly taking graduate courses and teaching at Santa Fe along with Gainesville natives Charles Gorton, Otis Stover, Joyce Kirkland, Sandra Hall Williams, and others; we formed a community-based Black organization called the Leagues of Blackness (LOB). We did guerilla theater pieces in community venues, started a free breakfast program on the Eastside, opened an office on 5th Avenue, and tried to help the winos get some decent facilities at the ABC Lounge. That latter was very interesting. Our clients—the regular winos—did not want our help and told us to take our goody two-shoes ideas back to one of the campuses. They just wanted to drink in peace, not to have protest marches for new seating facilities in the Lounge. Trying to mimic the Black Panther Party, we also started having political education classes for Eastside youth from the neighborhood.

Arrested: A Career in Law? Not!

When I got arrested in 1971, there were large, loud protest demonstrations at Santa Fe College, at UF, and in the Eastside community. The UF students in particular, as seen in Figure 2.2 below, were incensed, believing this was just a continuation of the week's attempt to muzzle student political activism. During the five days they had me in jail, members of the public—a sympathetic guard told me—overwhelmed the police switchboard with crank calls that blocked regular calls from coming through.

After the court dismissed the charges, I decided I'd be more effective in the community as an activist attorney, so I applied to law school at the University of Miami and, luckily, got accepted through the CLEO Program. I moved to Dade County and completed my first year, teaching at Miami-Dade College to finance myself. After successfully

Figure 2.2: UF students march to Alachua County Jail to free David Horne. (The Alligator. 4.16.1971)

completing that first year, I did an internship with a Gainesville law firm. We had a case in the Ocala Public Schools that changed my life. The Ocala Superintendent summarily expelled virtually all Black student seniors in 1972 to punish them for a "racial riot" at Ocala High. None of the white student participants were punished at all. Black students, some of whom had not even been on campus that day, were arrested, charged with criminal trespassing, and all of them lost any scholarships—athletic or academic—they had earned; they were even barred from attending graduation. The superintendent said that all the Black students had to publicly apologize to the citizens of Ocala, promise not to be violent anymore, and attend night school to finish their graduation requirements. The situation was so ridiculous that I lost my temper and almost blew my internship. I decided after I calmed down that being an attorney may not be my best option after all. I changed course one last time. I came back to UF and finished my master's thesis, applied to Boston University and UCLA, got accepted to both, and decided on the warm weather and larger graduate fellowship offer at UCLA. I left Florida and began matriculating at UCLA in the fall of 1973, and by 1984 had completed my dissertation and doctorate degree.

Chapter 2 Study Questions

1. What do you consider to be the substantive issues raised by the author in this chapter?
2. To what extent was the author influenced by his experiences as a Black student at UF in the 1960s?
3. How do you compare Black student life at UF today with that in the 1960s?

Chapter 3: Oral History, Democracy, and the Power of Memory by Paul Ortiz

Abstract: African American struggles from slavery to freedom in American history have helped to create viable and enduring Black institutions and communities. In many ways the reconstruction of the African American story has relied on oral history, deeply rooted in African oral tradition. And for the purpose of this chapter, oral history may be defined as the "collection and study of historical information about peoples of African descent in the Diaspora, and important events, using recording devices or transcriptions of interviews."

This essay argues that African American elders attempted to pass on to their children what will be referred to here as a "testimonial culture," a way of testifying to the struggles and dignity of individuals. This also illustrates the significance of oral history to African American Studies.

The research for this chapter mined the richness of the oral history archives at the University of Florida and at Duke University. It includes many interviews I have conducted with African American elders spanning nearly three decades between 1993 and 2020. In addition to weaving a historical narrative, I discuss methodological approaches to the study of African American history and oral history drawing on the works of James Baldwin, C.L.R. James, W.E.B. Du Bois and others. The essay is designed for use in African American Studies seminars that promote community-based public history and digital humanities learning and that facilitate collaboration between students and underserved communities.

> We should have likewise, days of bitter bread, and tabernacle in the wilderness, in which to remember our grief-worn brothers and sisters. They are now pleading with million tongues against those who have despoiled them. They cry from gory fields—from pestilential rice swamps—from cane break, and forests—from plantations of cotton and tobacco—from the dark holds of slave ships, and from countless acres where the sugar cane nods to the sighing winds. They lift up their voices from all the land over which

our country floats. From the banks of our silver streams, and broad rivers, from our valleys and sloping hills, and mountain tops!
—Rev. Henry Highland Garnet (1848; 2007)

Oral history is a testament to human survival, our aspirations for the future and the struggle to retain one's dignity in an uncertain world. We tell each other stories about our heritages and where we come from in order to affirm foundational values and to prove that our lives have meaning. Without our memories we have nothing to stand upon. Playwright August Wilson composed a cycle of riveting dramas to pose the question: "Can you acquire a sense of self-worth by denying your past?" (Heard and Wilson, 2001). This proverb is a preeminent theme of the African Diaspora. During the Middle Passage, enslaved African women collectively sung songs of cultures lost in order to steel each other to survive the horrific journey to the Americas. The British abolitionist Thomas Clarkson wrote of these women, "In their songs they call upon their lost Relations and Friends, they bid adieu to their Country, they recount the Luxuriance of their native soil, and the happy Days they have spent there" (Rediker, 2007).

Black bards used oral testimonies to preserve chronicles of the sacrifices needed to achieve—and to sustain—freedom. Work songs, ring shouts, religious sermons, jazz ensembles as well as Decoration Day lectures given by Civil War veterans bristled with lessons of faith, humility, and endurance. The characteristics that animated these diverse performative genres and made them powerful tools of community building included group participation, call-and-response cadences, and intense synergy between performers and observers (Levine, 1978). In James Baldwin's first novel, *Go Tell It on the Mountain*, the young minister in the story realizes that, for a sermon to be successful, he must move his congregation from being passive observers to active listeners and actual participants in the liturgy (Baldwin, 1952). Like the oral history encounter between interviewer and interviewee, audiences and performers in these sacred and secular encounters engaged in *dialogical* learning where new meanings and forms of knowledge were being created and recreated. In *Sonny's Blues*,

Baldwin describes how a group of musicians led by a fiddler named "Creole" tell the story of their people's painful and exultant histories in a small Harlem nightclub. They do so without uttering a single word. The narrator observes:

> He and his boys up there were keeping it new, at the risk of ruin, destruction, madness, and death, in order to find new ways to make us listen. For while the tale of how we suffer, and how we are delighted, and how we may triumph is never new, it always must be heard. There isn't any other tale to tell, it's the only light we've got in all this darkness (Baldwin, 1957).

It finally dawns on Sonny's brother—a member of the audience—that this is a *reciprocal* performance that demands participation from all: "Freedom lurked around us and I understood, at last, that he [Sonny on keyboards] could help us to be free if we would listen, that he would never be free until we did." Once again, the watchers become interlocutors and stamp their own collective historical meanings on an intimate blues performance (Baldwin, 1965). African American storytellers in the antebellum period tried as best as they could to preserve spaces to dream of liberation in a nation bent on aggressively expanding slavery (Kelley, 2003). Born in Baltimore in 1825, Frances Ellen Watkins Harper's career as an abolitionist, Underground Railroad conductor, poet, and co-founder of the National Association of Colored Women spanned seven decades. Harper wrote "Bury Me in a Free Land" in 1858 as a poetical sanctuary for all African Americans as they fought to defend their communities against torrents of white terror:

> Make me a grave where'er you will,
> In a lowly plain, or a lofty hill;
> Make it among earth's humblest graves,
> But not in a land where men are slaves.
>
> I could not rest if I heard the tread
> Of coffee gang to the shambles led,

And the mother's shriek of wild despair
Rise like a curse on the trembling air.

If I saw young girls from their mother's arms
Bartered and sold for their youthful charms,
My eye would flash with a mournful flame,
My death-paled cheek grew red with shame.

I ask no monument, proud and high.
To arrest the gaze of passers-by;
All that my yearning spirit craves.
Is bury me not in a land of slaves (Harper, 1858).

Black intellectuals toiled to remind each other of the egalitarian dimensions of their battles for emancipation. This is where African American Studies and oral history practices intersect. The emphasis in both disciplines is on the role of so-called ordinary people in remaking and redeeming the world. What Cedric Robinson called the "Black Radical Tradition" emphasized mass, collective struggles while critiquing top-down models of leadership favored by the dominant society (Robinson, 1983). Hence, W.E.B. Du Bois argued in *Black Reconstruction* (1935) that the self-activity of enslaved African Americans was the key to winning the American Civil War. In a speech given in the midst of the most perilous weeks of the conflict, Frederick Douglass made it clear that Lincoln's leadership would not win the Civil War: "We are not to be saved by the captain this time, but by the crew. We are not to be saved by Abraham Lincoln, but by the power behind the throne, greater than the throne itself" (Douglass, 1863). In the same vein, C.L.R. James (1938) stated that the enslaved Africans in Haiti learned through hard experience not to trust their leaders to carry out the revolution needed to achieve independence from the French empire. While the figure of General Toussaint L'Ouverture, "one of the most remarkable men of a period rich in remarkable men," towers over the transatlantic war to end slavery in the Americas, James urges his readers to understand, "Yet Toussaint did not make the revolution. It was the revolution that made Toussaint. And even that is not the whole truth" (James, 1938).

W.E.B. Du Bois, C.L.R James, Frederick Douglass, and other activist intellectuals understood that placing the African Diaspora at the center of global history was a way of anchoring Black labor, identities, and social movements to demonstrate that people of African descent were integral to the emergence of democracy in the modern world (Kelley, 1999). Realizing that he was delivering one of the final speeches of his life, Frederick Douglass asked his enthusiastic audience at the 1893 World's Columbian Exposition in Chicago to view their experiences as one of the great epics of world history. As Douglass recounted pivotal moments of the abolitionist movement, his "spectators" became active participants in the creation of a global origin narrative of liberation from the grassroots:

> Speaking for the Negro, I can say, we owe much to Walker for his appeal; to John Brown [applause] for the blow struck at Harper's Ferry, to Lundy and Garrison for their advocacy [applause], We owe much especially to Thomas Clarkson, [applause], to William Wilberforce, to Thomas Fowell Buxton, and to the anti-slavery societies at home and abroad; but we owe incomparably more to Haiti than to them all. [Prolonged applause.] I regard her as the original pioneer emancipator of the nineteenth century. [Applause.] (Ortiz, 2018)

As Douglass well knew, history was one of the nation's fiercest battlegrounds. At Emancipation Day celebrations, African Americans invoked memories of building the nation's wealth to emphasize their claims on citizenship while white Americans doctored history to claim that Black people had done nothing to earn a stake in the society. Prominent academics produced a white nationalist literature heavily influenced by eugenics and social Darwinism (Gould, 1983). Slavery was presented as a benevolent institution and Reconstruction after the Civil War as a tragic descent into "Negro Misrule." Public school books in Florida taught that newly freed African Americans acted like buffoons. A typical primer read: "Many of the negroes [sic] loved their old masters and stayed on the old plantations, but others wandered away. Some thought that because they were free, they would never need to work anymore, so they dressed up in their best clothes and went to picnics and had a good time" (Fairlie, 1935).

African Americans countered this propaganda by sharing and passing down oral traditions of achievement and striving through family circuits of memory; this is the paramount theme in Pauli Murray's autobiography *Proud Shoes: The Story of an American Family*. The future civil rights attorney and minister grew up in the West End neighborhood of Durham, North Carolina in the early twentieth century. While achieving a modicum of economic success, Pauli Murray's community experienced a tremendous amount of anti-Black racism in a city known as "The capital of the Black Middle Class." The future NAACP lawyer noted, "… the somber fact remained that until the three Negro schools of Durham in my childhood—West End, East End and Whitted—all burned to the ground mysteriously one after the other, the colored children got no new buildings" (Murray 1999). Refusing to let fear paralyze her, Murray drew on the stories that her elders told her to instill a pride that carried her through a city cemetery spiked with Confederate flags in order to plant a solitary Union banner on her grandfather's grave every Memorial Day. The story of Murray's grandfather Robert Fitzgerald's service in the Civil War, indeed the service of a quarter of a million African American soldiers in freedom's cause, was nowhere to be found in the history textbooks of Durham—or of any town in the South—in those days. It was a history that Pauli Murray's family had to teach and pass down to each other via oral history. There was no other way to tell the story.

Unfortunately, most Americans have no access to these historical memories. The result is a troubling disconnect between centuries-long struggles against white supremacy and efforts today to challenge systemic racism at universities, workplaces, and the broader society. This is why the craft of oral history is more important than ever, especially in the age of Black Lives Matter. Oral history done well establishes dialogues between past and present via intergenerational conversations between elders and younger people that can pierce the veils of silence and obfuscation that protect systems of power and hegemony.

Take for instance the issues of racism and racial re-segregation. Too often, a mere mention of the terms *racism* and *segregation* elicits hurried remarks by teachers, politicians, and others to the effect: "That's just the way things were *back then* and thank heavens that we've advanced beyond that." This Orwellian effort to protect the present from the past is self-defeating. In 2002, Pulitzer-Prize winning journalist Leonard Pitts, Jr., asked "Is there really a need to defend the idea that the evil of that day [the segregation era] impacts the struggles of this one? I can't imagine any intelligent observer would think there is." Pitts, however, understands that there are many Americans who religiously claim: "But slavery ended a long time ago," asserting that racism has been on the demise since Emancipation. "If I could," Pitts continues, "I'd buy each of those people a copy of the new *Remembering Jim Crow...Remembering* is a book and, more important, a two-CD set, of oral history straight from the mouths of those who came of age in the segregation era. Witness testimony from men and women reared in the days when drinking water came in black and white" (Pitts, 2002). These witnesses, according to Pitts:

> ...talk about lynching, of course, the bestial mob murders to which whole families flocked as entertainment. And they discuss the registrars who conspired to rob black people of their right to vote, the mendacity of the sharecrop bosses, the facilities that were separate, yet never equal (Pitts, 2002).

Leonard Pitts suggests *Remembering Jim Crow* as an antidote for those who ask, "Why is race still an issue?"

I was a co-editor of *Remembering Jim Crow* and, as a graduate student, I conducted many of the oral histories that appear in the book. The interviews featured in *Remembering Jim Crow* were done primarily by graduate students during the 1990s as part of a National Endowment for the Humanities-sponsored oral history project based at Duke's Center for Documentary Studies titled "Behind the Veil: Documenting African American Life in the Jim Crow South." This effort was launched by a consortium of scholars from Duke as well as Historically Black

Colleges and Universities including North Carolina Central University, Clark-Atlanta University, and Jackson State University. According to the project's initial brochure, the major goal of Behind the Veil (BTV) was to "recover the documentary base for understanding the experience of Jim Crow before this invaluable opportunity is lost." Directed by the historians William H. Chafe, Raymond Gavins, and Robert Korstad, BTV interviews also generated primary historical data instrumental in creating new college-level curriculum on African American Studies, courses on oral history, documentary photography and other fields. The entire Behind the Veil collection, consisting of approximately 1,300 interviews, family photographs, and other documents, is housed at the John Hope Franklin Research Center for African and African American Documentation at Duke University Libraries.

I brought these experiences in coordinating the BTV project to the University of Florida when I became director of the Samuel Proctor Oral History Program (SPOHP) in 2008. In the remainder of this essay, I will tell the story of the making of the Joel Buchanan Archive of African American Oral History at the University of Florida. I will discuss the many facets of oral history that have made it an integral aspect of African American Studies scholarship and praxis. This essay will also consider some of the obstacles that SPOHP has encountered along the way in creating this collection. The Joel Buchanan Archive (JBA) has recently surpassed 1,000 oral histories with African American elders in Florida, the Gulf South, the Mississippi Delta, and other parts of the United States. These interviews are now being used by students, scholars, filmmakers, and playwrights in senior theses, dissertations, documentaries, books, and stage productions. The historical information generated by the interviews has provided original content for new African American Studies courses in high schools, colleges, and universities.

Students, staff, and volunteers at the Proctor Program began gathering, preserving, and promoting oral histories with African American elders in earnest during the spring academic semester of 2009. In retrospect, this was not the most promising time to launch an oral history project.

Upon arriving at the University of Florida, the first official message I received from the Dean's office at the College of Liberal Arts and Sciences was that SPOHP's equipment and staffing funds were being cut 90% due to budget pressures generated by the Great Recession. (These funds have never been restored.) My position, as well as that of SPOHP's office manager, were both protected from the cuts.

It was at this inauspicious moment that Gainesville civil rights movement icon Joel Buchanan (Figure 3.1) requested a meeting with me to discuss organizing a major interview initiative on African American history. I had first met Mr. Buchanan in the summer of 1996 when I traveled to Gainesville to do oral history interviews for my doctoral dissertation. This dissertation, which eventually grew into my first monograph, *Emancipation Betrayed*, focused on the Black Freedom Struggle in Florida. Joel (as he preferred to be called) literally took me under his wing and introduced me to a remarkable array of people in Gainesville's African American neighborhoods. Joel welcomed me into the fraternity of local historians, archivists, and Black storytellers in Alachua County. He took me to meet Reverend Thomas A. Wright (Figure 3.2), then pastor of Mt. Carmel Baptist Church and a legendary activist who helped organize the St. Augustine civil rights movement in the early 1960s.

Figure 3.1: UF President Machen presents Black History Award to Civil Rights Movement Icon Joel Buchanan at SPOHP's "Florida Black History Program," 2009. (SPOHP)

Figure 3.2: *The Reverend Thomas T. A. Wright, pastor of Mt. Carmel Baptist Church, is a legendary activist who helped organize the St. Augustine Civil Rights Movement in the early 1960s. He relocated to Gainesville when he was forced to flee St. Augustine in fear of his life.* (SPOHP)

Joel shared with me the story of how he had been in the first cohort of four courageous Black pupils who integrated Gainesville High School in 1964. (Rev. Wright often drove the students to school in the mornings.) Journalists have often romanticized the experiences of African American children in cities like Little Rock, Arkansas, who were the first to attend historically all-white schools. In contrast, Buchanan emphasized the terrible psychological costs paid by Black students of his generation, who were insulted by white students, staff, and faculty and told that they did not belong in white-majority public schools.

Joel gave me a crash course on Gainesville's importance. He proudly called the city, "The key to Black history in the entire state of Florida." He was a great storyteller, and his narratives always had a purpose. Some stories were designed to explain the enduring power of racism in the United States. In contrast to many scholars who taught that "race relations weren't as bad in Florida as in other states," Buchanan was the first person to tell me that Florida had the highest per-capita lynching rate in the country, a statistic I later verified through quantitative research for *Emancipation Betrayed*. Joel Buchanan also told stories designed to heal terrible divisions in a town and campus suffering from UF's denial of its origins as a university built upon the exploitation of Black workers and the dispossession of Native Americans. Joel told me on many occasions that his goal as a historian was to teach all of us how to treat each other with dignity and respect.

Joel Buchanan was also an excellent organizer. As a librarian at UF's Smathers Libraries Special Collections Department, he brokered several discussions between SPOHP, library staff, and then-UF President Bernie Machen about the prospects of beginning an oral history project with an intensive focus on African American life and experiences in Florida. Joel insisted that the work begin with a focus on local Black history, and President Machen agreed with this emphasis. In the course of these dialogs led by Joel, a research agenda began to take shape. According to my notes of a meeting that included Joel Buchanan, Bernie Machen, and me on January 30, 2009:

> An overarching theme of the research proposal is to interview African Americans who came of age in the era prior to *Brown v Board of Education*. (However, we will also pose questions relevant to the 1960s and 1970s as well. One area of obvious focus is the various ways that African Americans encountered UF as staff, students, etc., etc.) Along with the oral histories, an emphasis will be on collecting extant papers, documents, and 'ephemera' related to Black History and getting those to the archives before they are lost (Ortiz, 2009). This included two female Korean War Veterans, Ernestine Dave and Dorothy Marshall, narrating their experiences (Figures 3.3. and 3.4).

Figure 3.3: SPOHP Narrator Korean War Veteran Ernestine Dave. (SPOHP)

Figure 3.4: SPOHP Narrator Korean War Veteran Dorothy Marshall. (SPOHP)

Equally important, when I asked Dr. Machen if UF's support for this endeavor "...would extend to a financial commitment he did not flinch. He invited me to submit a brief proposal to the President's Office. So, here we go!" (Ortiz, 2009). Along the way, critical research partners such as Jim Cusick and Carl Van Ness from Smathers Libraries and Marna Weston, a doctoral student at UF, joined what became known as the African American History Project (AAHP). Marna became AAHP's first graduate research coordinator. His stature as an organizer and educator in Alachua County was key to the initiative's successes. The Office of the Provost has provided steady funding for AAHP since the fall semester of 2009. This funding has allowed SPOHP to hire graduate students as well as undergraduates to do the interviews as well as to transcribe and to produce podcasts, mini-documentaries, and public programs on African American history.

Drawing on the traditions of community engagement and activism shared by African American Studies and oral history, AAHP's launch event was a public history program titled: "Florida Black History: Where We Stand in the Age of Barack Obama," held on March 17, 2009 at Smathers Libraries East. The event was co-sponsored by a wide array of campus and community-based organizations. We designed the event to honor the African American historical tradition of encouraging maximum public participation while avoiding the pedantic practices of university events where a single speaker lectures to an immobile audience. High school and university students gave interpretive dance, choral, and written performances steeped in Black history. UF rising senior Khambria Clarke recited James Weldon Johnson's "Fifty Years," a poem written in 1913 to commemorate the 50th anniversary of the Emancipation Proclamation. In front of an audience of over 300 people, Joel Buchanan moderated a panel composed primarily of African American informants who discussed issues of systemic racism at the University of Florida and the broader society. Speakers included US Senator Bill Nelson via a recorded video (Figure 3.5), Mrs. Evelyn Marie Moore Mickle (Figure 3.6), the first Black graduate of the UF College of Nursing, and Student Nonviolent Coordinating Committee veteran and UF African American Studies professor Gwendolyn Zoharah Simmons (Figure 3.7). An energized audience punctuated each presentation with applause and acclamations (Samuel Proctor Oral History Program, 2009).

Figure 3.5: U.S. Senator Bill Nelson was one of the panelists at the AAHP launch event in 2009, "Florida Black History: Where We Stand in the Age of Barack Obama." (SPOHP)

Figure 3.6: Evelyn Mickle, first Black graduate of the UF College of Nursing, was also a panelist at the AAHP event. (SPOHP)

This bridge-building open event proved to be the ideal vehicle for the Proctor Program to launch AAHP. Subsequently, Black history public programs featuring interviewees and involving town-gown partnerships have helped us to maintain the project's momentum and accountability to African American communities that sustain our work. In addition, the university's willingness to begin an oral history project critical of its own history has been vitally important to the initiative's successes. African Americans who have toiled for generations as the university's essential workers are used to a university environment where issues of racism and inequality remain unaddressed and ignored. In contrast, "Florida Black History: Where We Stand in the Age of Barack Obama," began with panelists questioning the institution's commitment to equality and social mobility for all. This spirit of self-criticism helped us to form key partnerships with African American churches, neighborhood associations, museums, labor unions and other organizations who in turn helped to recruit AAHP's initial cohort of interviewees (hereinafter referred to as narrators).

Figure 3.7: UF Professor Dr. G. Zoharah Simmons, a national Civil Rights Activist in the 1960s-1970s, provided her perspectives on the AAHP Panel. (SPOHP)

After a decade of field work and over 1,000 interviews completed, this classroom-ready archive is bursting with paradigm-shifting testimonies. The Joel Buchanan Archive of African American Oral History features family histories of slavery, resistance to segregation, anti-Black racial violence, the creation of African American businesses, the founding of churches, and educational achievements during legal segregation. Narrators recount the first time they dared to vote in the 1960s, as well as their initial thoughts on learning that Barack Obama had been elected President of the United States. Interviews with veterans of the historic Tallahassee Bus Boycott, organizers of the 1964 St. Augustine civil rights protests, founders of the Deacons for Defense and Justice in Louisiana as well as activists with Mississippi Freedom Summer have challenged our understandings of the origins of the modern Civil Rights Movement. Columbia Oral History Program student Benji de la Piedra wrote an overview of the collection after attending SPOHP's three-day public symposium, "From Segregation to Black Lives Matter," in 2019. Benji observed that the Joel Buchanan Archive is especially strong in narratives of "Life under Jim Crow, including institution building, educational philosophies and methods, food security, community based-healthcare, support and service organizations, displacement and dispossession, labor, armed self-defense, and tactics of resistance..." (de la Piedra, 2019).

Narrators including Laura Dixie (Figure 3.8), known as "The Mother of the Tallahassee Movement," Congress of Racial Equality leader Patricia Stephens Due (Figure 3.10), and author Nikki Giovanni (Figure 3.9) highlight the central roles of African American women in politics, protests, and the arts. Mrs. Dixie was a rank-and-file organizer of the Tallahassee Bus Boycott and the founding union president of the American Federation of State, County, and Municipal Employees (AFSCME), for healthcare workers in Tallahassee. Mrs. Dixie carried out both open and subtle struggles against segregation. She recalled:
I had a long fingernail file and they had these signs also where ... they had the patients segregated. They had a white wing, black wing, white bathroom, colored bathroom, white eating dining room, colored dining room, and so I took my fingernail file and went 'round and unscrewed every one of those segregation signs off the door (Ortiz 2017).

Figure 3.8: Laura Dixie, known as the "Mother of the Tallahassee Movement," spoke at the SPOHP Symposium: "From Segregation to Black Lives Matter," in 2019.

Figure 3.9: Renowned Poet Nikki Giovanni was featured at the symposium in 2019.

Figure 3.10: The symposium also featured Patricia Stephens Due, prominent leader of the Congress of Racial Equality (CORE), a major civil rights organization in the 1960s.

The Joel Buchanan Archive (JBA) also features stories from the first generation of African American students at the University of Florida, the creation of the Mississippi Freedom Democratic Party, as well as narratives of Black and Latinx intersectionality, among many other topics. Most of these testimonies are transcribed and "text searchable" in order to make them easier to adopt for use in classrooms, podcasts, blogs, scripts, and other outcomes. In addition to interviews, the JBA collection consists of scores of Black history-themed public programs, university seminars on African American studies, conference presentations, and Black History workshops across the country. Elements of the JBA archive especially useful to educators and to students in Black Studies include the two-day symposium and celebration of the 50th anniversary of African American Studies at UF (Samuel Proctor Oral History Program, 2020) as well video footage of "From Segregation to Black Lives Matter," the three-day national academic conference that SPOHP organized to formally open the JBA collection in 2019. The first panel of this conference featured four former SPOHP graduate research assistants and interviewers who discussed the topic: "Conducting the Oral Histories: Challenges, Impacts and Legacies" (Samuel Proctor Oral History Program, 2019). Many of these aforementioned symposiums, interviews, and workshops are already being used by high school teachers, university instructors, public radio producers, and filmmakers to create new African American Studies-themed classes, podcasts, and documentaries.

The Proctor Program has provided the institutional base of the Archive of African American Oral History from the outset. Founded in 1967 by UF University Historian Dr. Samuel Proctor, SPOHP has long specialized in gathering, preserving, and promoting oral narratives from individuals from all walks of life. The program's oral archives, housed at the University of Florida Digital Collections (UFDC), include one of the nation's foremost collections in Native American history, extensive testimonials on environmental and water issues in Florida, student movement organizing, as well as the National Women's March on Washington Archive. As an interdisciplinary research center, SPOHP has worked assiduously with colleagues and students from African American Studies, Women's Studies, Anthropology, Latin American Studies, African Studies, Journalism, Performance Arts, and many other fields to conduct and to support ethnographic fieldwork throughout the world.

The Proctor Program practices a community-based model of oral history encouraging students to conduct research projects outside of the campus where they listen to elders, organizers, and groups that are engaging in a broad array of struggles (Figure 3.11). SPOHP's social justice-centered approach holds that all learning is experiential. Drawing from the methods of Italian oral historian Allesandro Portelli, SPOHP teaches students to learn from the neighborhoods they work in rather than studying them as if they were examining people through a microscope (Portelli, 1997). The most important oral history skills taught in SPOHP workshops include the art of listening, humility on the part of the interviewer, and—to reiterate a central point drawn from African American history—the ability to approach the interview as an open-ended discussion where narrator and interviewer are engaged in the *dialogical* or mutual creation of knowledge.

Figure 3.11: SPOHP students interview Anthony Ray Hinton at the Equal Justice Initiative in Montgomery, Alabama in 2015. Mr. Hinton's story was told in 2019's Just Mercy.

The Proctor Program has received numerous national academic accolades including the Oral History Association's Stetson Kennedy Award for outstanding achievement in using oral history to create a more humane and just world, as well as the Society of American

Archivists' Diversity Award for SPOHP's relentless pursuit of community knowledge, local voices, and academic transformation, and has created a monumental program that has impacted the lives of countless people in Florida and across the nation. The Doris Duke Charitable Trust conducted an external review of SPOHP in 2020. The report concluded, "The program's social justice research methodologies are the focus of scholars and oral history programs across the globe" (Duke Charitable Trust, 2020).

In the Black Lives Matter era, well-planned oral history projects may enable institutions of higher learning to better address the forces of systemic racism including economic inequality, mass incarceration, housing discrimination, and (in some colleges) declining enrollment of African American students and students of color. Accustomed to acting rather than listening, universities often ignore the roles they play in exacerbating systemic racism—by paying workers low wages, promoting the clustering of student housing in working-class neighborhoods adjacent to campuses, and robbing towns of precious revenues by taking property of off tax rolls. In turn, these behaviors lead to intergenerational poverty, gentrification, and the displacement of African American and Latinx neighborhoods.

Oral history dialogues in the form of interviews, public programs, workshops, and other formats may illuminate dissenting voices and show academic institutions how to fight inequalities. This is where oral history and African American Studies' traditions of emphasizing civic engagement meld. SPOHP's former interim director, Dr. Ryan Morini (Figure 3.12) notes that the Proctor Program's public programs do not merely present information, but instead strive to create space for dialogue, exchange, and a sense of collective ownership over the historical narrative among audience members. He concluded that these critical spaces for public dialog "might be achieved by putting local community members or activists on the same panel as credentialed scholars...Or it might be done by honoring someone who the university community should know about...someone who will wake up a student audience" (de la Piedra, 2019).

Figure 3.12: Ryan Morini, a founding member of the Joel Buchanan Archive (JBA) research team conducts an oral history interview in Baker County, Florida.

Vivian Filer (Figure 3.13), a longtime civil rights organizer in Gainesville, often plays this role during SPOHP public programs. In a panel focusing on town-gown relations held during the 50th anniversary celebration of African American Studies at UF, Filer and other discussants called upon the university to stop promoting gentrification in adjacent neighborhoods and for students to be more engaged in community organizing. Other panelists called upon the university to promote sustainable economic development, career opportunities for local people, and living-wage jobs. Audience members pointed out that UF

Figure 3.13: Vivian Filer has guided the JBA project since its inception. She is the Chair and Director of the Cotton Club Museum and Cultural Center (CCMCC) in Gainesville.

has conducted numerous studies on economic inequality over the years; however, none of these studies has led to action or changes in university behaviors. This fruitful exchange reminds us of the positive benefits of authentic public dialog.

The Joel Buchanan Archive features numerous oral history interviews with generations of African American staff, faculty, students, and alumni who founded and sustained programs at UF that have promoted diversity and inclusion for all. Notable narrators include legendary African American Studies lecturer, filmmaker, and community activist Dr. Patricia Hilliard-Nunn; Dr. G.W. Mingo, founder of the UF Upward Bound Program; Mrs. Evelyn Mickle, the first Black graduate of the UF College of Nursing; and Betty J. Stewart-Fullwood, a student organizer during the Black Thursday protests. Dr. Stewart-Fullwood returned to the university to serve students for three decades as a beloved lecturer, counselor, and director of the Student Enrichment Services Program at the College of Liberal Arts and Sciences.

As UF's African American History Project enters into its second decade, where do we go from here? As the program's reputation has grown, SPOHP has become increasingly active nationally in supporting efforts at historical truth and reconciliation initiatives arising from incidents of anti-Black lynching and racial pogroms. SPOHP is participating in several historical endeavors to commemorate the victims of lynching and anti-Black violence. These include the City of Ocoee, Florida's 100th Anniversary of the Ocoee Election Day Massacre and the Elaine, Arkansas Legacy Center's project to document the 1919 Elaine Massacre. Since 2009, the Proctor Program has provided support for continuing efforts to educate students and individuals about the 1923 Rosewood Massacre. SPOHP staff, students and volunteers have provided research support for the Alachua County Remembrance Committee and the City of Newberry's Newberry Six Remembrance Project. Both of these collaborations are connected with the Equal Justice Initiative's efforts to memorialize the victims of anti-Black violence and to use these histories to inform reform efforts within the nation's deeply flawed criminal justice system.

The Joel Buchanan Archive of African American Oral History has built upon traditions of African American Studies that emphasize community-based research, democratic dialogue, the importance of documenting "ordinary people doing extraordinary things," as well as the centrality of social-justice oriented research. This collaborative initiative has demonstrated the power of oral history to contribute to discussions of how to challenge systemic racism by privileging the voices of Black elders and others who have battled white supremacy their entire lives.

Chapter 3 Study Questions

1. "The African American struggles from slavery to freedom in American history have helped to create viable and enduring Black institutions and communities in America." Discuss.
2. What is the significance of oral history and oral traditions in African American Studies and in American history?
3. Discuss some of the methodological approaches to the study of popular culture, drawing from W.E.B. Du Bois, C.L.R. James, and James Baldwin.

References

Baldwin, J. (1952). *Go Tell It on the Mountain*. Doubleday & Company, pp. 102-106.

Baldwin, J. (1965). *Going to Meet the Man*. Dial Press, pp. 119-122.

Chafe, W., Gavins, R., Korstad R., Ortiz, P. (Eds.). (2001). *Remembering Jim Crow: African Americans Tell About Life in the Segregated South*. New Press.

The Doris Duke Charitable Foundation. (2020). *Samuel Proctor Oral History Program, University of Florida*, p. 3.

Du Bois, W.E.B. (1935). *Black Reconstruction in America: An Essay Toward a History of the Part Which Black Folk Played in the Attempt to Reconstruct Democracy in America, 1860-1880*. Meridian Books.

Fairlie, M. (1935). *History of Florida*. Kingsport Press.

Garnet, H. and Royster, P. (1848). The Past and Present Condition, and the Destiny, of the Colored Race. [Address to Female

Benevolent Society]. Electronic Texts in American Studies (Paper 13). University of Nebraska-Lincoln. Retrieved from http://digitalcommons.unl.edu/etas/13

Gould, S.J. (1983). *The Mismeasure of Man*. W.W. Norton.

Harper, F.E.W. (1858). Bury Me in a Free Land. Academy of American Poets. Retrieved from https://www.poets.org/poetsorg/poem/bury-me-free-land

Heard, E.J., and Wilson, A. August Wilson on Playwriting: An Interview. *African American Review*, 35(1), 93-94. https://doi.org/10.2307/2903337

James, C.L.R. (1938). *Black Jacobins: Toussaint L'Ouverture and the San Domingo Revolution*. Vintage Books.

Kelley, R.D. 'But a Local Phase of a World Problem': Black History's Global Vision, 1883-1950. *The Journal of American History*, 86(3), pp. 1045-1077. https://doi.org/10.2307/2568605

Kelley, R.D. (2003). *Freedom Dreams: The Black Radical Imagination*. Beacon Press.

de la Piedra, B. (2019). Dispatch from Florida: A Celebration of African American Oral History in Gainesville, in *The Samuel Proctor Oral History Program: From Segregation to Black Lives Matter*, p. 4.

Levine, L. (1978). Black Culture and Black Consciousness: Afro-American Folk Thought from Slavery to Freedom. Oxford University Press.

McCarthy, Kevin and Stewart-Fullwood, Betty J., *African Americans and the University of Florida* (University of Florida, 2003).

Murray, P. (1999; 1956). Proud Shoes: The Story of an American Family. Beacon Press.

Ortiz, P. (2005) Emancipation Betrayed: The Hidden History of Black Organizing and White Violence in Florida From Reconstruction to the Bloody Election of 1920. University of California Press.

Ortiz, P. (2009, January 30). Notes from meeting with Joel Buchanan and Bernie Machen. In author's possession.

Ortiz, P. (2017, December 6). Laura Dixie: Remembering a 'Mother of the Movement.' Retrieved from https://www.facingsouth.org/2017/12/laura-dixie-remembering-mother-movement

Ortiz, P. (2018). An African American and Latinx History of the United States. Beacon Press, p. 31.

Pitts, L. (2002, February 23). Recalling Jim Crow Like it Was Yesterday. The Miami Herald, p. 1E.

Portelli, A. (1997). The Battle of Valle Giulia: Oral History and the Art of Dialogue. University of Wisconsin Press.

Rediker, M. (2007). The Slave Ship: A Human History. Penguin Books, p. 284.

Robinson, C. (Ed.). & Kelley, R.D.G. (Foreword). (1983; 2000). Black Marxism: The Making of the Black Radical Tradition. University of North Carolina Press.

Samuel Proctor Oral History Program. (2009). Florida Black History: Where We Stand in the Age of Barack Obama [Video]. https://www.youtube.com/watch?v=mkeBwBeKY7A&t=2658s

Samuel Proctor Oral History Program. (2019). From Segregation to Black Lives Matter [Video]. http://ufl.to/tu

Samuel Proctor Oral History Program (2020). African American Studies, Year 50 at UF: Community Celebration [Video]. https://www.youtube.com/watch?v=NP1BmkFUo14&list=PLzMFflzfI0ESQ-YvZ2HuRGsnA_gE_NsOO

Chapter 4: African American Library Collections and Services at the University of Florida by Stephanie Birch

Abstract: This chapter provides an overview of the University of Florida Libraries' efforts to collect and maintain materials to support the advancement of research and instruction in African American Studies. It offers insight into the role and function of the library system at the University of Florida, concentrating on the evolving practices of academic librarianship and long-term support for African American Studies. The Libraries' collection development efforts began in the 1970s, with a more robust collection program beginning in the early 2000s. Today, the Libraries manage substantial holdings in African American Studies in the special, circulating, and online collections, which are enriched by cross-campus and community-oriented collaboration.

The African American Studies Program at the University of Florida is supported by the University of Florida Libraries' robust collection development and management programs, through which Library personnel strive to the meet the information needs of a campus-wide network of interdisciplinary students, faculty, and staff researching Black experiences, histories, and cultures. Like other modern academic libraries, the University of Florida library system sits at the epicenter of academic life, delivering far more than books on shelves. This chapter explores the many ways in which the UF Libraries have and continue to support the advancement of African American Studies, through collection management, research support services, instruction, grantsmanship, public programming, and community engagement.

Overview of the University of Florida Libraries

The University of Florida's library system is a consortium of disciplinary-focused and multi-disciplinary library branches, providing continuous access to primary, secondary, and tertiary sources to support curricular and research needs across the institution. The library system maintains seven on-campus libraries and two off-site storage and office facilities. The de-centralized organization of the UF Libraries' on-campus branches expands the spatial reach of the library personnel and collections. The branches of the UF Libraries are Architecture and Fine Arts, Education, Health Sciences, Humanities and Social Sciences, Law, Science and Engineering, and Special and Area Studies. The UF Libraries employ over 80 faculty librarians, each leveraging subject and/or functional expertise to enhance research and learning at the University of Florida.

The UF Libraries off-site facilities provide temporary and permanent storage for collection materials, as well as space for behind-the-scenes library units, including Preservation and Digital Support Services. The Libraries' off-site facilities also house the Florida Educational Repository Collection (FLARE), a "statewide shared collection of low use print materials from academic libraries in Florida ("Florida Academic Repository," n.d.). In addition to physical collections and spaces, the UF Libraries maintain the UF Digital Collections (UFDC) platform, hosting "more than 300 digital collections, containing over 14 million pages ("University of Florida Digital Collections," n.d.). UFDC hosts major digital collections like the Samuel Proctor Oral History Program Archive and the UF Institutional Repository. It also provides permanent, shared access to digital content at other institutions, such as the Digital Library of the Caribbean (DLoC).

Library Operations

The University library system is comprised of complex ecosystem of front-end and back-end operations. Front-end services focus on patron services, such as circulation, reference and research assistance, instruction, course and electronic reserves, exhibits, and outreach. Throughout the years, the library system has continuously evolved and expanded to support established and emerging scholarly disciplines, while also integrating and adapting to advancements in library practices and technologies.

History of the Libraries

The University Library system dates to 1905. At that time, there were two library collections maintained in Thomas Hall: the main collection and an agricultural collection. Within a few years, the University Library expanded to include disciplinary collections in education, law, botany, zoology, physics, and engineering (Kisling, n.d.-c). In 1925, the University's first library building was erected (Kisling, n.d.-b). Today, the original building is known as Smathers Library, which houses the Special Collections and Area Studies Department.

In the post-war era, the scope of the Libraries' collections rapidly broadened in tandem with the expansion of the University's curricular offerings. At this time, the Libraries developed new collections for rare book, archival, and Latin American and Caribbean materials (Kisling, n.d.-c). In 1967, the Graduate Research Library opened and was renamed as Library West in 1970. Today, Library West houses the Humanities and Social Sciences collections, as well as several administrative departments. Later, in 1987, several departmental library branches were combined into one Central Science Library, now called the Marston Science Library (Kisling, n.d.-a). The University Libraries continued to expand in the 1980s through the development of the African Studies and Judaica Libraries. The University's first digital library collection launched in 2000, laying the foundation for the UF Digital Collections (UFDC) that exist today.

AFRICAN AMERICAN COLLECTIONS HISTORY

The collection of African American library materials did not begin until the 1970s. According to a survey of library holdings from 1974, the UF Libraries' African American Collection consisted of then-current "monographs and scholarly publications on Black music, theatre, and literatures" with an emphasis on Black popular culture and—specifically—reflections on the Harlem Renaissance (Renz, 1974, p. 28). The early collection prioritized Humanities research but did include some major Social Science materials. Some of the major microfilm acquisitions at the time were from the Schomburg Collections and long-standing Black newspapers from Detroit and Baltimore, as well as several "radical" Black newspapers.

According to University Historian Carl Van Ness, during the 1970s library workers transferred African American Studies materials from the circulating collection to rare books (Van Ness, personal communication, 2020, February 6). The apparent reason for the transfer was to protect these materials from being stolen, defaced, or destroyed. Some of these titles remain in the Rare Books Collection today and are now considered to be rare or uncommon books. In the early 2000s, the Libraries gained significant momentum to further develop its African American Special Collection holdings.

Influential Librarians, Archivists, and Curators: Past & Present

Since the early 2000s, the Libraries have allocated resources to develop collections in the field of African American Studies. These resources include the appointment of dedicated subject experts. Over the two decades, expert librarians, archivists, and curators have shaped the Libraries' collections, as well as programs centered around instruction and outreach. In turn, these individuals have (and continue) to influence and bolster African American Studies research and instruction at UF.

JOEL BUCHANAN (2004 – 2010)

Joel Buchanan worked for the UF Libraries in the Special Collections and Area Studies Library. He was instrumental in cultivating relationships with local community members and organizations to ensure the preservation of Gainesville's African American histories and archival materials. In addition to his leadership in the collections development, Joel also supported African American Studies faculty and students through research assistance, lectures, and public programs.

Today, the Libraries host a digital archive of African American Oral History named in Joel's honor. The Joel Buchanan Archive is comprised of recordings and transcripts from the Samuel Proctor Oral History program. His work with the Program in the 1980s to record interviews with local African American residents laid the foundation for the vast collection that exists today, which to date contains over 1,000 interviews.

JANA RONAN (2010 - 2016)
After 2010, Jana Ronan served as the Libraries' liaison to the African American Studies Program until 2016. Her work contributed to the development of a robust interdisciplinary circulating collection, which was largely concentrated in Library West (Humanities and Social Sciences). Ronan was later appointed Chair of Library West. Today, she serves as the History Librarian and liaison to the University Honors Program.

STEPHANIE BIRCH (2016 - PRESENT)
Following the establishment of the African American Studies Bachelor's degree program in 2013, I became the University of Florida's first African American Studies Librarian. The creation of this position signaled a change in the Libraries' priorities towards the advancement of African American Studies as a field and commitment to increasing representation of African American experiences, histories, and cultures across the collections.

I employ a collaborative approach to supporting African American Studies and interdisciplinary scholarship at UF by partnering with my library colleagues within and beyond the institution. My professional responsibilities include collection development and management, research instruction, reference, and research consultation services, as well as community outreach and engagement to promote the Libraries' African American collections, resources, and programs.

FLORENCE TURCOTTE (2017 - PRESENT)
Since 2005, Florence Turcotte has served as the UF Libraries' Literary Collections Archivist in the Special Collections and Area Studies Department. During this time, Turcotte's role has expanded to include LGBTQ and Women's Studies Special Collections, and, in 2017, African American Special Collections. During her tenure, Florence has contributed to several major African American acquisition projects,

including the Bo Diddley and James Haskins Collections and the Zora Neale Hurston Papers. Under her careful stewardship, the African American Special Collections safeguard over 300 linear feet of archival materials and objects, organized into over 650 boxes. Included within these collections are numerous vulnerable and unique materials documenting African American communities and experiences across Florida.

Library Partners

While I serve as the African American Studies subject specialist and program liaison, I also actively collaborate with other library employees and departments to develop and manage the Libraries' African American collection holdings. Within the UF Libraries, there are more than 80 subject specialists, many of whom contribute their skills, expertise, and time to enhancing the Libraries' interdisciplinary collections. Access to collection materials is supported by library staff in a myriad of behind-the-scenes departments, which perform such essential duties as acquisitions, cataloguing, preservation, course reserves, user services, digital production services, and e-resources.

Collections Overview

The UF Libraries collections house a broad range of materials relating to African American experiences, including African American cultural materials and ephemera and African American Studies scholarship. African American experiences are presented in different formats, including print, digital, and microfilm/microfiche. The Libraries' collection holdings are dispersed across the Libraries' many branches and facilities. However, most information about African Americans is shelved in Library West (Humanities and Social Sciences) and Smathers Library (Special and Area Studies Collections). For the purposes of this chapter, I will be categorizing materials into collection type: general, special, and digital. Here, *general* collections refer to circulating and reserved materials, while *special* collections refer to distinguished circulating and non-circulating collections, many containing rare, archival, and/or manuscript materials.

General Collections

The general collection utilizes the Library of Congress Classification (LC and Library of Congress Subject Heading [LSCH]) systems. While systems support the discoverability of library materials, it also presents increasingly complex challenges for interdisciplinary scholars. The LC system was developing circa 1900 and is used widely by academic libraries (Howard and Knowlton, 2019, p. 74). This shared system allows institutions to link collections together to facilitate shared access and cross-institutional borrowing.

However, the LC system was not designed to support disciplines like African American Studies. The system is organized into 21 basic classes is based on an early 20th century understanding of the information universe. As such, the classes are organized around the fundamental disciplines of the time (for example, History, Philosophy, etc.). To put it simply, there is no class for African American Studies. Instead, information about and pertaining to African Americans and Black peoples are disbursed across the classes, though information is often concentrated within subclasses of Class E: History of the Americas (Department of Cataloging and Acquisitions, n.d.). Specifically, there are three call ranges where African American Studies materials are frequently catalogued:

- E184.5-185.98   Afro-Americans
- E185.2-185.89   Status and development since emancipation
- E185.96-185.98   Biography. Genealogy

While the concentration of these materials makes it easier for patrons to browse the shelves, information about African Americans that falls beyond the scope of the E Class and the Afro-American History subclass can be difficult to locate. This is where the Library of Congress Subject Headings (LCSH) come into play. Each catalogue record is assigned a unique call number, as well as list of subject headings. This creates what is called "linked data," which connects virtual threads across the catalogue and help users find related sources in different classes. The

LCSH system uses a "controlled vocabulary" or a shared, authorized system of language. This creates consistency in phrasing and spelling. To demonstrate the breadth and disbursal of the general collection holdings of African American Studies-related materials, I conducted a sample catalog search. I search the phrase "African American" (in quotation marks), using the subject heading search field in the UF Library catalogue. The search generated over 30,000 results, with over 28,000 titles available in UF library locations or online. (Note: Discrepancies in the visible search results versus actual print and eBook holdings is likely due to catalog records automatically populated through the Libraries patron-driven and demand-driven acquisitions systems, whereby eBook titles appear that are not yet owned by Library. The PDA and DDA systems trigger the purchase of titles once a patron(s) has viewed that record three times.) The sample search (see Table 4.1) provides a baseline understanding of the size of the Libraries' African American collection holdings and the different shelving locations.

Table 4.1: "African American" Subject Heading Sample Search Results.

Shelving Location	# of Records
Library West	12,610
eBook	7,628
Smathers Library	2,747
Education Library	1,201
Legal Information Center	1,044
Off-Site Storage	995
UF Lab School Library	861
Architecture & Fine Arts Library	740
Health Science Center Libraries	130
UFDC & Online Dissertations	128
Affiliate Libraries	43
Marston Science Library	14
Total	28,141

The records returned via the sample search each contain at least one subject heading with the phrase "African Americans." It is important to note that there are dozens of LC Subject Headings pertaining to information about African American histories, cultures, and experiences. Therefore, it is likely that not all pertinent catalog records appeared in the search results. The sample search excludes many of the archival and manuscript materials located in the Special Collections and Area Studies Department. The number of titles available and the number of records per shelving location will change as the collection grows and new titles are added. Each year, the general collection grows larger.

Major African American Special Collections

Separate from the general collection are special collection materials, which reside in Smathers Library. In total, there are 28 special collections within the "African American, Civil Rights, and Slavery" subject category. These collections vary greatly in size and scope. To access materials in these collections, patrons must browse the finding aid and contact the Special Collections and Area Studies Department (SASC) to plan a visit to the Smathers Library Grand Reading Room. Some of these collections have been partially or fully digitized and are available for free and open access via UFDC. The list of special collection finding aids is available on the SASC website.

The A. Quinn Jones Collection is named after a prominent African American educator who lived and worked in Gainesville, Florida from 1921 until his passing in 1997. It documents his work and life, "concentrating on Lincoln High School and the Great Bethel AME Church" (Douglas, 2017). The collection also contains papers relating to the Florida State Teachers Association and the National Association of Teachers in Colored Schools, among others. The collection documents Black life in Gainesville and Florida from 1901 to 2007, as recorded in newspaper clippings, correspondence, family papers, photographs, memorabilia, and more.

The Papers of the Black Student Union (BSU) Collection documents the organizational history of the BSU. Established in 1968, the BSU was "founded as a support system and social organization" for Black students at the University of Florida (Coates, 2019). In 1971, BSU students took historic action at the University to demand, among other things, increases in Black student enrollment, support for Black Studies education, and the recruitment of Black faculty, staff, and administrators. On April 15, 1971, BSU students organized protests and sit-ins that led to the arrest and suspension of 60 students. These events are now remembered as the Black Thursday protests. The BSU Collection is comprised of organizational records from 1974-2010. It includes documents pertaining to organizational business, such as financial records and budgets, meeting minutes and agendas, and sponsored events.

The James S. Haskins Collection contains the personal and professional papers of the prolific African American author for whom it is named. In addition to his rich literary career, Haskins worked as a professor in the UF Department of English from 1977-2005. The collection contains copies of his published works and original manuscripts, unpublished manuscripts, essays and speeches, and correspondences, as well as his personal library collection (Duckworth, 2015). Some of Haskins' most noteworthy works are *Diary of a Harlem Schoolteacher* (1969), *Cotton Club* (1977), and his many biographies on African American public figures.

The Papers of Zora Neale Hurston Collection contains a wealth of documentation pertaining to Hurston's life and work. Today, Hurston is heralded as a renowned author, folklorist, and anthropologist. However, her final days were marred by hardship and poverty. Tossed into a fire, Hurston's papers were badly singed and nearly lost altogether. Most of the collection is in fragile condition from the fire damage and has been encapsulated in velum to prevent further deterioration (Special and Area Studies Collection, 2008). The collection includes correspondences, manuscripts, fieldnotes, and biographical materials. The UF Libraries does not maintain the only Zora Neale Hurston archival and manuscript collection. Other collections of varying sizes and scopes are maintained by the New York Public Library, the Library of Congress, and Yale University Libraries.

Special Collections with Significant African American Holdings

In addition to the 28 African American Special Collections, there are many other special and area studies collection with materials pertaining to African Americans. While these collections are not directly focused on acquiring information about or by African Americans, they do include relevant subcollections or significant holdings.

The Baldwin Library of Historic Children's Literature is a world-class collection of historic and contemporary children's books, including a robust selection of works by Black authors and illustrators writing for children and young adult audiences. It also includes historic books from the 18th and 19th centuries which depict racist representations of African and African-descended peoples. The collection of these controversial materials is important to research in the development and perpetuation of racial stereotypes through popular literature. Materials in this collection are non-circulating, but many titles exist in the public domain and are digitized in UFDC.

The Latin American & Caribbean Studies Collection (LACC) maintains both circulating general collection materials and a few special collections pertaining to African Americans and the African Diaspora. The general collection supports interdisciplinary and transnational Black Studies scholarship. African American, Afro-Caribbean, and Afro-Latinx materials are integrated into the LACC circulating collection, thus bolstering the visibility of Black histories, experiences, cultures, and identities within Latin American and Caribbean Studies scholarship. LACC also contains four separate colonial archival collections pertaining to slavery in the Caribbean, with papers from Saint Dominique, Haiti, and France ("Latin American and Caribbean Collection," n.d.).

The Popular Culture Collections contains two subcollections significant to African American Studies. Firstly, the Jim Liversidge Collection focuses on American pop culture history from 1900-2013. It contains documents, audiovisual materials, and memorabilia from many African American films, television shows, and theatrical productions ("Jim Liversidge Collection," n.d.). Secondly, the Belknap Collection for Performing Arts is an archival collection of 19th and 20th century music and theater ("Belknap Collection," n.d.). The collection includes creative works by African Americans such as playbills, sheet music, recordings, and more.

The Rare Books Collection is an eclectic mix of unique and hard-to-find materials. This collection contains the early African American Studies Collection, which was relocated and removed from circulation in the 1970s for the protection of these materials. Today, the Rare Books Collection selection of African American materials "traces Black experiences in literature, culture, and politics from the eve of the American Revolution to the present day" (Weijer, n.d.). The selections are categories into two broad themes: early African American literature and African American political culture.

Online Resources

With advancements in library technologies, much of the African American Studies research conducted at the University of Florida is supported by digital resources. These resources include digitized and born-digital content.

DIGITAL COLLECTIONS

The UF Digital Collections (UFDC) are comprised of over 300 digital collections. Within UFDC, there are several subcollections pertaining to African American Studies including digitized Special and Area Studies Collection content. UFDC hosts several collections relevant to African American Studies research and curriculum. Among these collections is the Samuel Proctor Oral History Program Collection, which contains the Joel Buchanan Archive of African American Oral History. The Buchanan Archive is an ever-growing collection of near

1,000 interview recordings and transcripts on African Americans experiences in the Gulf South. Another substantial collection is the Digital Library of the Caribbean (DLoC), a cooperative digital library of Caribbean resources supported by 82 partnering institutions. DLoC provides digital access to a wide range of subcollections, including the Vodou Archive and the U.S. Virgin Islands History and Culture Project. UFDC also hosts the Florida Digital Newspaper Library, which contains historic African American newspapers from Jacksonville and Tampa.

DATABASES & JOURNALS

Among the most in-demand library resources are online databases and journals. Access to these resources is available to University affiliates (including students, faculty, and staff) through subscriptions and access fees paid by the Libraries. Numerous African American Studies journals (for example, *The Black Scholar* and *the Journal of Black Studies*) are available through large multidisciplinary databases, like EBSCO, Academic Search Premier, JSTOR, and ProQuest. Additionally, the Libraries subscribe to specialty databases focused on African American experiences, such as the African American Biographical Database, 19th Century African American Newspapers, and the Black Studies Center.

Research Support Services and Instruction

Since 2016, with the creation of the African American Studies Librarian position, library patrons have been able to consult a subject specialist for assistance in locating resources and information in this area. In my four years at UF, I have supported African American Studies research by faculty, students, and staff through in-depth research consultations, library instruction sessions, and the development of a comprehensive library research guide.

For underrepresented and marginalized users, academic libraries at predominantly white institutions can be uninviting places where oppressive systems are replicated. My role as the African American Studies Librarian compels me to consistently combat user's library anxiety through strategic and purposeful librarianship practices. Users experience library anxiety for many reasons, one source being the professional standards of organizing and classifying information. The disbursal of materials across the LC classes often leads to confusion and makes the search process time consuming and labor-intensive. Additionally, when employing search techniques, users often encounter (and are compelled to use) racially and culturally insensitive subject heading terms and phrases. The centralization of whiteness within the LC systems contributes to the library anxiety that users, especially African American and underrepresented students, frequently experience when doing research (Howard and Knowlton, 2019, p. 78). As a result, my approach to instruction, consultation, and resource development is always shifting to adapt to users' unique and evolving needs.

Each semester, I facilitate library research instruction sessions and workshops with African American Studies and cross-listed courses. Using student-centered pedagogies, my instruction sessions aim to foster students' confidence in their abilities to navigate the research process and produce high-quality, independent scholarship (Campbell & Birch, 2018). My instruction sessions are informed by the Association for College and Research Libraries (ACRL) *Framework for Information Literacy for Higher Education* (2015), as well as student-centered and democratic teaching practices. Within these sessions (Table 4.2), students gain a fundamental understanding of the library system, what resources and information are available to users, and how to access that information for their projects. Students also learn about the social science research process, as well as strategies to manage their projects and avoid information fatigue. Each session is tailored to address course themes and assignments.

Library instruction sessions are a powerful tool for building a rapport with African American Studies students. As a result, these sessions often lead to one-on-one research consultations after the fact, in which students receive direct support. Students are also often referred directly to me from their instructor. Alternatively, I work directly

Table 4.2. African American Studies & Interdisciplinary Library Instruction Statistics, 2016-2020.

Academic Year	Sessions Taught
2016-2017	6
2017-2018	7
2018-2019	10
2019-2020	5
Total	28

with course instructors to coordinate an embedded librarianship experience whereby I engage with students at multiple points during the semester and/or students are required to seek consultation as part of their grade.

Through research consultations (Table 4.3), students can workshop their ideas and receive individualized assistance in crafting and executing their research assignments. The research consultation is my opportunity, as a librarian, to teach library-searching skills and build students' confidence and comfortability as library users. This process is collaborative, whereby students are treated as experts in their own learning. Their expertise is complemented by my own subject and professional expertise. This approach to consultations shifts the power dynamic away from me as the librarian and establishes an even playing field for discussing and exploring research ideas, thus helping the students to understand that research is a conversation and to find their scholarly voice (Ford, 2019, p. 605).

My instructional and consultation pedagogies greatly inform my approach to developing online African American library resources. Libraries often utilize LibGuides (also called library or research guides) to compile themed content to help users quickly locate library information and resources. Over the years, I have created multiple LibGuides on various topics, including mass incarceration, oral history, and open resources for K-12 teachers on African and African American experiences. However, my primary LibGuide is the African American

Table 4.3: Research Consultation Statistics, 2016-2020.

Academic Year	Consultation Conducted
2016-2017	40
2017-2018	81
2018-2019	29
2019-2020	45
Total	195

Library Resource Guide, which is a one-stop shop for accessing African American library collections and materials, as well as core African American Studies databases and journals.

The LibGuide also replicates some information introduced to students through instruction or research consultation sessions. It includes a page on the research process and resources for project, time, and citation management. During the COVID-19 pandemic and the transition to remote learning, usages statistics for the African American Library Resources Guide has dramatically increased from the previous year (Table 4.4).

Table 4.4: African American Library Resource LibGuide Usage Statistics, 2016-2020.

Academic Year	LibGuide Views
2016-2017	1,212
2017-2018	1,417
2018-2019	1,560
2019-2020	3,727
Total	7,916

The guide also features project exploration resources for students struggling to identify a topic of interest to them. One particularly unique feature of this LibGuide is the "Community Resources" page, which connects students to campus and local services (for example, mental health resources, crisis centers, reproductive health clinics, and food pantries) to support their overall wellbeing. The LibGuide is intended to teach students who have not participated in an African American Studies library instruction or research consultation session.

Grantsmanship

In addition to collections management, research support services, and instruction, the UF Libraries are actively engaged in grant-seeking to facilitate the exploration of innovative research and collaborative opportunities. Under the leadership of the Libraries' Grants Manager, Bess de Farber, library faculty and staff have won numerous awards to advance the African American library collection's development, research, and outreach. Librarians also frequently serve as principal investigators and project team members for internal and external grant projects. Leveraging their subject expertise, practical skillsets, and a wide-casting net of professional relationships, librarians are key partners in the development and implementation of successful grant projects.

ENHANCING THE LEGACY DIGITAL COLLECTIONS OF THE SPOHP FOR IMPROVED USER ACCESS

This 2019-2020 project was funded by the Libraries' Strategic Opportunities Grant to comprehensively optimize the content discoverability of the Samuel Proctor Oral History Programs' collection in UFDC (Birch, 2019). The project team developed and implemented a new collection structure and metadata scheme to support the rapidly growing collection, which contains a substantial number of digitized and born-digital African American oral histories. As a result of this project, the project team developed a model for re-structuring ineffective digital collections while also laying the groundwork for major external grant-seeking efforts.

DIGITAL PUBLISHING ON BLACK LIFE AND HISTORY COLLABORATIVE MEETING

This 2019-2020 pilot project leveraged the positionality of the UF Libraries to connect people with Black heritage information and digital humanities resources. The focus of the project was to facilitate collaborative encounters in a workshop environment between scholars, cultural heritage professionals, and community members towards the development of a sustainable and community-centered Black digital humanities pedagogy (Birch, 2020). Funded by a Libraries' Strategic Opportunities Grant, the project was a partnered effort between the UF Libraries, the AFRO Publishing Without Walls initiative at the University of Illinois at Urbana-Champaign, and the Florida African American Heritage Preservation Network.

FILM ON A BOAT: DIGITIZING HISTORICAL NEWSPAPERS OF THE CARIBBEAN

This ongoing project is funded by the Council on Library Information Resources' Digitizing Hidden Collections grant program, which has awarded approximately $20 million in aid since 2015 ("Digitizing Hidden Collections", n.d.). In partnership with the University of Puerto Rico-Rio Piedras, the UF Libraries is engaged in a three-year project to digitize Caribbean newspaper content published in Antigua, the Bahamas, Barbados, Dominica, Guyana, St. Lucia, Trinidad and Tobago, and Puerto Rico (Durant et al., 2018). Digitized content will be hosted in UFDC with free open access and will support transnational Black Studies scholarship.

INTERSECTIONS: RESEARCH-INTO-TEACHING GRANTS

In 2018, the UF Center for the Humanities and the Public Sphere and the UF Libraries awarded in $120,000 in re-granted funds from the Andrew W. Mellon Foundation. In total, four projects were awarded, each including librarians as key leaders or partners (Center for the Humanities and the Public Sphere, n.d.). Two of the awarded projects relate to African American Studies research and curriculum at UF: Intersections on Black & Latinx Global Identities and Intersections on Mass Incarceration.

Exhibitions

The UF Libraries' exhibitions program provides an opportunity for members of the local and campus communities to engage with library resources and materials in new ways. The purpose of the Libraries' exhibition program is to "promote interdisciplinary approaches to research and teaching and stimulate intellectual curiosity ("Exhibits," n.d.). Led by Exhibits Director, Lourdes Santamaria-Wheeler, the UF Libraries offer a robust annual program of physical and online exhibits. Since 2018, there have been several exhibitions focused on African American histories.

Racism, Representation, and Resistance in Children's Literature, 1800-2015 (Alteri et al., 2018) examines the perpetuation of racial stereotypes as presented in historical children's literature through derogatory modes of illustrations, characterization, and dialect. It also explores the impact of Black authors who challenged and subverted prevailing racist representations and ideologies in the early 20th century. Initially displayed in the Smathers Library gallery from August 13 to October 5, 2018, this exhibition continues to be available in an online format. It features materials from the UF Baldwin Library of Historic Children's Literature.

The Black Florida Educators: Secret Social Justice Advocates, 1920-1960 (Houchen et al., 2018) exhibition (see Figures 4.1 and 4.2) was a curatorial collaboration between the UF Center for the Study of Race and Race Relations (CSRRR), the City of Gainesville's A. Quinn Jones Museum and Cultural Center, and the UF Libraries. The exhibition was on display in the Smathers Library gallery from October 22 to December 18, 2018 and is accessible as an online exhibition. It commemorates the 60th anniversary of desegregation at the University of Florida and celebrates the hidden histories of Black educators under de jure segregation.

Black Thursday: UF's Black Campus Movement (Birch et al., 2020) is an online-only exhibition that was launched in June 2020. It details an organized sit-in by the UF Black Student Union in 1971, as documented in the UF student newspaper, *The Alligator*. The UF Libraries maintains a full run of *The Alligator* (now *The Independent Florida Alligator*) from 1912 to the present in print, microfilm, and/or digitized formats.

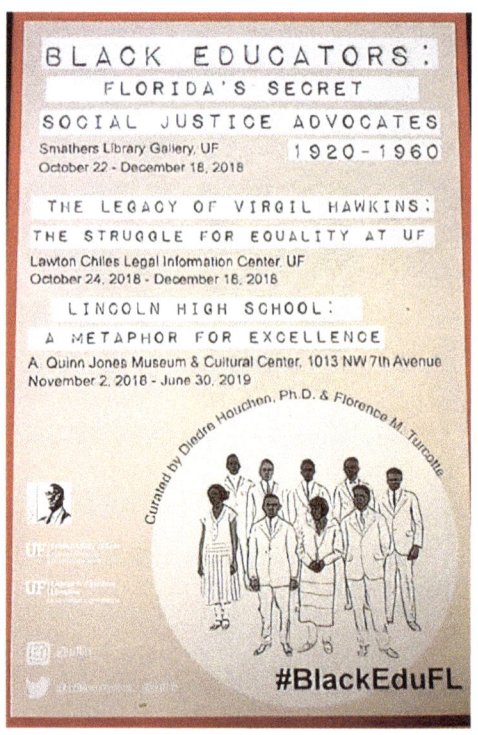

Figure 4.1: 4.1 Exhibition poster, "Black Educators: 1920-1960," created by Dr. Deidre Houchen, UF Law School, and Florence Turcotte, UF Libraries' Literary Collections Archivist. (UF Library Archives)

Figure 4.2: Black Florida Educators attend conference at A. Quinn Jones School, 1925. (*UF Library Archives*)

The Libraries' exhibition program aims to support course curricula and student learning. African American Studies classes have toured library exhibitions to engage with primary archival resources and enhance classroom discussions of course topics and themes. While most of the Libraries' exhibitions are curated by library and teaching faculty and showcase library resources and materials, the Libraries also partner with outside organizations to bring traveling exhibitions to the University.

Looking Forward

In the next 50 years, the Libraries will remain a key partner in the advancement of African American Studies research and instruction at the University of Florida. Through collections, resources, services, and collaborative research, the UF Libraries ensure continued support for African American Studies Program faculty, students, and staff, as well as the broader campus and local communities. Ongoing and increased collaboration between library specialists and African American Studies personnel will be an essential component in the Program's transition to a departmental structure. As African American Studies continues to grow and flourish at UF, the Libraries' collections must grow in tandem to support emerging research, the expansion of undergraduate course offerings, and the eventual establishment of graduate degree programs. Through transformative collaboration with instructional faculty and the community-at-large, the Libraries will continue to pursue several ongoing initiatives and objects. Through the annual acquisitions program, I seek to increase the representation of Black voices within the Libraries' collections. The Libraries will also continue to enhance the visibility of its African American collections and resources through the curation of physical and online exhibitions, the coordination and facilitation of dynamic public programs, and the pursuit of digital library and scholarship initiatives.

Chapter 4 Study Questions

1. The Libraries at the University of Florida serve as the major research infrastructure. Explain.
2. The African American Studies Collections at the University of Florida Library are substantial, special, circulating, online, and enriched by cross-campus, and community-oriented collaboration. What has been your experience in accessing African American Studies materials?
3. What do you consider to be the importance of African American Studies Collections to your field of studies at the University of Florida?

References

Alteri, S., Birch, S., Huet, H., & Santamaria-Wheeler, L. (2018). *Racism, Representation, and Resistance in Children's Literature, 1800-2015*. University of Florida Libraries. http://exhibits.uflib.ufl.edu/RacismRepresentation/

Baldwin Library of Historic Children's Literature (n.d.). University of Florida Libraries. https://library-baldwin.sites.medinfo.ufl.edu/

Belknap Collection for the Performing Arts (n.d.). University of Florida Libraries. https://library-popular.sites.medinfo.ufl.edu/performing-arts-collection/

Birch, S. (2019). *Fixer-Uppers: Restructuring an Inefficient Digital Collection* [Conference presentation]. Digital Library Federation Forum, Tampa, FL, United States.

Birch, S. (2020). *Digital Collaborations Workshop on Black History in Florida: Final Report*. University of Florida Libraries. https://ufdc.ufl.edu/IR00011157/00001

Birch, S. (n.d.). *African American Studies Library Resource Guide*. University of Florida Libraries. https://guides.uflib.ufl.edu/aas

Birch, S., Ronan, J., & Santamaria-Wheeler, L. (2020). *Black Thursday: UF's Black Campus Movement*. University of Florida Libraries. http://exhibits.uflib.ufl.edu/BlackThursdayUF

Campbell, L. & Birch, S. (2018) *Meeting Students' Goals: Practicing Learning-Centered Library Instruction* [Conference presentation]. Florida Association of College & Research Libraries Conference, Ft. Myers, FL, United States.

Center for the Humanities and the Public Sphere (n.d.) *UF Intersections*. University of Florida. https://intersections.humanities.ufl.edu/

Coates, S. (2019). *A Guide to the Black Student Union at the University of Florida Records*. University of Florida Libraries. http://www.library.ufl.edu/spec/archome/MS147.htm

Douglas, P. (2017). *A Guide to the A. Quinn Jones Collection*. University of Florida Libraries. http://www.library.ufl.edu/spec/pkyonge/jones.htm

Duckworth, S. (2015). *A Guide to the James S. Haskins Papers*. University of Florida Libraries. http://www.library.ufl.edu/spec/manuscript/guides/haskins.htm

Durant, F., Taylor, L. N., de Farber, B., Torres-Alamo, M., Vargas Betancourt, M., Reakes, P., Dinsmore, C., Van Kleeck, D., Hines, A., Huet, H., Birch, S., Perry, L., de Roche, S., Renner, R., Soto, A., Moczygemba, S., Young, H., Millán Díaz, J. A., Ordóñez Mercado, M. E., & Torres, S. (2018). Film on a Boat: Digitizing Historical Newspapers of the Caribbean [Grant proposal]. University of Florida Libraries, University of Puerto Rico, and the Digital Library of the Caribbean. http://ufdc.ufl.edu/AA00064298/00001

Exhibits (n.d.). University of Florida Libraries. http://www.exhibits.uflib.ufl.edu

Florida Academic Repository (n.d.). University of Florida Libraries. https://flare.uflib.ufl.edu/

Ford, R. (2019, December). The Long Conversation: Reflections on Science Librarianship. *C&RL News*, 80(11), 604-605. https://crln.acrl.org/index.php/crlnews/article/view/24191/31989. https://doi.org/10.5860/crln.80.11.604

Framework for Information Literacy for Higher Education. (2015). Association of College & Research Libraries. http://www.ala.org/acrl/standards/ilframework

Houchen, D., Turcotte, F., Santamaria-Wheeler, L. (2018). *Black Educators: Florida's Secret Social Justice Advocates, 1920-1960.* University of Florida Libraries. http://exhibits.uflib.ufl.edu/FloridaBlackEducators

Howard, S.A. & Knowlton, S.A. (2018). Browsing through Bias: The Library of Congress Classification and Subject Headings for African American Studies and LGBTQIA Studies. *Library Trends,* 67(1), 74-88. https://doi.org/10.1353/lib.2018.0026

Latin American and Caribbean Collection (n.d.). University of Florida Libraries. https://library-lacc.sites.medinfo.ufl.edu/

Liversidge, J. (2008). *A Guide to the Jim Liversidge Collection.* University of Florida Libraries. http://www.library.ufl.edu/spec/belknap/liversidge.htm

Department of Cataloging and Acquisitions (n.d.) *Library of Congress Classification Outline: Class E-F – History of the Americas.* Library of Congress. https://www.loc.gov/aba/cataloging/classification/lcco/lcco_ef.pdf

Digitizing Hidden Collections (n.d.). Council for Library Information Research. https://www.clir.org/hiddencollections/

Kisling, Jr. V. N. (n.d.-a). *George A. Smathers Libraries History: Electronic Era, 1984-2003.* University of Florida Libraries. https://communications.uflib.ufl.edu/at-a-glance/smathers-library-history/electronic-era-1984-2003/

Kisling, Jr. V. N. (n.d.-b). *George A. Smathers Libraries History: First Library and Professional Development, 1918-1937.* University of Florida Libraries. https://communications.uflib.ufl.edu/at-a-glance/smathers-library-history/first-library-and-professional-development-1918-1937/

Kisling, Jr. V. N. (n.d.-c). *George A. Smathers Libraries History: Genesis: The University Libraries, 1905-1918.* University of Florida Libraries. https://communications.uflib.ufl.edu/at-a-glance/smathers-library-history/genesis-the-university-libraries-1905-1918/

Kisling, Jr. V. N. (n.d.-d). *George A. Smathers Libraries History: Resurgence and Growth, 1946-1967.* University of Florida Libraries. https://communications.uflib.ufl.edu/at-a-glance/smathers-library-history/resurgence-and-growth-1946-1967/

Rare Books Collection (n.d.). University of Florida Libraries. https://library-rarebooks.sites.medinfo.ufl.edu/

A Guide to the Zora Neale Hurston Papers (n.d.). University of Florida Libraries. http://www.library.ufl.edu/spec/manuscript/hurston/hurston.htm

Renz, J. H. (Ed.) (1974). *A survey of the holdings of the University of Florida Libraries.* University of Florida. 28-29.

University of Florida Digital Collections (n.d.). University of Florida Libraries. https://ufdc.ufl.edu/

Weijer, N. (n.d.). *African American Studies Library Resources Guide: Rare Books.* University of Florida Libraries. https://guides.uflib.ufl.edu/aas/rarebooks

Chapter 5: Selected Works of African American Studies Faculty at the University of Florida by Sharon D. Wright Austin

Abstract: One of the primary functions of the Institutions of Higher Education is research, "the systematic investigation and study of materials and sources in order to establish facts and reach new conclusions." As a part of the academic mission of the University of Florida, this chapter examines the contributions of the faculty in African American Studies at the University. While the faculty has an impressive list of research production since the establishment of the African American Studies Program in 1969, the focus in this chapter is on selected major research publications that have attracted national and international recognitions and awards. It also documents other major publications by the faculty towards knowledge production and the advancement of African American Studies.

Introduction

The stature of African American Studies programs and departments is primarily based on the research of their faculty members, especially at Research I universities like the University of Florida. The core faculty of the UF African American Studies Program have done an enormous amount of prestigious research on various topics. Many are also sought-after public intellectuals who have appeared on television and print outlets. In this chapter, I will discuss the impact of this research since the program's inception in 1969. This research includes a diverse array of theories and methodologies pertaining to the study of African Americans. Some faculty members have also conducted research on their community service, experiential educational, and social justice activities. Others have published books and articles that compared and contrasted the experiences of people of African descent in the United States to those in the wider African Diaspora. Finally, the faculty has co-authored research with undergraduate and graduate students. While the faculty has an impressive list of research production since the program's establishment, the focus in this chapter is on selected major research publications that have attracted national recognition. It also documents other major publications by the faculty towards knowledge-production and the advancement of African American Studies. The selected publications by the affiliate faculty of the African American Studies Program at UF are included in the Appendix. I will begin with a discussion of the program's origin and evolution.

The Early Years of the UF African American Studies Program

After the April 1968 assassination of Dr. Martin Luther King Jr., African Americans, including college students, increasingly participated in demonstrations of massive civil unrest to demand that America make good on its promises of democracy and equality. Part of the change demanded was greater access to higher education. Many Predominately White Institutions (PWIs) responded by granting symbolic access to Black students. Once on campus, students again protested for substantial inclusion in curriculum and increased presence of Black students, staff, and faculty. Responding to increasing nationwide student activism, President Robert Smith announced the creation of a Black Studies Department at San Francisco State University in September 1968. This is recognized as the first such department in the nation. Dr. Nathan Hare, a sociology professor, was named Acting Chair.

In November 1968, students at the University of Florida went on strike against the administration and demanded, among other things, inclusion of Black Studies courses as a part of a Black Studies Program with the capacity to grant Bachelor's Degrees in Black Studies, as well as increased admission of Black students and creation of positions for Black faculty members. Similar student strikes took place at many other institutions. Thus, it is clear that the development of the African American Studies Program at the University of Florida was part of a worldwide push for enfranchisement by Africans throughout the Diaspora, and a national development of student activism for equality and equity in higher education.

Key figures in the establishment of the African American Studies Program at UF included administrators: Dr. Manning J. Dauer, Chairman, Social Sciences Division; Dr. Harry H. Sisler, Dean, College of Arts and Sciences; and Dr. Harold Stahmer, Associate Dean, College of Arts and Sciences. The faculty who assisted in the earliest development of the program included: Dr. Hunt Davis, Jr., (History Professor); Dr. Seldon Henry, (History), Dr. Steve Conroy, (Social Sciences), Dr. James Morrison (Political Science); and Dr. Augustus M. Burns (Social Sciences, History). The students who played a role in the program's development include Samuel Taylor (the President of Black Student Union in 1970 and the first Black Student Government President in 1972), David Horne (Doctoral candidate in History), Emerson Thompson (Undergraduate student), and Larry Jordan (Undergraduate student).

The Program was established in 1969 and enrolled its first students during the Fall 1970 semester. In 1971, the Program awarded the first certificate in African American Studies, but during that year UF only had three African American faculty members out of a total 2,600 faculty members and only 387 Black students, including "foreign" Black students. In 2006, the Program began offering an African American Studies minor and began offering an African American Studies major in the Fall 2013 semester. After many years of efforts, the University now has a Black student enrollment of less than 10% and a Black faculty presence of less than 5%. Although many things have been accomplished in the Program and concerning the increased enrollment and employment of African American students, faculty, and staff, many challenges remain.

Since 1970, the following individuals have served as Director of the UF African American Studies Program: Dr. Ronald C. Foreman, 1970-2000, Ph.D. in Mass Communications, University of Illinois; Dr.

Darryl M. Scott, 2000-2003, Ph.D. in History, Stanford University; Dr. Marilyn M. Thomas-Houston, 2003-2004, Ph.D. in Cultural Anthropology, New York University; Dr. Terry Mills, 2004-2006, Ph.D. in Sociology, University of Southern California; Dr. Faye Harrison, 2006- 2010, Ph.D. in Anthropology, Stanford University; Dr. Stephanie Evans, 2010- 2011, Ph.D. in African American Studies, University of Massachusetts, Amherst; Dr. Sharon Austin, 2011- 2019, Ph.D. in Political Science, The University of Tennessee, Knoxville; and Dr. David Canton, 2020-Present Ph.D. in History, Temple University.

Many African American Studies departments have achieved distinction because of their emphasis on certain types of research. For example, Temple University has been known for the Afrocentric paradigms developed by Dr. Molefi Asante. While some programs and departments such as Harvard merge the study of Africans with the study of Africans (that is, the African Diaspora), others such as UCLA primarily emphasize the study of African Americans. UF's African American Studies Program integrates knowledge about African Americans with information about African descendants in other diasporic situations within the Americas, the Afro-Atlantic, and the broader African World. Using and reworking the theories of traditional academic disciplines, the African American Studies Program at UF specializes in disseminating knowledge about African descendants in the United States (encompassing African Americans, African Caribbeans, Afro-Latinos, and African immigrants [sometimes all labeled African American in the pan-ethnic sense]) as well as in other diasporic settings. In this section of the chapter, I will examine the selected works of UF African American Studies core faculty members listed in alphabetical order as follows: Dr. Sharon Wright Austin, Dr. David A. Canton, Dr. Manoucheka Celeste, Dr. Stephanie Evans, Dr. Faye V. Harrison, Dr. Ibram X. Kendi, Dr. Ashely Robertson Preston, Dr. Daryl Michael Scott, Dr. Gwendolyn Zoharah Simmons, and Dr. Marilyn Thomas-Houston. A display of faculty books was organized by African American Studies Librarian Stephanie Birch at the Smathers Library for the AASP 50th Anniversary Commemorations (Figure 5.1.).

Figure 5.1: Books published by AASP faculty were on display at Smathers Library during the 50th Anniversary Commemoration. (Photo by B. M. Gordon)

The Contemporary Research of African American Studies Core Faculty Members

DR. SHARON AUSTIN'S RESEARCH ON SOUTHERN AND URBAN POLITICS

Dr. Austin's career began at the University of Florida in 2001. She worked as both an affiliate faculty member, core faculty member, and Director of the African American Studies Program. During her eight-year tenure as Program Director, the Program gained approval for its major and had the largest number of majors of any African American Studies entity in the country. In addition, she heavily emphasized both undergraduate and graduate research by encouraging students to coauthor research with their professors and present their research at academic conferences.

Dr. Austin's research focuses on African American women's political behavior, African American mayoral elections, rural African American political activism, and African American political participation. She is the author of three books. Her first, *Race, Power, and Political Emergence in Memphis* (Garland 2000), examines Black political behavior and empowerment strategies in the city of Memphis. Each chapter of the text focuses on three themes: mobilization, emergence, and incorporation. By analyzing the effects of race on Black political development in Memphis, scholars will be able to examine broader questions about its effects in other cities. How do political machines use substantial Black electorates to their advantage? What forms of protest do Black communities conduct to rebel against machine rule? What primary mobilization tactics have Black citizens used during the different periods of their political development? Why do Blacks mobilize more quickly in some cities? In cities with large and predominantly Black populations, what elements prevent Black candidates from winning citywide races? What constraints do newly elected Black mayors face? What benefits do Black citizens gain from their representation? After a predominantly Black governing coalition is elected, what obstacles remain? Can Black citizens translate proportional representation into strong political incorporation? How much power can African Americans realistically expect to gain in cities? This book is the most comprehensive case study of the city's political scene written to date. The text primarily shows that white racism is not the only obstacle to Black political development. Black citizens can have population majorities but lose elections for other reasons. Their ability to win elections and gain full incorporation depends heavily on whether they minimize internal conflict and establish coalitions with middle-class citizens and the business establishment.

Dr. Austin's second book, *The Transformation of Plantation Politics in the Mississippi Delta: Black Politics, Concentrated Poverty, and Social Capital in the Mississippi Delta* (State University of New York Press 2006), explores the effects of Black political exclusion, the sharecropping system, and white resistance on the Mississippi Delta's current economic and political situation. Her interviews with residents of the region shed light on the transformations and legacies of the Delta's political and economic institutions. While African Americans now hold most of the major political offices in the region and are no longer formally excluded from political participation, educational opportunities, or lucrative jobs, Wright Austin shows that white wealth and Black poverty continue to be the norm partly because of the deeply entrenched legacies of the Delta's history. Contributing to a greater theoretical understanding of Black political efforts, this book demonstrates a need for a strong level of Black social capital, intergroup capital, financial capital, political capital, and human capital in the form of skilled, educated workers.

Her third book, *The Caribbeanization of Black Politics: Race, Group Consciousness, and Political Participation in America* (State University of New York Press 2018), explores the impact of ethnic diversification in African American communities on the prospects for Black political empowerment. Focusing on Boston, Chicago, Miami, and New York City—cities that for the last several years have experienced an influx of Black immigrants—she surveyed more than 2,000 African Americans, Cape Verdeans, Haitians, and West Indians. Although many studies conclude that African American's group consciousness causes them to participate in politics at higher rates when socioeconomic status is controlled for, Wright Austin analyzes whether this is true for other Black groups. She assesses the current political incorporation of these groups by looking at data on public officeholders and by examining political coalitions and conflicts among the groups; she also discusses the possible future of Black political development in these cities.

Her latest edited book is entitled *Political Black Girl Magic: The Elections and Governance of Black Female Mayors* (Temple University Press, unpublished manuscript) and examines the experiences of Black female mayors from two perspectives--the acquisition of power (their campaigns) and the actual exercise of power (their governance). The main research questions are, "What is the influence of race, gender, or the combination of both on the mayoral campaigns and governance of Black women?" and "What are the most significant obstacles for Black women when running for mayoral offices and governing as mayors?" The chapters will assess the campaigns and governance of Black female mayors in several cities including Atlanta, Baltimore, Charlotte, Chicago, Flint, Pontiac, Rochester, San Francisco, Tacoma, and Washington, D.C. She is also coauthoring a book with Dr. Angela K. Lewis-Maddox of the University of Alabama, Birmingham on Black women and the presidency. Using the intersectionality framework that examines the impact of both racism and sexism on Black female candidates, Austin and Lewis-Maddox examine, first, what racial and gender barriers have Black women encountered in seeking the vice-presidential and presidential offices? Second, what impact have Black female voters had on presidential election outcomes? These will be the first books examining Black women as mayors and presidential candidates and as a distinct constituency with the power to determine election results.

DR. DAVID CANTON AND AFRICAN AMERICAN HISTORY

David Canton began his service as the current Director of the African American Studies Program during the Fall 2020 semester. He is currently working diligently toward the goal of attaining departmental status for the program. Dr. Canton is the author of *Raymond Pace Alexander: A New Negro Lawyer Fights for Civil Rights in Philadelphia* (University Press of Mississippi 2010) and several other scholarly works. In his book, Dr. Canton discusses the life and work of Raymond Pace Alexander (1897-1974), an African American Philadelphia attorney. A Harvard Law School graduate, Alexander was motivated to engage in activism after enduring vehement racial discrimination.

In the book, Professor Canton details Alexander's tireless participation in the National Bar Association, which is the oldest and largest association of African American lawyers and judges. Raymond Alexander cooperated with prominent attorneys such as Charles Hamilton Houston, William Hastie, and Thurgood Marshall in the fight for civil rights both in Philadelphia and nationwide. Although Hamilton Houston and Marshall achieved prominence because of their work that set the stage for the *Brown v. Board of Education of Topeka, Kansas* (1954) case and for other civil rights cases, few people are familiar with the contributions of Pace

Alexander. All of the aforementioned men believed that racial equity and change could be accomplished via the litigation strategy.

In the book that was an expansion of his doctoral dissertation, Professor Canton refers to Pace Alexander as a "New Negro lawyer." During the World War I period, the New Negro lawyers advocated for civil rights, economic independence, and integration while also emphasizing Black pride (Canton, 2001). These individuals played a major role in the civil rights struggle by working for the National Association for the Advancement of Colored People (NAACP) and other civil rights organizations. Although they mostly worked in Northern cities, their efforts had implications in cities all over the country (Canton, 2001). Alexander was heavily influenced by Booker T. Washington's self-help concept with W.E.B. Du Bois' agitation theories. During the height of his activism, most of Alexander's clients had connections with Black businesses, churches, and fraternal organizations (Canton, 2010).

Raymond Pace Alexander achieved several civil rights accomplishments before the height of the modern civil rights movement. For example, his collaborations with civil rights organizations resulted in the desegregation of an all-white elementary school in Berwin, Pennsylvania during the 1930s. After World War II, some Black activists had Communist affiliations because of the Party's emphasis on racial equality. However, he became an anti-Communist activist who cooperated with both white and African American activists in the struggle for civil rights. During the sixties, Alexander criticized the rhetoric used by Black Power activists, but agreed with their focus on Black political empowerment, economic self-sufficiency, and the need to study Black history. Although he spent decades fighting for racial justice, some of the younger Black Power activists criticized his tactics and those of other older Black civil rights activists. Dr. Canton wrote a fascinating account of an unsung hero who fought for rights that many Americans sometimes take for granted.

DR. MANOUCHEKA CELESTE AND TRAVELLING BLACKNESS

In 2018, *Race, Gender, and Citizenship in the African Diaspora: Travelling Blackness* (Routledge Press 2017) won the National Communication Association's Diamond Anniversary Book Award. With the exception of slave narratives, there are few stories of Black international migration in U.S. news and popular culture. This book is interested in stratified immigrant experiences, diverse Black experiences, and the intersection of Black and immigrant identities. Citizenship, as it is commonly understood today in the public sphere, is a legal issue, yet scholars have done much to move beyond this popular view and situate citizenship in the context of economic, social, and political positioning. The book shows that citizenship in all of its forms is often rhetorically, representationally, and legally negated by Blackness, and considers the ways that Blackness, and representations of Blackness, impact one's ability to travel across national and social borders and become a citizen. This book is a story of citizenship and the ways that race, gender, and class shape national belonging, with Haiti, Cuba, and the United States as the primary sites of examination.

After an introduction, the book includes chapters entitled "Framing Cubans and Haitians in *The New York Times*: Enduring Imprints of Political History"; "Communists and Immigrants: Images of Cubans and Haitians"; "Negotiating Media Representations and Cultural Icons: Audience and Group-Identity"; and "A Love Story: Media and an (New) Exceptional Haitian-American Political Subject, and a Conclusion." Dr. Celeste's other publications appear in journals and book chapters including *Black Camera* and *Feminist Media Histories*. She is committed to critical scholarship on representations of Blackness, including public scholarship, with her work published in *The Seattle Times*, The Dart Center for Journalism & Trauma, and *Spark: Elevating Scholarship on Social Issues*. Dr. Celeste is currently working on a second book project, *The Wailing Black Woman: Interrupting Narratives of Life, Death, and Citizenship in Media and the Public Sphere*, where she centers Black women to examine media portrayals of Black notions of life, death, and criminality, exploring the implications of such representations.

DR. STEPHANIE Y. EVANS' INNOVATIVE RESEARCH ON BLACK WOMEN

Dr. Evans has authored or edited six books on topics ranging from Black women's intellectual history to their mental health. In 2007, her first book, *Black Women in the Ivory Tower, 1850-1954*, was published by the University Press of Florida while she served as an Assistant Professor of African American Studies and Women's Studies. Her comprehensive historiography primarily emphasizes the educational contributions of Drs. Anna Julia Cooper and Mary McLeod Bethune. Dr. Cooper was an Oberlin College graduate and also earned a doctorate from the Sorbonne in Paris. Despite her extensive educational record, she spent much of her career teaching high school, but authored A *Voice from the South* in 1892, a book which some refer to as the first Black feminist text. On the other hand, Dr. Bethune founded a small school for Black girls that later evolved into the coeducational Bethune-Cookman College, even though she never attended college herself. She was also a member of President Franklin D. Roosevelt's Black Cabinet. Professor Evans also traces Black women's higher educational experiences from 1850 to the beginning of the modern civil rights movement more generally. The book has two major sections that address their "Educational Attainment" and "Intellectual Legacy." Professor Evans also mentions other Black female educational pioneers such as Fanny Jackson Coppin, Lena Beatrice Morton, and Pauli Murray. One review of her book mentions the significance of these women as the "first of their race and gender to prevail in formerly all-white academic spaces, as well as some of the personal travails they experienced, including rejection and ridicule" (McCluskey, 2008).

Her other research reveals the manner in which Africana women's life writings serve as paradigms for social justice education and portraits of historical wellness, while modeling a sustainable struggle for human rights. Along with Andrea D. Domingue and Tania D. Mitchell, Dr. Evans edited *Black Women and Social Justice Education: Legacies and Lessons* (SUNY Press 2019). In addition, Professor Evans' research has addressed issues involving community engagement. In 2014, SUNY Press published her book *Black Passports: Travel Memoirs as a Tool for Youth Empowerment*. Along with Colette Taylor, Michelle Dunlap, and DeMond Miller, she edited *African Americans and Community Engagement* (SUNY Press 2019). More recently, Dr. Evans has examined the manner in which African American memoirs are guides to self-care, inner peace, and stress management, particularly for survivors of sexual violence. With Kanika Bell and Nsenga Burton, Professor Evans edited *Black Women's Mental Health: Balancing Strength and Vulnerability* (SUNY Press 2017). Her two forthcoming books are *Black Women's Yoga History: Memoirs of Inner Peace* (SUNY Press 2021) and *Black Women's Public Health: Regenerative History, Practice, and Planning* (SUNY Press 2021). She is also the editor for a book series on Black women's wellness for the State University of New York, Albany Press.

THE PIONEERING RESEARCH OF DR. FAYE V. HARRISON

Dr. Faye Venetia Harrison is one of the nation's most accomplished anthropologists and has achieved international acclaim for her pioneering research. For 10 years, she was Professor of Anthropology and African American Studies at UF and also served as Program Director for three years. She served as President of the International Union of Anthropological and Ethnological Sciences from 2013 to 2018. In 2010, she received the Legacy Scholar Award from the Association of Black Anthropologists. Throughout her distinguished career, her research has examined political economy, race, and power in the United States, the United Kingdom, and Jamaica ("Faye V. Harrison," n.d.). This research agenda includes an analysis of the gendered division of labor within Jamaica's urban informal economy; the interplay of gangs, crime, and politics in Jamaica; the impact of neoliberal globalization on everyday life in Jamaica, Cuba, and the United States; racism, antiracism, and human rights in the global context; and critical race feminist methodology as a tool for global research ("Faye V. Harrison," n.d.).

From 2004 to 2014, Dr. Harrison published one single-authored book (*Outsider Within: Reworking Anthropology in the Global Age*, 2008) and two edited books (*Resisting Racism & Xenophobia: Global Perspectives on Race, Gender & Human Rights*, 2005, and the third edition of *Decolonizing Anthropology: Moving Further toward an Anthropology for Liberation,* 2010). The three books reflect her interest in antiracism as a site of human rights struggle (*Resisting Racism*) and in pursuing a critical anthropology of anthropology as a discipline to be "reworked," "decolonized," and "transformed"— untethered from its Eurocentric, white supremacist, colonial past and the afterlife of that history of knowledge and power (*Decolonizing Anthropology* and *Outsider*). *The Routledge Companion to Contemporary Anthropology* describes *Decolonizing Anthropology: Moving Further toward an Anthropology for Liberation* as a «key moment of re-invention» for American anthropology encouraging the re-centering of anthropological work by people of color ("Faye V. Harrison," n.d.).

In *Outsider*, Dr. Harrison reflects on her years of research in African American, African Caribbean, and Afro-Caribbean/Black British Diasporic contexts to inform an anthropological analysis of the forms of structural power and structural violence that shape African descendants' lives, agency, and knowledge production. The book brings a critical anthropological project into a crossroads of knowledge with insights and tools from African American studies, Caribbean studies, and gender/women's studies. *Outsider Within* presents an approach to critically reconstructing the anthropology discipline to better encompass issues of gender and race. Among the nine key changes to the field that Faye V. Harrison advocates are researching in an ethically and politically responsible manner, promoting greater diversity in the discipline, rethinking theory, and committing to a genuine multicultural dialogue. In drawing from materials developed during her distinguished 25-year career in Caribbean and African American studies, Harrison analyzes anthropology's limits and possibilities from an African American woman's perspective, while also challenging anthropologists to work together to transcend stark gender, racial, and national hierarchies. Professor Tony Whitehead noted that: *Outsider Within* is a real winner. The anthropology field has been waiting over three decades for new scholarship on the African diaspora to the New World. This book is a masterpiece of broad scholarship that covers the field›s multiple lineages and legacies, and also draws on literature from a range of other fields: sociology, psychology, women's and feminist studies, popular literature, political science, cultural studies, and more (Whitehead, n.d.).

Audrey Smedley, professor emerita of anthropology at Virginia Commonwealth University, called Harrison, "One of the most gifted and profound writers in anthropology today, it is imperative that her corpus of materials be shared (n.d.)." Finally, Professor Lee D. Baker, author of *From Savage to Negro: Anthropology and the Construction of Race, 1896-1954* said, "Harrison provides a bold vision for anthropology in the twenty-first century. She calls for a collective reworking of anthropology so we can be more responsive to issues of race, gender, and inequality in this century than we were in the last (n.d.)."

In addition, Professor Harrison has published many articles, chapters, encyclopedia entries, review essays, and even some blog posts on issues such as racism and antiracism as sites of struggle within the international human rights regime and the transnational human rights movement. Her research on the Diaspora, particularly the African Diaspora and more recent migrations propelled within it, examines a variety of topics. For example, her work has examined the "gendered activism" of African Diasporic women in the fight for human rights; their racial, gendered, and class consciousness; and their overall fight against racism in groups such as the Network of Afro-Latin American, Afro-Caribbean, and Afro-Diaspora Women. Her work uses conceptual, theoretical, and methodological perspectives to research the national and transnational solidarities and coalitions among Black American, Caribbean, and Latin American women.

Throughout her career, Professor Harrison has contributed to several other important anthologies on the African Diaspora, among them: *Afro-Descendants, Identity, and the Struggle for Development in the Americas*; *Transnational Blackness: Navigating the Global Color Line*; *Afro-Atlantic Dialogues: Anthropology in the Diaspora*; and *Blackness in Latin America and the Caribbean*. Her writings also appear in several significant feminist collections, among them: *Third World Women & the*

Politics of Feminism; Women Writing Culture; Situated Lives: Gender & Culture in Everyday Life; Gender & Globalization: Women Navigating Cultural & Economic Marginalities; and, most recently, Feminist Activist Ethnography (for which she wrote the foreword).

STAMPED FROM THE BEGINNING AND THE RESEARCH OF DR. IBRAM X. KENDI

Dr. Ibram X. Kendi is now one of the nation's foremost authorities on issues pertaining to race. Before arriving at UF, Professor Kendi published the Black Campus Movement book that won the W.E.B. Du Bois Award. While employed as an Assistant Professor of African American Studies and History at UF in 2016, Professor Kendi won the National Book Award, winning for his #1 New York Times bestselling book Stamped from the Beginning: The Definitive History of Racist Ideas in America. At 34 years old, he was the youngest-ever winner of the National Book Award for Nonfiction.

In Stamped from the Beginning, Kendi argues that racism is still prevalent in American society. Although some believe that we live in a post-racial society, he argues that racist beliefs are more thinly veiled and covert, but remain just as insidious as in the past. In Stamped, Professor Kendi chronicles the extensive history of racist ideas in America. The book analyzes the life histories of five major American intellectuals: Puritan minister Cotton Mather, Thomas Jefferson, abolitionist William Lloyd Garrison, W.E.B. Du Bois, and Angela Davis. Professor Kendi explains that racist ideas do not result from ignorance or hatred, but instead are used by society's elites to justify discriminatory policies and to maintain the nation's racial inequities.

After winning the National Book Award for Stamped, Professor Kendi authored two additional #1 New York Times bestsellers How to Be An Antiracist and Stamped: Racism, Antiracism, and You (co-authored with Jason Reynolds). The New York Times referred to How to Be An Antiracist as "the most courageous book to date on the problem of race in the Western mind" (Stewart, 2019). Kendi has published 14 academic essays in books and academic journals, including The

Journal of African American History, *Journal of Social History*, *Journal of Black Studies*, *Journal of African American Studies*, and *The Sixties: A Journal of History, Politics and Culture*. He also coedits the Black Power Series at NYU Press with historian Ashley Farmer. Then and now, he was a contributor writer for The Atlantic and a popular media analyst and public intellectual whose op-eds have appeared in numerous periodicals, including *The New York Times*, *The Guardian*, *The Washington Post*, *London Review*, *Time*, *Salon*, *Diverse: Issues in Higher Education*, *Paris Review*, *Black Perspectives*, and *The Chronicle of Higher Education*. He commented on a series of international, national, and local media outlets, such as CNN, ABC, CBS, MSNBC, NPR, Al Jazeera, PBS, BBC, Democracy Now, OWN, and Sirius XM. A sought-after public speaker, Kendi has delivered hundreds of addresses over the years at colleges and universities, bookstores, festivals, conferences, libraries, churches, and other institutions in the United States and abroad.

DR. ASHLEY ROBERTSON PRESTON EXPLORES LIFE AND LEADERSHIP OF DR. MARY MCLEOD BETHUNE

Dr. Preston is former Curator and Director of the Mary McLeod Bethune Foundation National Historic Landmark at Bethune-Cookman University. She is a lecturer in African American Studies at UF. In her book, *Mary McLeod Bethune in Florida: Bringing Social Justice to the Sunshine State* (2015), Dr. Preston explores the life, leadership, and amazing contributions of this dynamic activist.

Mary McLeod Bethune was often called the "First Lady of Negro America," but she made significant contributions to the political climate of Florida as well. From the founding of the Daytona Literary and Industrial School for Training Negro Girls in 1904, Bethune galvanized African American women for change. She created an environment in Daytona Beach that, despite racial tension throughout the state, allowed Jackie Robinson to begin his journey to integrating Major League Baseball less than two miles away from her school. She was an advocate for issues including educational funding, access to affordable housing, and equitable healthcare in her local community. As she rose nationally and internationally as an influential voice on politics, education, and women's rights, she continued to fight for justice within her state also. Today, her legacy lives through a number of institutions, including Bethune-Cookman University and the Mary McLeod Bethune Foundation National Historic Landmark.

DR. DARYL MICHAEL SCOTT: CHALLENGING BELIEFS ABOUT THE HISTORY OF DAMAGE IMAGERY

Dr. Daryl Michael Scott is a historian of Black-white relations in America since the Civil War, Southern history, and African American history. He is also the author of *Contempt and Pity: Social Policy and the Image of the Damaged Black Psyche, 1880–1996* which won the Organization of American Historian's 1998 James Rawley Prize for the best work in race relations. For over a century, the idea that African Americans are psychologically damaged has played an important role in discussions of race. In this provocative work, Daryl Michael Scott argues that damage imagery has been the product of liberals and conservatives, of racists and antiracists. While racial conservatives, often playing on white contempt for Blacks, have sought to use findings of Black pathology to justify exclusionary policies, racial liberals have used damage imagery primarily to promote policies of inclusion and rehabilitation. In advancing his argument, Scott challenges some long-held beliefs about the history of damage imagery. He rediscovers the liberal impulses behind Stanley Elkins' Sambo hypothesis and Daniel Patrick Moynihan's *Negro Family* and exposes the damage imagery in the work of Ralph Ellison, the leading anti-pathologist. He also corrects the view that the Chicago School depicted Blacks as pathological products of matriarchy. New Negro experts such as Charles Johnson and E. Franklin Frazier, he says, disdained sympathy-seeking and refrained from exploring individual pathology. Scott's reassessment of social science sheds new light on *Brown v. Board of Education*, revealing how experts reversed four decades of theory in order to represent segregation as inherently damaging to Blacks. In this controversial work, Scott warns the Left of the dangers in their recent rediscovery of damage imagery amidst an age of conservative reform.

DR. GWENDOLYN ZOHARAH SIMMONS' SCHOLAR ACTIVISM

Gwendolyn Zoharah Simmons is a scholar activist who has devoted her life to the fight for social and human rights justice. A native of Memphis, Tennessee, Dr. Simmons experienced vehement racism. A gifted scholar, she eventually graduated from Spelman College. While there, she became heavily involved in the modern civil rights movement, especially in the Student Nonviolent Coordinating Committee, after hearing Dr. Martin Luther King Jr. speak.

During the 1964 Freedom Summer in Mississippi, Dr. Simmons (whose name was Gwendolyn Robinson at the time) worked mostly in Laurel, Mississippi because it was "too dangerous to send whites" there ("Gwen Robinson [Zoharah Simmons]," n.d.). In Laurel, Robinson organized 23 volunteers who built Freedom Schools and a library, conducted a literacy program and mock voter registration project, and rallied for integration of local restaurants and schools. She was arrested after a march in Jackson and was beaten and tortured for 15 days in the fairgrounds, an open area where livestock were usually kept. Robinson then left Laurel and briefly worked with the Friends of SNCC in New York before heading to Atlanta ("Gwen Robinson [Zoharah Simmons]," n.d.).

She later became a member of the Nation of Islam and continued her community, human rights, and international activism. After earning a doctorate in Religion at Temple University and before her retirement, Professor Simmons taught in both the African American Studies Program and the Religion Department. Her diverse research focuses on the position of women in Islamic Sharia Law—especially their quest for gender equality and their fight against patriarchy.

In "From Muslims in America to American Muslims," Dr. Simmons gives an historical overview of Islam in America by focusing on the three largest American Muslim groups—African American, Arab, and South Asian. As part of her analysis, she explores the tensions among these communities, which undermine the unity of these adherents and their potential influence on the United States' domestic and foreign policies. She also explores the question many American Muslims ask themselves: are they "Muslims in America" or are they "American Muslims?" She concludes the articles by suggesting ways that all three Muslim communities can find ways to unite.

DR. MARILYN THOMAS-HOUSTON STARTED A *FIRE!!!*

In 2012, the inaugural issue of *Fire!!!: The Multimedia Journal of Black Studies* was published. Sponsored by the Association for the Study of Afro American Life and History, *Fire!!!* was conceptualized by Drs. Marilyn Thomas-Houston, Abdul Alkalimat, and Ron Bailey, who also founded the eBlack Studies Consortium, and the late Gloria Dickerson. Former UF African American Studies Program Director and Associate Professor of History Daryl Michael Scott was also involved in its inception. Along with Professor Thomas-Houston, Professor Scott was co-editor of the journal's first issue. *Fire!!!* was named after a short-lived Harlem Renaissance journal edited by Wallace Thurman and participated in by other legendary literary figures, including Langston Hughes and Zora Neale Hurston (Harold 2012). As a strictly online journal, it contributes to the eBlack Studies movement (Association for the Study of African American Life and History, 2012).

During the summer of 2010, Dr. Thomas-Houston continued her research on Black female basket makers from Nova Scotia. She interviewed Clara Gough, a descendent of a long line of Black female basket makers who took the craft to Nova Scotia as refugees from the War of 1812. Marilyn also created a documentary (*From These Roots: Taking Up the Basket*) and an exhibit (From These Roots: Clara Gough's Split Maple Baskets) at Savannah State University's Social Science Gallery. The exhibit was there for one month and was sponsored by a grant from the Institute of Museum and Library Services and hosted by the Project to Build Capacity of African American Museums. Professor Thomas-Houston began work on these projects while serving as a Fulbright Research Chair for Globalization and Cultural Studies and studying issues of identity, citizenship, and cultural studies in Nova Scotia with a base at Dalhousie University in Halifax. She also conducted research on the descendants of Black Loyalists, Jamaica Maroons, and refugees from the War of 1812 as a Fulbright Fellow ("Mary M. Thomas-Houston, PhD," n.d.).

In her first book *Stony the Road to Change: Black Mississippians and the Culture of Social Relations*, Dr. Thomas-Houston examines the impact of history, memory, space, and the concept of belonging on the social structure of a small-town, Black Southern community (Cambridge University Press 2005). Using the Civil Rights Movement of the 1960s as the point of departure for a critique of the culture of social relations among Blacks, it also proposes to provide an example of activist, native ethnographic research in a complex society. In her second book, Dr. Thomas-Houston and Mark Schuller edited *Homing Devices: The Poor as Targets of Public Housing and Practice* (Lexington Books 2006). This collection of ethnographies addresses the problem associated with the provisions of affordable housing in America and in other countries. These ethnographies cut across national and cultural borders, offering a diverse look at housing policies and practices as well as addressing the problems associated with providing or obtaining affordable housing. The studies incorporate perspectives of both policymakers and recipients and as such provide comparative insight into public housing policy programs and practices based on qualitative research. The collected experts provide an analysis of such problems as displacement, resettlement, policy implementation, collaborative planning, exclusionary practices, environmental racism, and silencing the voices of dissent. Editors Schuller and Thomas-Houston have assembled a strong volume that offers a fresh approach to discussing policy while bringing the particular problem of *housing* to the forefront in a way that will appeal to scholars of anthropology and social science, governmental policy departments, and activists from the general public across the nation.

Conclusion: If Only and the Issue of Retention

The African American Studies faculty have published groundbreaking interdisciplinary research over the years. This chapter has mostly focused on their research over the last 20 years. When thinking about the depth of this research and the talent of the many scholars who have taught in the program, one must question why so many left the University of Florida. Could the University have done anything to retain talented scholars who now teach at other universities? If the University had succeeded in retaining these scholars, would it already have an African American Studies department rather than still being a program? These are questions that one cannot answer, but the University must do more than just recruit gifted faculty members, it must also find ways to retain talented Black scholars.

Chapter 5 Study Questions

1. Based on the materials in this chapter, to what extent has the faculty in African American Studies contributed to the Mission of the University of Florida as a Research Institution.
2. In what ways has the African American Studies faculty contributed to knowledge production and the advancement of African American Studies?
3. List and briefly review what you consider to be the two most relevant research publications by the African American Studies faculty at the University of Florida.

References

Association for the Study of African American Life and History. (2012). *Fire!!!: The Multimedia Journal of Black Studies* 1(1). Retrieved on November 13, 2020, from JSTOR: https://www.jstor.org/stable/pdf/10.5323/fire.1.1.fm.pdf.

Austin, S.D.W. (2018). *The Caribbeanization of Black Politics: Race, Group Consciousness and Political Participation in America*. State University of Albany Press.

Austin, S.D.W. (2006). *The Transformation of Plantation Politics in the Mississippi Delta: Black Politics, Concentrated Poverty, and Social Capital in the Mississippi Delta*. State University of New York Press.

Austin, S.D.W. (Ed.). (2019). *Political Black Girl Magic: The Elections and Governance of Black Female Mayors*. Temple University Press. Manuscript under contract.

Canton, D. (2010). *Raymond Pace Alexander: A New Negro Lawyer Fights for Civil Rights in Philadelphia*. University Press of Mississippi. https://doi.org/10.14325/mississippi/9781604734256.001.0001

Celeste, M. (2017). *Race, Gender, and Citizenship in the African Diaspora: Travelling Blackness*. Routledge Press. https://doi.org/10.4324/9781315691824

Celeste, M. (2018). "What Now?": The Wailing Black Woman, Grief, and Difference. *Black Camera* 9(2), 110-131. Retrieved March 22, 2021, from: https://www.muse.jhu.edu/article/694970. https://doi.org/10.2979/blackcamera.9.2.08

Celeste, M. (2018). Black Media Studies. *Feminist Media Histories* 4(2), 38-42. https://doi.org/10.1525/fmh.2018.4.2.38

Evans, S.Y. (2019). *Regeneration: Healing and Self-Care in Black Women's Centenarian Memoirs*. State University of New York Press. Manuscript under contract.

Evans, S.Y. (2014). *Black Passports: Travel Memoirs as a Tool for Youth Empowerment*. State University of New York Press.

Evans, S.Y. (2007). *Black Women in the Ivory Tower, 1850-1954: An Intellectual History*. University Press of Florida. https://doi.org/10.5744/florida/9780813032689.001.0001

Faye V Harrison. (n.d.) Department of African American Studies. Retrieved March 19, 2021, from https://afro.illinois.edu/directory/profile/fvharrsn

Gwen Robinson (Zoharah Simmons). (n.d.). *SNCC Digital Gateway*, SNCC Legacy Project and Duke University. Retrieved March 22, 2021, from: https://snccdigital.org/people/gwen-zoharah-simmons-robinson/

Harold, C. (2012). "Introducing Fire!!!: The Multimedia Journal of Black Studies." Black Fire at UVA. Retrieved November 13, 2020, from: https://blackfireuva.com/2012/03/01/introducing-fire-the-multimedia-journal-of-black-studies/

Harrison, F.V. (Ed.). (2010). *Decolonizing Anthropology: Moving Further Toward an Anthropology for Liberation*, (3rd ed.). American

Anthropological Association.

Harrison, F.V. (2008). *Outsider Within: Reworking Anthropology in the Global Age.* University of Illinois Press.

Harrison, F.V. (Ed.). (2005). *Resisting Racism: Global Perspectives on Race, Gender, and Human Rights.* AltaMira Press.

Kendi, I.X. (2019). *How to Be an Anti-Racist.* Random House.

Kendi, I.X. (2016). *Stamped from the Beginning: The Definitive History of Racist Ideas in America.* Nation Books.

Mary M. Thomas-Houston, PhD. (n.d.) *College of Liberal Arts and Sciences*, University of Florida. Retrieved on March 22, 2021 from: http://users.clas.ufl.edu/marilynm/home.html

McCluskey, A. (2008, April). Review of Evans, Stephanie Y., *Black Women in the Ivory Tower, 1850-1954: An Intellectual History.* H-SAWH, H-Net Reviews.

Preston, A.R. (2015). *Mary McLeod Bethune in Florida: Bringing Social Justice to the Sunshine State.* Acadia Publishing.

Rogers, I. (2012). *Black Campus Movement: Black Students and the Racial Reconstitution of Higher Education, 1965-1972.* Palgrave.

Scott, D.M. (1997). *Contempt and Pity: Social Policy and the Image of the Damaged Black Psyche, 1880–1996.* University of North Carolina Press.

Simmons, G.Z. (2008). From Muslims in America to American Muslims. *Journal of Islamic Law and Culture*, 10(3), 254-280. https://doi.org/10.1080/15288170802481145

Stewart, J.C. (2019, August 20). Fighting Racism Even, and Especially, Where We Don't Realize It Exists. *The New York Times.* Retrieved March 22, 2021, from https://www.nytimes.com/2019/08/20/books/review/how-to-be-an-antiracist-ibram-x-kendi.html

Thomas-Houston, M. (2005). *'Stony the Road' to Change: Black Mississippians and the Culture of Social Relations.* Cambridge University Press. https://doi.org/10.1017/CBO9780511614149

Thomas-Houston, M. & Schuller, M. (Eds.). 2006. *Homing Devices: The Poor as Targets of Public Housing and Practice.* Lexington Books.

Wright, S.D. (2000). *Race, Power, and Political Emergence in Memphis.* Garland Press.

Chapter 6: University of Florida and Black Community Engagement by Barbara McDade Gordon, Gwenuel W. Mingo, and Sherry Sherrod DuPree

Abstract: A review of the literature in Community Engagement provides the conceptual framework for documenting the University of Florida's engagement with the Black communities in Gainesville. Community Engagement may be defined as a dynamic relational process that facilitates communication, interaction, involvement, and exchange between an organization and a community for a range of social and organizational outcomes. As a concept, Engagement features attitudes of connection and interacting participation. It is in this context that selected major engagements between the University and the local Black communities are examined. It focuses on three relational Community Engagement Models: Faculty Research & Service, Educational Outreach, and Religious Connections. The Chapter concludes with outcome-based strategies for future stronger Community Engagement Networks.

Section 1: Faculty Research and Service — Missions of a Public University by Barbara McDade Gordon

According to its mission statement, the University of Florida is a comprehensive learning institution dedicated to excellence in education and research to shape a better future for Florida, the nation, and the world. The three interlocking elements—teaching, research, and service—represent the University's commitment to serve the state of Florida, the United States, and the global community. Central to the mission is the commitment to share the benefits of UF research and knowledge for the public good.

This chapter highlights research and service activities by UF faculty members that involve the African American/Black communities in the Gainesville area. The selections are organized by UF colleges and departments. Selections were made from perusing the faculty websites that showcased their research interests and activities; contacting Department Chairs and colleagues; discovering relevant presentations; and browsing the UF website, faculty publications, and reports of community activities. Research by faculty members is ongoing and continuous. Therefore, information in this publication may be updated, as necessary.

COLLEGE OF AGRICULTURE AND LIFE SCIENCES

SALLY K. WILLIAMS, PH.D. ASSOCIATE PROFESSOR, DEPARTMENT OF ANIMAL SCIENCES

Dr. Williams' primary subject area is on poultry research in Florida, and she has also done work in Africa. She is one of a few African American faculty members in the College of Agriculture and Life Sciences and has been awarded for her mentorship service in the UF Multicultural Mentoring Program for students of color. Through her sorority, Delta Sigma Theta, she has worked with girls and young women in Gainesville area, particularly encouraging them to consider and prepare for careers in the STEM fields. Dr. Williams often serves as a judge at science and engineering fairs hosted by Alachua County Public Schools. She also mentors students in these schools.

COLLEGE OF ARTS

DIONNE NICOLE CHAMPION, PH.D. RESEARCH ASSISTANT PROFESSOR, CENTER FOR ARTS IN MEDICINE

Dr. Champion's work focuses on the design and ethnographic study of learning environments that blend STEM and creative embodied educational activities, particularly for children who have experienced feelings of marginalization in STEM settings (for example, African Americans and girls).

She works with youth, K-12, and college students. Dr. Champion is currently developing a research program that studies ways to engage children in authentic STEM experiences and works with African

Figure 6.1.1: Dr. Dionne Champion, Research Assistant Professor, Center for Arts in Medicine, blends STEAM (Science-Technology-Engineering-Mathematics) in learning environments.

American children at the UF Virtual Creative Arts Academy (VCAA). The VCAA successfully launched a pilot program with Gainesville's Howard Bishop Middle School's summer enhancement program (HBVCAA) and has received funding to help implement a one-year, in-school version of the program. She said that Howard Bishop administration actually reached out to VCAA to help design a program that would help students adjust and become more productive in the virtual classrooms which the Alachua County School District adopted as safety precautions due to the coronavirus pandemic. There are 17 total schools in Florida's community partnership network who are becoming aware of the project. The program was a brainchild of the College of the Arts (COA) Center for the Arts, Migration, and Entrepreneurship (CAME), led by Director Osubi Craig. Her program with the COA/CAME/School of Music has procured the old fire station on Main Street as a location for community activities. They will work with people in the community to enable them to conduct their own research and evaluation to develop solutions to issues in the community. For more information you may visit the VCAA online: www.UFVCAA.com.

WELSON ALVES TREMURA, PH.D. PROFESSOR, SCHOOL OF MUSIC AND CENTER FOR LATIN AMERICAN STUDIES

Dr. Tremura organized a program of concerts held at the Bo Diddley Plaza in downtown Gainesville and other open spaces in the city, such as parks, to provide the community with the opportunity to intersect with the Arts at the University of Florida and to facilitate new possibilities for collaboration. He and another UF faculty member, Dr. Larry Crook, coordinated these concerts with the City of Gainesville Cultural Affairs Department. Students and local artists were invited to assist in the production and to perform at the concerts. As an ethnomusicologist, he explores the possibilities of acculturation among Latin American, African, and World Music an essential step towards building good communities. The following links are to concerts at the Bo Diddley Plaza in downtown Gainesville:

- https://www.youtube.com/watch?v=5cn6fhh6JkA. World Music Fest. October 14, 2011.
- https://www.youtube.com/watch?v=nbOkdiwHsas. World Music Concert. December 22, 2013.

JOAN FROSCH, PH.D. PROFESSOR, SCHOOL OF THEATRE AND DANCE; DIRECTOR OF THE CENTER FOR WORLD ARTS

Dr. Frosch founded the Center for World Arts (CWA) with Dr. Larry Crook, an ethno-musicologist in the School of Music. She describes it as a living laboratory exploring the interface of arts and society. Her primary research and teaching are in African contemporary dance. The CWA links local artists from the Gainesville communities (African American and others) with global communities to expand the international reach and artistic breadth of UF's academic programs. Recognizing the diverse and interconnected nature of the contemporary world, the Center tests new paradigms of research, curriculum, cultural programming, and public outreach. The CWA seeks to integrate a socio-artistic aesthetic into practice and study of the arts, exploring issues of identity, migration, race, gender, and privilege through the lens of the arts. More information on the CWA: https://arts.ufl.edu/centers/center-for-world-arts/about.

THE HARN MUSEUM

ERIC JEFFERSON SEGAL, PH.D. DIRECTOR OF EDUCATION AND CURATOR OF ACADEMIC PROGRAMS

Dr. Segal (see Figures 6.1.2 and 6.1.3) is responsible for designing the Harn Museum programs that engage faculty and students at UF, Santa Fe College, and other area colleges. According to the Harn website, "As Director of Education, Segal leads a remarkable staff of educators who develop innovative and sustainable programs supporting learning for diverse audiences, including families and children and diverse community leaders" (Harn Museum of Art, n.d.).

Figure 6.1.2: Dr. Eric Segal, Director of Education at the Harn Museum, brings students from East Gainesville and other areas of the city to experience art at the museum.

For many years, Bonnie Berneau, M.S., now retired, was Education Curator of Community Programs and was very much involved with Friends of Elementary Arts. The organization raises funds to support field trips to attend events at the Philipps Center for the Performing Arts and to the Harn Museum by school children in the Gainesville area.

Below are some of the outreach programs conducted by the Harn Museum that serve the African/American Black communities in the Gainesville area.

Exhibitions

- Exhibition Advisory groups that include members of Gainesville's African American communities.
- Jacob Lawrence Exhibition and Community Day. *History Labor Life – Prints of Jacob Lawrence*. 2018
- *I, Too, Am America*. 2019

Programs with schools in largely African American neighborhoods or with diverse populations.

- Early Learning at the Harn Museum
- Science Night with Florida Museum of Natural History
- Eastside High class tours.
- Collaborations with Nicole Harris, English and African American History teacher at Gainesville High School: The Harn has facilitated art gallery tours for her classes and plans to collaborate with her in the future on programming.

Outreach

- Tabling and engagement at Fifth Avenue Arts Festival
- Art kits (individual backpacks with art supplies and projects) distributed through SWAG Family Resource Center and by the Gainesville Chapter of the Links (working with Rawlings and Caring and Sharing schools).
- Program with PACE Center for Girls (currently paused due to the pandemic).
- Elementary Art at the Library – program for Head Start Program 4-year-olds to visit the Harn, make art, and enjoy parent engagement activity.
- Program with Reichert House School for at-risk boys (discontinued).
- Tours – free tours for K-12 schools; support for field trip busses; digital educator resources; virtual tours developed and distributed during COVID-19 pandemic.

Figure 6.1.3: These young children listen to a docent explain a popular painting at the Harn Museum.

COLLEGE OF BUSINESS

HECTOR H. SANDOVAL, ASSISTANT PROFESSOR. DIRECTOR, ECONOMIC ANALYSIS PROGRAM AND BUREAU OF ECONOMIC & BUSINESS RESEARCH

Sandoval, H. (Project Director). (2018 January). Understanding Racial Inequity in Alachua County. Prepared by the University of Florida Bureau of Economic and Business Research (BEBR). The report provides a baseline of racial disparity data in the county, showing differences between whites and four minority groups: Blacks, Hispanics, Asians, and other. The report was commissioned by Alachua County, Alachua County Public Schools, City of Gainesville, Gainesville Area Chamber of Commerce, Santa Fe College, UF Health, and the University of Florida.

COLLEGE OF DESIGN, CONSTRUCTION, AND PLANNING

RUTH STEINER, PH.D. PROFESSOR, DEPARTMENT OF URBAN AND REGIONAL PLANNING. DIRECTOR, CENTER FOR HEALTH AND THE BUILT ENVIRONMENT

KRISTIN E. LARSEN, PH.D., AICP. PROFESSOR, DEPARTMENT OF URBAN AND REGIONAL PLANNING. DIRECTOR, SCHOOL OF LANDSCAPE ARCHITECTURE AND PLANNING

KATHRYN FRANK, PH.D. ASSOCIATE PROFESSOR, DEPARTMENT OF URBAN AND REGIONAL PLANNING

LAURA J. DEDENBACH, PH.D., AICP. LECTURER, DEPARTMENT OF URBAN AND REGIONAL PLANNING

The research included here about Gainesville's African American communities has often been a collaborative effort among Drs. Larsen, Frank, Dedenbach, and Steiner:

- Frank K., Larsen K., Dedenbach L., Redden T., & Wright, S. (2018). Neighborhoods as Community Assets: The Porters Community, Gainesville, Florida. Grant-funded Research Report (Figures 6.1.4 and 6.1.5).

Figure 6.1.4: UF Faculty Team who worked on Porters Neighborhood Project. Left to Right: Drs. Tyeshia Redden, Kristin Larsen, Laura Dedenbach, and Kathryn Frank. Photo credit: Joseph Mazzaferro.

Figure 6.1.5: Kindergarten to 5th grade students at Porters Community Center design neighborhood boxes in a class project taught by Dr. Laura Dedenbach, UF faculty member in Urban and Regional Planning. Photo credit: *Gainesville Sun*. 9.20.2017

- Dedenbach, L. J. (2019). A Report on UF-Gainesville Collaborative Engagement Initiatives. Technical Report.
- Larsen, K. (2002). Housing Studio, Duval Neighborhood, Gainesville, Florida. A housing plan for this African American majority community. Unfunded Research.
- Larsen, K. (1990). *The Low-Income Housing Tax Credit: Examining an Incentive for the Productive of Affordable Housing in Gainesville's Pleasant Street District*. [Master's thesis, University of Florida].
- Steiner, R. (Principal Investigator). (n.d.) Safe Routes to School Technical Assistance Phase 2. Department of Urban and Regional Planning. Director, Center for Health and the Built Environment. [Ongoing project].

COLLEGE OF EDUCATION

THOMASENIA LOTT ADAMS, PH.D. PROFESSOR AND ASSOCIATE DEAN FOR RESEARCH AND FACULTY DEVELOPMENT, OFFICE OF EDUCATIONAL RESEARCH

Dr. Adams' (Figure 6.1.6) specialty is Mathematics Education in the COE School of Teaching and Learning. She submitted the following publications about research about African American/Black students in Gainesville.

Research with African American female students at Howard Bishop Middle School:
- West-Olatunji, C., Yoon, E., Shure, L., Pringle, R., & **Adams, T. L.** (2020). Exploring how school counselors position low-income African American girls as mathematics and science learners: Findings from two-year data. In B. Polnick & B. Irby (Eds.), *Girls and Women of Color in STEM: Navigating the Double Blind in K-12 Education* (pp. 205-225). Information Age Publishing.
- Pringle, R. M., Brkich, K. M., **Adams, T. L.**, West-Olatunji, C., & Archer-Banks, D. A. (2012). Factors influencing elementary teachers' positioning of African American girls as science and mathematics learners. *School Science and Mathematics*, 112(4), 217-229.

Figure 6.1.6: Dr. Thomasenia Adams. "Making sense of mathematics" for elementary school students, particularly girls, has been the focus of some of her research.

- West-Olatunji, C., Shure, L., Pringle, R., **Adams, T. L.**, Lewis, D., & Cholewa, B. (2010). Exploring how school counselors position low-income African American girls as mathematics and science learners. *Professional School Counseling*, 13(3), 184-195.
- West-Olatunji, C., Pringle, R., **Adams, T. L.**, Baratelli, A., Goodman, R., & Maxis, S. (2008). How African-American middle school girls position themselves as mathematics and science learners. *International Journal of Learning*, 14(9), 219-228.
- **Adams, T. L.**, Laframenta, J., Pringle, R., & West-Olatunji, C. (2010). The positionality of African American girls toward mathematics. *Proceedings of the 31st annual meeting of the North American Chapter of the International Group for the Psychology of Mathematics Education*, Atlanta, GA., Vol. 5, pp. 477-482.

The following research programs were conducted with an African American teacher and her students at Duval Elementary School:
- **Adams, T. L.**, & Bonner, E. (2018). Distinguishing features of culturally responsive pedagogy related to formative assessment in mathematics instruction. In E. A. Silver & V. L. Mills (Eds.), *A fresh look at formative assessment in mathematics teaching: Leveraging*

- connections to tasks, discourse, equity, and more. (pp. 61-79). National Council of Teachers of Mathematics.
- Peterek, E., & **Adams, T. L.** (2009). Meeting the challenge of engaging students for success in mathematics by using culturally responsive methods. In D. Y. White & J. S. Spitzer (Eds.), *Responding to diversity, grades preK-5* (pp. 149-160). National Council of Teachers of Mathematics.
- Bonner, E., & **Adams, T. L.** (2012). Culturally responsive teaching in the context of mathematics: A grounded theory case study. *Journal for Mathematics Teacher Education*, 15(1), 25-38. https://doi.org/10.1007/s10857-011-9198-4.

VICKI VESCIO, PH.D. CLINICAL ASSOCIATE PROFESSOR, SCHOOL OF TEACHING AND LEARNING

Dr. Vescio's doctoral dissertation, awarded by the University of Florida (2010), was about 4th grade African American boys and their identification with academics. When asked about this research, she answered as follows:

> I came to this topic because I had spent a lot of time working in the East side elementary schools during my doctoral studies and was disheartened by patterns that I saw in how Black boys were being treated…It was an enriching experience for me, but it was not without its difficulties as I struggled with "taking" from the boys and the community for my research and wondered what I was giving back. In recent years, I have been trying to find the 6 boys whom I worked with who are now young college-aged men. I have had success in connecting with people who know where a few of them are but I have not actually had the chance to connect with any of the young men who were in my study when they were 10 years old—although I will continue to try (Vescio, 2018).

COLLEGE OF ENGINEERING

JUAN E. GILBERT, PH.D. THE BANKS PREEMINENCE CHAIR IN ENGINEERING, DEPARTMENT OF COMPUTER & INFORMATION SCIENCE & ENGINEERING. (CISE)

Dr. Gilbert's research and outreach have not focused specifically on the Black communities in Gainesville. However, he specializes in human-centered computing and artificial intelligence and has committed himself to increasing diversity in the STEM field and supporting and empowering other Black scientists in the scientific community. He created a set of guidelines to structure and support inclusion in the CISE department at UF. One of the guidelines is to engage the local community. Seek opportunities to engage the local Black community in research and development. Offer technology learning classes, provide broadband access, etc. Work with them as partners not as subjects.

Like many in the Gainesville Black communities, Dr. Gilbert was the first person in his family to go to college and he was the only African American in his Computer Science Ph.D. program at the University of Cincinnati. This and other experiences have led him to become not only an advocate, but a leader at UF and nationally. According to his website, in 2006 Gilbert launched Applications Quest, a software tool which uses artificial intelligence in evaluating and comparing student's applications to increase diversity without sacrificing quality. Most recently, he created the Prime III Software Voting System as a model to make elections more secure, equitable, and inclusive. His inventions were used in recent elections in several states. In order to help students to expand their awareness of opportunities in computer science engineering, he regularly speaks to students at local schools, and particularly aiming to inspire African American/Black students.

CHRISTINA GARDNER-MCCUNE, PH.D. ASSISTANT PROFESSOR, COMPUTER & INFORMATION SCIENCE & ENGINEERING
Dr. Gardner (Figure 6.1.7) has been engaged in the African American/Black Communities in Gainesville over the past six years since she came to UF. She has also involved her graduate students in project design and implementation. In response to our inquiry, she submitted the following research publications and outreach service projects.

Publications that have resulted from this community engagement:
- Aggarwal, A., Gardner-McCune, C., & Touretzky, D. S. (2017, March).

Figure 6.1.7: Dr. Christina Gardner-McCune works with African American and other youth in Gainesville to break down barriers to entry in studying computer science and technology.

Evaluating the effect of using physical manipulatives to foster computational thinking in elementary school. In *Proceedings of the 2017 ACM SIGCSE Technical Symposium on Computer Science Education* (pp. 9-14).

- Rivera, R., Gardner-McCune, C., & McCune, D. B. (2017, June). Engagement in Practice: University & K-12 Partnership with Robotics Outreach. In *2017 ASEE Annual Conference & Exposition*.
- Jester, E. (2014, December 11) Students get early glimpse at the joy of computer coding. *Gainesville Sun*. https://www.gainesville.com/article/LK/20141211/news/604159224/GS
- Isaac, J., Yerika Jimenez, Y., and Gardner-McCune, C. (2020). (In Press) Engaging 4th and 5th Grade Students with Cultural Pedagogy in Introductory Programming. *2020 Research on Equity and Sustained Participation in Engineering, Computing, and Technology* (RESPECT), Portland, Oregon.

Outreach Events reported by Dr. Gardner-McCune:
- In 2014, we collaborated with Eastside High School and conducted an all-day Hour of Code for CS Education Week for over 1000 students.
- In 2015, we offered a Cybersecurity Summer Camp in collaboration with Gainesville Parks and Recreation at McPherson Community Center. We had 15 AA students grades 4th through 7th participate.
- In 2015-2016, I participated in the Alachua County School District's Vex Robotic program training undergraduate STEM (mostly engineering) students in how to teach robots. We were in several of the elementary and middle schools including Lincoln Middle School.
- In 2016, we ran a six-week after-school program in collaboration with the Passage Christian Academy with 10 African American students in elementary and middle schools.
- Two of my Ph.D. students, Yerika Jimenez and Joseph Isaac, Jr., have run six-to-eight week summer programs in 2019 and 2020 for 50 4th and 5th graders at Caring and Sharing Learning School's STEM Summer Camp.
- From 2015-2019, I have worked with eight African American small businesses owners and entrepreneurs to build web applications for their businesses through my software engineering course.

COLLEGE OF HEALTH AND HUMAN PERFORMANCE (CHHP)

BERTHA CATO, PH.D. ASSOCIATE PROFESSOR EMERITUS, DEPARTMENT OF TOURISM, RECREATION, AND SPORT MANAGEMENT

As the principal investigator, Dr. Cato received a $434,000 grant from the U.S. Department of Juvenile Justice and Delinquency Prevent and the state of Florida Juvenile Justice Department. Known as Project WISE-UP this case study used a logic model to plan and evaluate an intervention project for African American students at a Gainesville middle school. The aim of the project was to reduce the risk of using drugs and alcohol and becoming involved in criminal activities. The study considered a continuum of integrated interactive activities that

comprised the students' environment: community, school, peer group and family. Two of the publications from this research:
- Chen, W. W., Cato, B. M., & Rainford, N. (1999, January). Using a Logic Model to Plan and Evaluate a Community Intervention Program: A Case Study. *International Quarterly of Community Health Education*. Retrieved from: https://journals.sagepub.com/doi/10.2190/JDNM-MNPB-9P25-17CQ
- Cato, B. (2006). Enhancing Prevention Programs' Credibility through the Use of a Logic Model. *Journal of Alcohol and Drug Education*. 50(3), 8-20.

DELORES C. S. JAMES, PH.D. ASSOCIATE PROFESSOR, DEPARTMENT OF HEALTH EDUCATION AND BEHAVIOR

Dr. James' (Figure 6.1.8) research lays the groundwork for understanding how African Americans use technology to improve their health, their motivations for (and barriers to) to participation in mHealth interventions, as well as recruitment strategies and desirable program elements for mHealth interventions. The National Institutes of Health (NIH) defines mHealth as "the use of mobile and wireless devices (cell phones, tablets, etc.) to improve health outcomes, health care services, and health research (n.d.)." Dr. James' current research focuses on creating and sustaining online health communities. She created a blog and website, *Keep It Tight Sisters*, https://keepittightsisters.com, and Facebook page focused on Black women's health issues. She also uses the social media platform Pinterest as a digital clearinghouse for resources on self-care and wellness. In response to our inquiry about her research and service involving the Black/African American communities in Gainesville, Dr. James sent an extensive list of publications conducted in Gainesville over more than 20 years. In addition to her academic research and service, she has served the community as Chair of the Affordable Housing Advisory Committee for the City of Gainesville.

Five topic areas of her research are presented below. Because of space limits of this chapter, two of Dr. James' publications in each topic were selected.

Figure 6.1.8: Dr. Delores James' research promotes healthy eating, exercise, and lifestyles particularly among African Americans in the Gainesville communities.

Health, Social Media, and Technology Use and Access among African Americans
- James, D.C.S. (2019). Willingness of African American men to participate in mHealth weight management programs. *International Journal of Health Sciences*, 7(4), 13-21.
- James, D.C.S., Harville, C. (2019). Online Health Information Seeking among African Americans. *International Journal of Health Sciences*, 7(3), 19-32.

Health Issues among African American Women.
- James, D.C.S., Harville, C. (2017, June 1) Electronic publication ahead of print: Smartphone Usage, Social Media Engagement, and Willingness to Participate in mHealth Weight Management Research

among African American Women. *Health Education & Behavior.* http://journals.sagepub.com/doi/full/10.1177/1090198117714020
- James, D.C.S., Pobee, J., Brown, L., and Oxidine, D. Using the Health Belief Model to Develop Culturally Appropriate Weight Management Materials for African American Women. *Journal of the American Academy of Nutrition and Dietetics.* 2012 112: 664-670.

Health Literacy and eHealth Literacy and African Americans. Health literacy is a key social determinant of health.
- James, D.C.S. and Harville, C. (2016). Assessment of eHealth Literacy, Online Help-seeking Behavior, and Willingness to Participate in mHealth Chronic Disease Research among African Americans, Florida, 2014-2015. *Preventing Chronic Disease,* 13, https://doi.org/10.5888/pcd13.160210
- James, D.C.S., Harville, C., and Efunbumi, O. (2015). Health Literacy and Online Health-Seeking Behaviors among African Americans. *The Health Education Monograph Series,* 32(2), 22-32.

Cultural Influences on the Diets of African Americans.
- James, D.C.S. (2009). Cluster Analysis Defines Distinct Dietary Patterns for African American Men and Women. *Journal of the American Dietetic Association,* 109(2), 255-262.
- James, D.C.S. (2004). Factors Influencing Dietary Intake among African Americans: Application of a Culturally Sensitive Model. *Ethnicity and Health,* 9(4), 349-368.

Development of Culturally Relevant Health Education Messages and Programs.
- James, D.C.S. (2013). The Right Size for Me: A Weight Management Guide for African American Women. *The American Dietetic Association.*
- James, D.C.S. (2000).*The Temple Project: A Spiritually Based Health and Wellness Curriculum.* Florida Department of Health.

COLLEGE OF LIBERAL ARTS AND SCIENCES

PATRICIA HILLIARD-NUNN, PH.D. SENIOR LECTURER, AFRICAN AMERICAN STUDIES PROGRAM

Dr. Hilliard-Nunn (1963-2020) passed during the Fall Semester. In tribute to her organized by the College of Liberal Arts & Sciences (CLAS), she was lauded for bridging the gap between the University and the local communities through her research and service activities. She worked in several different media. Her research addresses Africana history and culture, media representations, the history of Blacks in Gainesville and Alachua County, lynching in Alachua County, Black Seminoles, and African Cultural Retentions. Her most recent article, "The Agency of Black Female Protagonists in Haile Gerima's Bush Mama and Sankofa," is in *African American Cinema Through Black Lives Consciousness* (Reid, 2019).

She researched and produced 100 *Years of Gracious Dignity: The Chestnut Funeral Home (Gainesville, FL)* [DVD] (2014), *45 Years of Triumph and Struggle: African American Studies at UF* [DVD] (2014), and *First Footsteps: The Struggle for Racial Desegregation at UF* [DVD] (2012) for the Levin College of Law. She also researched and wrote the script for *In the Shadow of Plantations*, a video about enslaved laborers in Alachua County that was produced by the Alachua County Communications Office. With a mini grant from the Florida Humanities Council, she collaborated with Kenneth Nunn to write and produce the *Sankofa Black History Flash* radio spots which aired on Magic 101.3 in Gainesville, FL. She served as the first host of the Alachua County NAACP public affairs radio program called *The Voice*.

KEVIN M. MCCARTHY, PH.D. PROFESSOR EMERITUS, DEPARTMENT OF ENGLISH

Dr. McCarthy has published over 35 books, the majority of which deal with Florida history and culture. Relevant to this chapter are his books on African American History and Culture (Figures 6.1.9 and 6.1.10).

Figure 6.1.9: Dr. Kevin McCarthy has published many books on African American history.

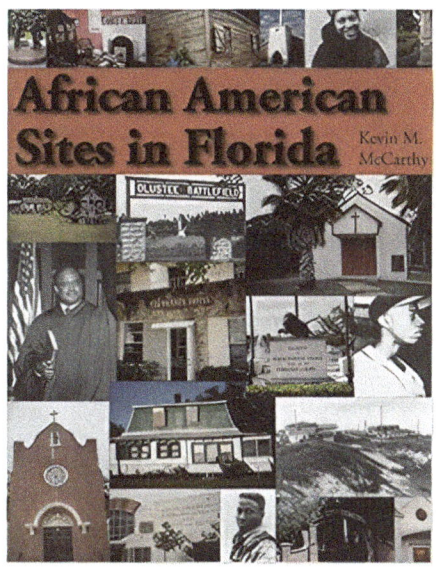

Figure 6.1.10: Gainesville's African American community is featured in Dr. McCarthy's book that takes a geographical tour of Florida's counties.

- McCarthy, K. M. (2019). *African American Sites in Florida*. Pineapple Press, Inc. (Original work published 2014).
  In this book, Dr. McCarthy alphabetically organizes Florida's 67 counties. Alachua County—in which Gainesville is located—is the subject of the book's first chapter. It covers major historical figures such as Josiah Walls, the first Black Congressman from Florida, after whom the Supervisor of Elections office in Gainesville—among other things—is named.

- McCarthy, K. M. (1995). *Black Florida*. Hippocrene Books, Inc.
  This book is a city-by-city guide to churches, schools, homes, and other significant sites in more than 70 towns across Florida, including Gainesville.

- Jones, M. D. & McCarthy. K. M. (1993). *African Americans in Florida*. Pineapple Press.

This book tells the story of 400 years of African American presence and contributions to the state beginning with "Estevanico the Black" who arrived in 1528 as an explorer to 20th century discussing Floridians such as musician Ray Charles and author Zora Neale Hurston.

- Jones, M. D. & McCarthy, K. M. (2014). *Teachers' Manual for African Americans in Florida.* Pineapple Press, Inc. (Originally published 1993).

- White, A. and K. M. McCarthy. (2012). *Lincoln High School: Its History and Legacy.* Pineapple Press, Inc.

HEIDI LANNON, PH.D. ADJUNCT PROFESSOR, DEPARTMENT OF GEOGRAPHY

Dr. Lannon worked on a four-year National Science Foundation grant to recruit, retain, and transfer local high school students from underrepresented groups, including but not exclusively for African Americans in the local community. The grant was a joint effort between UF and Santa Fe College. Students took basic geography courses, did research with UF faculty, and participated in a summer internship at the Orlando Science Museum. Four students currently enrolled in the UF Geography Department were participants in the NSF grant. She is currently working with an African American student from Gainesville who graduate from Santa Fe College and will apply for admission to UF.

Dr. Lannon is developing a service-learning course for the UF Geography curriculum. She believes that it has much potential for students taking the course to work with local African American organizations and encourage youth members to consider careers in geography. The aim of service-learning is to extend traditional classroom-based education by placing students into the community. The objectives of the class (GEO/GEA 2000 or 3000) are: enhanced civic responsibility, citizen engagement with geography, awareness of career interests and opportunities in service, science, public policy, and the environment. Focus areas include Medical Geography/Global Health, Sustainability/Global Environmental Change, Geopolitics, and the Global Economy.

Dr. Lannon also assists geography teachers in local high schools, particularly those that offer AP Geography courses such as P.K. Yonge, Eastside, and Santa Fe.

GABRIELA HAMERLINCK, PH.D. LECTURER, DEPARTMENT OF GEOGRAPHY

Dr. Hamerlinck and Graduate Student Sarah VanSchoick have started an outreach initiative for local K-12 students. The aim is to increase enrollment in Geography Department and to reach out to students from diverse backgrounds. The project will connect with local schools, clubs, and programs to provide resources to inform the students about majors and careers in geography.

PAUL ORTIZ, PH.D. PROFESSOR, DEPARTMENT OF HISTORY AND DIRECTOR OF THE SAMUEL PROCTOR ORAL HISTORY PROGRAM (SPOHP)

See also Chapter 3.

The mission of SPOHP is to gather, preserve, and promote living histories of individuals from all walks of life: https://oral.history.ufl.edu.

The Proctor Program was founded in 1967 by University Historian Dr. Samuel Proctor. SPOHP engages students, scholars, and local communities throughout the world in gathering, preserving, and promoting living history through academic publications, public programs, electronic media, and other forums in order to document the human condition. Its motto: "One community, many voices."

The Joel Buchanan Archive of African American Oral History is an archive of 1,000+ oral history interviews conducted with African

Americans in Alachua County, as well as Florida, the Gulf South, and other parts of the nation. The Joel Buchanan collection is one of the premier archives of African American oral history in the United States. It also includes scores of public programs, symposia on Black history, oral history workshops, documentaries, and podcasts on many facets of African American Studies. The collection has been used by scholars, students, film makers, radio producers and many others: https://oral.history.ufl.edu/projects/aahp.

CAROLYN M. TUCKER, PH.D. PROFESSOR, DEPARTMENT OF PSYCHOLOGY.

Dr. Tucker (Figure 6.1.11) has over 40 years of experience in conducting community engaged and patient-centered research to promote health and culturally sensitive health care, particularly in racial/ethnic minority, low-income, and medically underserved communities. According to her website, she is the founder of the culturally sensitive

Figure 6.1.11: Dr. Carolyn M. Tucker's expertise in local African American communities in Gainesville and Jacksonville comprises a significant part of her research and service.

Health-Smart Program to Prevent and Reduce Obesity and Related Diseases. She uses an academic-community partnership approach and the community-based participatory research model.

She has over 140 published, refereed, research articles that span from 2020 to 1980. Her current research was featured on the UF Website in April 2020: "Golden Years. New Program Looks to Improve Lives of Seniors in Need." Led by Dr. Tucker, this community-based program provides resources that empower participants to improve their own mental, physical, and spiritual health (Figure 6.1.12). This project was initially launched in the Jacksonville area. Much of her life-long research and clinical work have embraced the Gainesville communities, both urban and rural.

Dr. Tucker's research publications span over 20 pages. A small sample of her most recent publications is provided here.
- Tucker, C. M., Roncoroni, J., & Buki, L. P. (2019). Counseling Psychologists and Behavioral Health: Promoting Mental and Physical Health Outcomes. *The Counseling Psychologist*, 47(7), 970-998.
- Tucker, C. M., Kang, S., & Williams, J. L. (2019). Translational research to reduce health disparities and promote health equity. *Translational Issues in Psychological Science*, 5(4), 297-301.

Figure 6.1.12: Dr. Tucker received a grant from The Humana Foundation to fund Health-Smart Holistic Health and Wellness Centers and provide resources that empower participants to improve their mental, physical, and spiritual health.

- Tucker, C. M., Kang, S., Nmezi, N. A., Linn, G. S., Disangro, C. S., Arthur, T. M., & Ralston, P.A. (2019). A culturally sensitive church-based health-smart intervention for increasing health literacy and health-promoting behaviors among Black adult churchgoers. *Journal of health care for the poor and underserved*, 30(1), 80-101.
- Wall, W. A., Tucker, C. M., Roncoroni, J., Guastello, A. A., & Arthur, T. M. (2019). Clinical staff's motivators and barriers to engagement in health-promoting behaviors. *Journal for Nurses in Professional Development*, 35(2), 85-92.
- Roncoroni, J., Tucker, C. M., Wall, W.A., Wippold, G., & Ratchford, J. (2019). Associations of health self-efficacy with engagement in health-promoting behaviors and treatment adherence in rural patients. *Family & Community Health*, 42(2), 109-116.
- Wippold, G.M., Tucker, C. M., Smith, T., Ennis, N., Kang, S., Guastello A.A., Morrissette T.A., Arthur, T.M., & Desmond, F.F. (2019). An examination of health-promoting behaviors among Hispanic adults using an activation and empowerment approach. *Progress in Community Health Partnerships: Research, Education, and Action*, 13(1), 7–18.
- Tucker, C. M., Roncoroni, J., Wippold, G. M., Marsiske, M., Flenar, D. J., & Hultgren, K. (2018). Health self-empowerment theory: predicting health behaviors and BMI in culturally diverse adults. *Family & Community Health*, 41(3), 168-177.
- Tucker, C. M., Smith, T.M., Hogan, M. L., Banzhaf, M., Molina, N., & Rodriguez, B. (2018). Current demographics and roles of Florida Community Health Workers: Implications for future recruitment and training. *Journal of Community Health*, 43(3), 552-559.
- Tucker, C. M., Roncoroni, J., Wippold, G. M., Marsiske, M., & Flenar, D. (2018). Health self-empowerment theory (HSET): Predicting health behaviors and BMI in culturally diverse adults. *Family & Community Health*, 41(3), 168-177.
- Wippold, G., Tucker, C. M., Smith T. M., Rodriguez, V., Hayes, L., & Folger, A. C. (2018). Motivators of and barriers to healthy health-promoting behaviors among culturally diverse middle and high school students. *American Journal of Health Education*, 49(2), 105-112.

BRIAN CAHILL, PH.D. LECTURER, DEPARTMENT OF PSYCHOLOGY
Dr. Cahill established a year-long internship with the Gainesville Public Defenders Office, exclusively for Psychology undergraduate students. Students will be working directly with lawyers who represent low-income clients facing criminal charges in Alachua County, both misdemeanors and felonies.

Summary

Research by faculty members is ongoing and continuous. Service activities respond to both faculty interests and community initiatives and needs. Therefore, information in this publication can be updated as faculty and community engagement inevitably continue. These activities are the human faces of the mission of the University of Florida as a public institution.

Chapter 6, Section 1 Study Questions

1. Discuss in 200-300 words what you consider to be three major substantive issues in this section.
2. How relevant are the research and services cited in this section to your studies and future career?
3. What is your overall assessment of the content in this section?

Section 2: Educational Outreach – The Upward Bound Program at UF by Gwenuel W. Mingo

Since the mid-1960s, institutions of higher education like the University of Florida have facilitated federally funded programs designed to serve low-income students from their local communities. Three initial programs were known as the TRIO programs: Upward Bound, Talent Search, and Supportive Educational Services. The Upward Bound Program was first and was created out of the Economic Opportunity Act of 1964 and the War on Poverty ("History of TRIO Programs," 2020). The Program serves students from low-income households and families in which neither parent holds a Bachelor's degree. Upward Bound (UB) is designed to provide the support necessary for low-income students to succeed in their high schools, graduate, then enroll in and earn a degree at a post-secondary institution.

From April of 1974 until he retired in June of 2003, Dr. Gwenuel W. (G.W.) Mingo directed the Upward Bound Program at UF. The reflections presented here represent that period. (For Directors after Dr. Mingo, see Notes #2). In applying for federal funds for this program, post-secondary institutions had to submit a proposal to the U.S. Department of Education (USDOE) specifying how they would provide academic instruction, counseling, tutoring, and educational and cultural activities for the students to facilitate success.

Funded institutions were not required to show how parents would be involved in Upward Bound, but parents played a critical role in the Program at the University of Florida, where Mingo created specific objectives regarding parental involvement. The Parent Advisory Board as outlined in Mingo's proposal reviewed policies, carried out fundraising activities, advocated for the Program and shared beneficial information to all of the families in the Program. The Parent Advisory Board also shared strategies and information between other Upward Bound Programs throughout the nation.

The Parent Advisory Board was designed to help the Director accomplish the Program's objectives more efficiently by providing guidance in locating and utilizing community resources. The Advisory Board consisted of elected officers, mainly a President, Vice President, Secretary, Assistant Secretary, Treasurer, Assistant Treasurer, and Chaplain. The officers and other parents were empowered and educated by the Director on matters impacting their children both in the classroom and in the community. The Parent Advisory Board was the primary source of community engagement between the University of Florida and the Black Communities in Gainesville. Although Upward Bound is open to all students, the majority of participants were Black.

Parents of students in the University of Florida's Upward Bound Program's engagement in the community included:

- Assisting in the mobilization of community resources for Upward Bound activities.
- Serving as the liaisons between the Program and community personnel.
- Recruiting volunteer services from individuals and agencies in the community.
- Assisting in finding solutions for families with problems such as housing, welfare, transportation, employment, legal, and social issues.
- Advising the University on issues that were confronting the Program.
- Assisting with the grant application.
- Providing suggestions for Program improvement.
- Suggesting ways of expanding the influence of the Program in the community.
- Conducting UB events at churches in the community.
- Conducting fundraising activities in the community.

During each academic year, parent meetings were scheduled at least once per month where the agenda items often included discussing Upward Bound Program activities, attending workshops, participating as chaperones on education and cultural field trips, as well as planning and implementing fundraising activities. The Parent Advisory Board was effectively leveraged by the Director to help minimize challenges by dealing with hostile parents and students, disciplining students who broke rules, discouraging drug and alcohol use, motivating unmotivated students, informing uninformed community members about the merits of the Program, and dispelling any negative publicity. Knowing the data, especially for the support of students in minoritized communities, and believing that parents should play an active role in the education of their children, the Director encouraged parents to be effective educational team members. This included partnering with teachers at Upward Bound and the high school their child attended, as well as the Upward Bound Staff (Director, Coordinator, and Counselors), and the students.

Expanding the Reach Through Fundraising

Mingo worked to establish a rapport and maintain open lines of communication with the parents over the years, which served as the basis for a helpful partnership. Parents and students had a clear understanding of the educational and cultural goals and objectives of the University of Florida's Upward Bound Program and they worked to help the Director achieve those goals by raising additional funds to supplement the resources from the federal government, creating avenues for their students to gain greater exposure. Table 6.2.1 lists annual fundraising activities that were executed by the UB Parent Advisory Board.

Table 6.2.1: *Upward Bound Fundraising Activities.*

Month	Fundraising Activities
September – November	Worked the Concession Stands at University of Florida Football Games Sold Sweet Potato Pies during Thanksgiving
December	Assembled Financial Aid Packets for the University of Florida
January	Conducted a Gospel Jubilee at Mt. Olive A.M.E. Church in Gainesville
March	Worked the Concession Stands at the Gator Nationals
April	Held a Fashion Show in the UF and P.K. Yonge Auditoriums Sold Candy tins
May	Held a May Day Festival at T.B. McPherson Center and Citizen's Field
June	Held Car Washes throughout the city

Mingo encouraged the parents to attend seminars and workshops at the University of Florida specifically targeted for the students including College/Career Fairs, Financial Aid Workshops or Recruitment Conferences that Upward Bound students attended. Parents were also taught techniques of effective communication so they could advocate on behalf of their students, they were given clarity on high school course requirements and college preparation strategies so their children would not only attend college, but successfully graduate from college. The exposure to higher education provided by Upward Bound was helpful in educating not only students—many of whom would go on to become first-generation college students—but also preparing parents to support their students' pursuit of higher education. By enthusiastically sharing the benefits—academic preparation, cultural expansion, and overall student success—gained through participation in Upward Bound, the Parent Advisory Board served as an effective recruitment vehicle for other parents and students in the community who were not familiar with the Upward Bound Program. As partners within the community, parents also assisted local groups in increasing attendance at events by distributing flyers and calling parents and students to publicize their programs.

The Parent Advisory Board and the Director regularly conducted workshops on parental involvement in high school (which could contribute to academic success), college admission procedures, and applying for financial aid. Recognized beyond the local arena for their strong impact with the program, occasionally, the Director would take a group of parents to State, Regional, and National TRIO Conventions to participate as presenters on parental involvement in the Upward Bound Program. The parents provided their own funding for the trips to the conventions.

Maintaining a clear and distinct financial separation between the Parent Advisory Board and the Upward Bound Program, the parents' funds were in a checking account at a local bank where they deposited funds from their fundraising events. The Treasurer kept records of all monies received as well as all monies dispersed. The President,

Secretary, and Treasurer had the authority to sign checks; two signatures were required for any checks written by the Treasurer.

Political Advocacy for Federal Funding and Support

During the 1982 academic year, Mingo submitted the proposal to the U.S. Department of Education (USDOE) for Upward Bound funding only to learn that the Program would not be funded. The Dean of the College of Liberal Arts and Sciences at the University of Florida, Charles F. Sidman, was informed of this matter and he informed Robert Bryant, the Vice President of Academic Affairs. Bryant responded, "I do not believe it is appropriate to use general revenue dollars to fund a Program that has as its participants people who are not students at this university or persons who may never enroll as students at this university." He went on to say that the University should make no attempts to restore the funding for the Upward Bound Program.

After calling the USDOE many times to inquire about the proposal, specifically the scores earned for each evaluated objective and the data which justified the need for the Program, the USDOE would not provide any information. It was suggested that the Director go to Washington, D.C. to meet with someone face-to-face. Understanding the importance of the Upward Bound Program to the community and the critical partnership with the parents, not only did Mingo prepare to go to Capitol Hill, but he also involved the parents.

Two parents, Mrs. Lucille Miles and Mrs. Deloris Johnson, who served as the Vice President and Treasurer of the Parent Advisory Board respectively, accompanied Dr. Mingo to Washington to meet with the Program Officer at the USDOE, who was responsible for the University of Florida Upward Bound Program. While in Washington, they went to the offices of Florida Congressional members including Senator Lawton Chiles to solicit their help before going to meet with the Program Officer. The parents prayed for guidance before the meetings. The parents were professionally dressed, and they asked direct and logical questions of those they met with. The USDOE officials thought that they were Upward Bound staff members. They were surprised to find out that parents used their limited resources to travel to Washington and obtain an explanation for the retraction of funding for the University of Florida's program.

The two Parent Advisory Board leaders—representing many other parents back in Florida—asked questions about the scoring process and how USDOE determined there was no longer a need for the Program in the Gainesville area. The parents cited the names of students from Gainesville who had gone to college who were now teachers, engineers, pharmacists, and productive citizens. The parents also conducted some research on their own while they were in the USDOE facility, which was used to appeal the decision to not fund the University of Florida's Program. After two days in Washington, the Director and parents returned to Gainesville and immediately sent a written appeal to the USDOE regarding the funding, which was successfully approved. The University of Florida's Upward Bound Program had been saved and the Parent Advisory Board played a significant role in this victory.

The parents in UB were active and involved citizens who understood the political and philosophical battles surrounding the funding of UB Programs, so they did not hesitate to participate in the letter writing campaigns or to place calls to the offices of Representatives. The Upward Bound parents at the University of Florida were definitely fighters seeking to expand the funding and benefits of all Upward Bound Programs. The experiences of the Upward Bound parents in writing to their senators and representatives concerning funding of the program was a real-life civics lesson that inspired and empowered them to use their voices in other ways to benefit their neighborhoods.

In 1987, President Reagan proposed a 44% cut to the funding of the Upward Bound Programs around the nation (Eksterowicz & Gartner, 1990). Students and their parents wrote letters asking their Congresspersons to increase funding for these programs rather than cutting them, as President Reagan proposed. With an introduction by Senator Lawton Chiles, G.W. Mingo made his first appearance before the Senate Subcommittee on Appropriations on May 5, 1987 in Washington D.C. testifying in support of the TRIO Programs and helping influence a positive funding outcome for Upward Bound Programs (see Notes #1). Galvanizing support of students, parents, and community members, the letter-writing campaigns of all Upward Bound Programs nationwide ultimately proved effective in increasing funding to the Programs. Both the Senate and House passed a Continuing Resolution for a 16.7% increase in the funding of the Upward Bound Programs for the 1988 Fiscal Year. While his testimony helped make the case for funding, Mingo is clear that the bombardment of heartfelt letters written by parents to their Congresspersons describing the impact of Upward Bound on their family undoubtedly had a greater effect than that of one person testifying before a committee.

Encouraging Political Involvement

In this day and time of volatile political activity, it is unthinkable and unwise not to write or call your Congresspersons to solicit their support for keeping legislation and appropriation favorable to the Upward Bound Programs. As modeled by Dr. Mingo during his tenure at the University of Florida, Program Directors should not be the only ones emailing, calling, texting, and faxing the Congressperson about Upward Bound matters. They should also enroll students, parents and guardians of the students, and friends of the Upward Bound Program to contact the Congresspersons from their districts and advocate for Upward Bound.

Mingo found that the first step in empowering parents to become politically active was getting them registered to vote. As registered voters, parents can be more effective advocates for political change. Upward Bound Directors and parents of the students can establish an effective political advocacy team in conjunction with the Upward Bound educational team.

Parents must be encouraged by the Directors to involve themselves in the political processes in their communities. Parents should be involved in political groups at the lowest levels, in areas such as crime watch groups, parent/teacher associations, school boards, city and county commissions, etc. Directors and parents should find ways to utilize their talents to form educational and political teams for the purpose of enhancing the services rendered to their children. A team consisting of parents and UB personnel who advocate for better education in their school districts can also be effective advocates for education on the national level.

Cultural Exposure Within and Beyond Gainesville

Participation in the Gator Homecoming parade was a major activity that the parents used to publicize the Upward Bound Program in the Gainesville community. Each year, the Program had a float in the parade with Mr. and Ms. Upward Bound and their royal court dressed in gowns and suits riding on the float, looking very distinguished. The parents secured a trailer from contacts in the community and the Chestnut Funeral Home donated garage space to allow the students and parents to build the float—in case of inclement weather. One year, the UF Student Government Association decided not to let the Upward Bound Program participate in the parade, and that made the parents upset. The Student Government Association was going to let groups not affiliated with the University (such as the Shriners) participate, but not the Upward Bound Program, which is an official University of Florida program. The parents and the Director told Student Government officials that if Upward Bound was excluded then the parade should be cancelled. After some heated discussion, the SGA allowed the UB Program back in the parade.

The Upward Bound parents were not only focused on helping to make a difference and positive impact in the Gainesville community, but they were also cognizant of helping others outside of their local community. In 1992, when Hurricane Andrew hit South Florida, the Upward Bound

Parent Advisory Board contributed $800 to the University of Miami's Upward Bound Relief Fund to help Upward Board families that suffered losses. In 1995, the parents sent $1,600 to the U.S. Virgin Islands to help Upward Bound families that were devastated when Hurricane Marylin hit their island.

Every summer, students from the University of Florida's Upward Bound participated in an educational and cultural field trip to various states around the country, Puerto Rico, Canada, Mexico, or the Caribbean (See Figures 6.2.1. to 6.2.4). Prior to departing on these trips, participants were given preparatory instructions or experiences to acquaint them with the people and their culture. These trips to exhilarating, exotic, and enchanting destinations were planned by the Director, but the students and parents voted on whether they wanted to go on the trips. However, without the fundraising efforts of the parents, the trips would have been limited to a 300-mile radius and students would not have gained the exposure the Director desired.

Figure 6.2.1: Students and chaperones listen intently to Dr. Wilhem Baan of the National Astronomy and Ionosphere Center at the Arecibo Observatory in Puerto Rico. 1987.

Figure 6.2.2: Upward Bound Director Dr. Gwenuel Mingo and parents organized trips to places such as Vancouver, British Columbia, Canada to expand students' knowledge and experiences beyond Florida. 1991.

Figure 6.2.3: Students and parents visit the World Trade Center, New York. 1997.

Figure 6.2.4: Upward Bound students pose at the U.S.-Mexico border before entering Tijuana. 2001.

Upward Bound students at UF travelled to the following destinations:
- Nassau, Bahamas – 1980, 1984, 1985, 1993, 1996
- Jamaica – 1986, 1999
- Puerto Rico – 1987, 1990, 1995, 2002
- U.S. Virgin Islands – 1990, 1995, 2002
- Florida to California (Cross-Country Tour) – July 17th – 31st, 1988
- Key West – 1982, 1984, 1991
- Seattle and Vancouver – 1991
- New York, Montreal, Quebec – 1989, 1992, 2000
- Tuskegee, Selma, Montgomery – 2000
- California, Mexico, Nevada – 2001

Whenever it was possible during the field trips, the Director made sure students stopped at institutions that had Upward Bound Programs. If the stop included an overnight stay, they coordinated with the directors of those programs to meet with their students and have a social activity. The following provides insight into the types of educational and cultural activities students engaged in during a domestic summer field trip.

Fourteen Days on the Road – A Cross-Country Tour

This 14-day "Marathon Tour" went from Florida to Alabama to Tennessee to Missouri, Colorado, New Mexico, Arizona, California, Texas, Mexico, Louisiana and then back to Gainesville, Florida. It was a trip to remember, and included stops in historic Tuskegee, Alabama, where students and parent chaperones toured Tuskegee University and the George Washington Carver Museum. In Memphis, all were respectfully silent when we visited the Lorrain Hotel where Dr. Martin Luther King, Jr. was assassinated.

Visits to colleges that students might want to apply included LeMoyne-Owen College in Memphis, Metro State Park City College, University of Colorado, the Community College of Denver, the Air Force Academy, Pike's Peak Community College, Colorado College, Northern Arizona State University, Arizona State University, University of Nevada-Las Vegas, and University of Southern California. Then the tour headed back east to Texas Southern University and Huston-Tillotson University. Then Dillard, Loyola, and Xavier Universities in New Orleans.

Highlights of the trip included the Grand Canyon, Pike's Peak, Chinatown, Beverly Hills, Los Angeles Philharmonic Concert, and a live TV viewing of the hit daytime program *Family Feud*. Then back to the Alamo in San Antonio, the high-tech Motorola Plant in Austin, and the Superdome in New Orleans.

The extensive coast-to-coast trip wound back to Panama City and Tallahassee before arriving on the 14th day in Gainesville.

This cross-country trip would not have been possible if it had not been for the Upward Bound parents. They raised a considerable amount of money for the trip and they served as outstanding chaperones for the duration of the 14 days on the road. In addition to the two Upward

Bound staff members, a total of five parents served as chaperones on this trip. In order to develop a strong Upward Bound Program, Mingo found that it was important to mobilize and utilize a wide variety of community resources including parents and guardians to facilitate an efficient and effective program.

Conclusion

As a clear marker of the program's success, 85% of the over-3,000 high school students from low-income or first-generation college backgrounds who participated in the University of Florida's Upward Bound Program while Mingo was the Director attended colleges and universities throughout the United States, with some electing to attend the University of Florida. Parental involvement made a difference not only while their children were high school students taking weekend and summer academic enrichment classes on the University of Florida campus, but it also prepared them to support their students as they pursued higher education. Some of the parents became inspired by their children to enroll in college, which resulted in many older adults earning Associate's and Bachelor's Degrees and establishing new legacies of academic achievement in their families. Some went on to work in local education systems as teacher's aides and office administrators in the Alachua County Public Schools.

The Upward Bound Parent Advisory Board at the University of Florida served as a model for increasing relational educational and community engagement for the Alachua County Public Schools, Santa Fe Community College, and the University of Florida to follow. Each year, parents, students, and staff cooperated in decorating a float in the UF Homecoming Parade which showcased Mr. and Miss Upward Bound (Figure 6.2.5). Upward Bound parents and key individuals in the community formed a natural communication bridge that created positive social capital for the educational institutions in the local area.

The Upward Bound parents functioned as an unofficial liaison from one Program at the University to churches, clubs, schools, and many social and fraternal organizations in Gainesville, particularly within the Black

Figure 6.2.5: Mr. and Miss Upward Bound and Court ride in University of Florida Homecoming Parade. Pictured left to right: Gregory Beard (Mr. Upward Bound), Raymond Washington, James Jackson, Keisha Strawder, Angel Johnson (Miss Upward Bound), and Tomeka Anderson. 1997.

community. The Parent Advisory Board provided the University of Florida with a great opportunity to connect with the Black community, but the University failed to recognize and utilize the talents and skills of the parents. Many educators and administrators tend to bypass direct contact with parents and did not solicit their input in matters related to educating their children.

During his tenure as Director, G.W. Mingo educated and empowered parents by including them in the planning and operation of the Program. Many of the parents personally benefitted from their involvement, with some becoming inspired to further their own educational pursuits and following in their children's footsteps to earn Bachelor's Degrees, which enabled them to increase their incomes with better job opportunities.

The parents in the University of Florida's Upward Bound Program through the Parent Advisory Board operated as an integral and critical component of the Program. The Advisory Board reviewed Program policies, carried out fundraising activities, and shared information beneficial to all families in the Program through a variety of official and semiofficial activities. The parents have been a great asset and a salient tool in fighting funding cutbacks. Their advocacy on the state, local, and national level has resulted in greater benefits for the low-income children and families connected to TRIO Programs in the United States.

Overall, the parents of the University of Florida's Upward Bound Program were dedicated advocates and partners in the educational, cultural, and community activities in Gainesville and the surrounding counties. Thus, the impact of the program on Black and low-income families and the Gainesville communities was significant. During the period of more than 38 years when Upward Bound was funded at the University of Florida, over 3,000 students were enrolled in this college preparation program.

Notes

1. G.W. Mingo testified before the U.S. Senate on two occasions in support of TRIO Programs on May 5, 1987 and June 7, 1988. The testimonies are recorded with the Department of Labor, Health and Human Services, Education and Related Agencies Appropriations in H.R. 3058 and H.R. 4783 during the first and second session of the 100th Congress for fiscal years 1988 and 1989 (the fiscal years end in September).
2. Dr. Mingo was succeeded as Director by Beatrice Peak (2003-2004), and Dr. Barbara McDade Gordon (2004-2012), who served with shared appointment as a faculty member in the Department of Geography and Center for African students. The Upward Bound Program was not funded by the USDOE after 2012.

Chapter 6, Section 2 Study Questions

1. Based on this essay and related materials—what, in your opinion, is the value of Upward Bound in American higher education?
2. Conduct interviews with at least three students to get their views about programs such as Upward Bound.
3. To what extent did the Upward Bound Program contribute to the University of Florida's mission as a public institution?

References for Chapter 6, Section 2

"History of Federal TRIO Programs." Retrieved August 10, 2020, from: https://www2.ed.gov/about/offices/list/ope/trio/triohistory.html.

Eksterowicz, A. J. and Gartner J. D. (1990, July). Funding the Department of Education's Trio Programs. *Public Affairs Quarterly*, 4(3), 233-247.

Section 3: Religious Connections – The Pentecostal Initiative at UF and the Community by Sherry Sherrod DuPree

The role of community engagement in developing information sources in the area of African American Studies, including historical primary sources, has not been well documented by scholars. This case study on community engagement focuses on the University of Florida's (UF) interactions with the African American Eastside communities in Gainesville, especially Seminary Lane. The new information sources, which were produced by the Pentecostal Initiative discussed herein, were the result of an ongoing dialogue and cooperation between university administrators, scholars, and community members. For the purposes of this paper, the term community engagement is defined as "the collaboration between institutions of higher education and their larger communities (local, regional/state, national, global) for the mutually beneficial exchange of knowledge and resources in a context of partnership and reciprocity" (Carnegie Classification, 2020, p.1). Since 1981, the University of Florida's Division of Sponsored Research (DSR) has supported grassroots research for the exploration and development of learning tools for students, scholars, church leaders, and laypeople who study Black Church history. By highlighting the process of building ties to the local Black communities and the eventual resulting scholarship in the area of Black Pentecostal church history and culture, this study may point the way toward a more inclusive approach to religious research in the United States and around the world.

UF Division of Sponsored Research: Pentecostal Initiative

In 1980, a building construction student came to the reference desk at UF's Library West asking for information on Rev. Charles Harrison Mason (1864-1961), the founder of the Church of God in Christ (COGIC) in Memphis, Tennessee. This male UF student, Mr. Lee, was studying to be a minister in the COGIC under Reverend Dr. D.R. Williams, pastor of Williams Temple COGIC, located on Seventh Avenue, in the Seminary Lane community. Lee was completing his studies at UF. A search of available religious, non-religious, and African American reference sources did not produce any results. Reference librarian Sherry DuPree asked him to allow a few days for the return of a query from academic and public libraries for a biography or other information on COGIC. These searches did not yield any new sources. A query was also sent to the UF interlibrary loan desk to African American librarian, Marva Coward. In two weeks, DuPree received a pamphlet from the church headquarters with a telephone number that DuPree called to speak with the assistant. The next week, she received an envelope with several items which were given to the student. Lee took the items to his COGIC class. Next, DuPree received a telephone call from Williams, thanking the UF library for help. He shared the documents with his class and invited DuPree and family to visit his church.

The problem in researching early African American church leaders of the African American Holiness Pentecostal Movement, such as Mason, is that scholars found sources were not available, especially sermons. The primary and secondary sources often contain claims that were difficult to substantiate, since they were usually republished stories with little or no research to clarify claims. (DuPree, 1990, p.3). In the process of aiding this information-seeking student, DuPree realized that a lacuna in African American religion research needed to be filled. Therefore, DuPree spoke to Dr. William Simmons, Director of the Institute of Black Culture (IBC) about establishing a Pentecostal research project. Although the history and culture of Baptist and Methodist African American churches have been documented, information about Holiness Pentecostal churches was omitted in academic literature due to the fact that they have been considered a subculture. In order to rectify this omission, Simmons, a Methodist minister, agreed to bring awareness to this specific area of religious culture. Simmons and DuPree spoke to Dr. James Scott and Dr. Art Sandeen of the Division of Student Services (DSS), about conducting and engaging UF in this research. Scott put Simmons and DuPree in contact with Vice President Donald Price in the Division of Sponsored Research (DSR). A meeting was held with Dr. Samuel S. Hill, Professor of Religion and Social Ethics (RSE). As a result of these interactions, DuPree wrote a proposal for a research study, with an emphasis on COGIC and founding of the African American Pentecostal Movement in the United States. The proposed study resulted in providing a reference book that included the locations of items from other academic institutions. UF administrators approved the research study and encouraged IBC to include the African American Studies Program and the Eastside African American communities in Gainesville. A pilot study with a DSR grant of $500 included funding to carry out a survey. From that survey, DuPree and Simmons learned they needed to communicate with church historians, such as Dr. Ithiel Clemmons, the COGIC historian in Greensboro, North Carolina. In addition, the pastor of Mount Carmel Baptist Church in Gainesville, Rev. Dr. T.A. Wright, directed the project to Howard University Divinity School Director, Dr. N. Jones, and Dr. James S. Tinney, of Howard's journalism department, for their far-reaching contacts and support communities. The initial report convinced those involved at DSR to continue the African American Pentecostal research. Several grants were written, and funds were received from the Howard University School of Divinity, the National Humanities Council, International Business Machine Corporation (IBM), the National Council of Churches, the Southern Regional Education Board, and the Lilly Foundation. Each grantor provided funds of between $1,000 to $15,000, which were used for recording equipment, travel, and archival supplies. Additional funding from the UF Gatorade Trust were used to hire and pay data entry clerks to enter items on spreadsheets. UF African American students were hired part-time, and tasked with the responsibilities to send letters, return phone calls, acquire items, and conduct other office duties under the supervision of Ms. Alma Johnson Small, the IBC administrative assistant. Many oral interviews of family members in Pentecostal churches were conducted by DuPree and other African American researchers. A Pentecostal clearinghouse of materials was formed with scholars contributing and requesting information from all over the world, including Canada and London, England.

DuPree asked the National Archives and Records Administration in Washington, DC to detail the existing scholarship, in order to provide a historical overview of the African American Pentecostal movement that would provide sources for scholars. That question was the genesis of what became the Holiness-Pentecostal Movement Initiative, out of which came a network of supporters. Several major project goals were agreed upon by project stakeholders. The goal of the project was to promote gathering documentation from Black organizations, religious institutions, and individuals. Secondly, the project joined other academic institutions in encouraging scholarship on Pentecostalism. Third, the project explored both primary and secondary resources in academic settings and in the possession of individuals. Fourth, the project examined the academic perspective of students and scholars, who would use the information to produce theses and dissertations. This was in keeping with the realization that Holiness Pentecostals are a diverse group. Finally, organizers were committed to the idea of making this collection accessible to the general public. (DuPree, 1988, p.10-12).

As the existence of this project became known, many more African American Pentecostal organizations donated documents. In 1996, *African-American Holiness-Pentecostal Movement: An Annotated Bibliography* was published by Garland Publishing, for which Hill at RSE wrote a two-page preface. He mentions that one of the major repositories for the Pentecostal movement in the American Black Church was the Federal Bureau of Investigations. "A trip to the nation's capital to see FBI reports belongs on your research trip itinerary" (DuPree, 2013, p.vii).

The Pentecostal Initiative produced A *Biographical Dictionary of African-American Holiness-Pentecostals 1880-1990*, printed in Washington, DC by the Middle Atlantic Regional Press, 1989. In the foreword written by Simmons at IBC, he observed,

> It is surprising to learn that Pentecostalism in America began with an African American preacher in Los Angeles, California. From this publication, Pentecostals, as well as other Black Denominations, will gain pride in the knowledge that the Black church was in the forefront of a multi-ethnic religious movement in America. This dictionary should stimulate research and encourage our youth to gain a greater appreciation for the many contributions of Blacks in America (DuPree, 1989, p.vii).

After years of data collection and archival research, the question raised by a UF engineering student about the founding of the Black Pentecostal church can be answered, thanks to the cooperative effort known as the Pentecostal initiative. It all started with Rev. C.H. Mason.

Rev. Charles Harrison Mason, Founder of COGIC

Mason (Figure 6.3.1) was raised in a rural area, near Pine Bluff, Arkansas to a family of ex-slaves. Mason was not allowed to have a formal education; he worked on farms. Yet, Mason learned to read, write, and understand the Bible (Stewart et al., 2017, p.42). Mason was raised in the Baptist Church and involved in the Sanctified Holiness Movement with Rev. Charles Price Jones (who died in 1949) in Los Angeles, California. Mason heard about the baptism of the Holy Ghost and he along with Rev. D.J. Young and Rev. J. Jeter traveled from Mississippi to Los Angeles, California, to learn and receive this New Testament blessing. Mason received his baptism in the Holy Ghost at the famous Azusa Street Mission Revival, under leader Rev. William

Figure 6.3.1: The Revered C. H. Mason was founder of the Church of God in Christ (COGIC) in Memphis, Tennessee. (www.cogic.org; see References: Chapter 6, Section 3)

Joseph Seymour (1870-1922) in March 1907 (Stewart et al., 2017, pp. 22-24).

The Azusa Street, Apostolic Faith Gospel Mission, Revival signaled a new approach to religion, and a new oral tradition of speaking in tongues or glossolalia. Historian and President of the William Seymour College and Educational Foundation, Estrelda Y. Alexander, stated Seymour changed his approach to worship to a personal relationship with Jesus Christ, using scripture from Acts 2:4 (Alexander, 2011, pp.124-125).

After Mason returned from Los Angeles to Mississippi, he was disfellowshipped (similar to being shunned) by Jones and others. Mason

Figure 6.3.2: The Reverend William J. Seymour was a leader in the Church of God in Christ (COGIC) in the early 1900s. (https://commons.wikimedia.org; see References: Chapter 6, Section 3)

and his followers changed COGIC from Holiness (living a clean life, set apart from worldly processions) to Pentecostal. Until 1916, Mason had integrated congregations in COGIC, but after the film Birth of A Nation, which opened in 1915, societal racism caused COGIC to become a predominantly Black Church (Stewart, et al., 2017, p.42). At COGIC churches, members were baptized in the name of the Father, the Son, and the Holy Ghost, known as the Holy Trinity. Baptism in the Holy Ghost is the evidence of speaking in unknown tongues. Pentecostals believe they should share, love and be led in brotherhood with all men and women from all cultures (Faulkner & Smith, 2017, pp.58-60).

Because few early Pentecostal church records were saved, one of the most important government sources on Mason and others in Black

Figure 6.3.3: The Azusa Street Mission and Revival signaled a new approach to religion, and the oral tradition of speaking in tongues or glossolalia. (https://commons.wikimedia.org; see References: Chapter 6, Section 3)

church history have been Federal Bureau of Investigation (FBI) reports, which were written (often daily) surveillance notes that are accepted by scholars as factual. It is through the FBI primary documents from 1917 about Pentecostal leader Mason that scholars have been able to verify he was opposed to COGIC participating in World War I (DuPree, 2013, p.412). Aided by increased access to archival documents, research continues to bring to light a more nuanced understanding of the founding of African American Pentecostalism and the context from which it sprung.

Community Engagement Outcomes

UF students and senior leadership have periodically forged bonds with Black community organizations which may not be directly connected to the Pentecostal Initiative. For instance, campus members took part in a broader coalition to encourage Gainesville City Commissioners and others to consider saving the remainder of the Black Historic neighborhood, Seminary Lane, an area close to UF's campus. UF African American leaders, faculty and students have connected with this neighborhood to save Gainesville's oldest underserved Eastside community. Furthermore, UF scholars created a UF African American studies community syllabus and shared it with African American community network leaders. Other UF affiliated groups have identified immediate COVID-19 pandemic educational needs, such as after-school tutoring to support secondary students in these challenging times.

Although UF and local African American communities have co-existed for decades in the adjacent neighborhoods, the Seminary Lane community housing issues have been problematic. Gentrification has caused Black families to lose their homes vis-à-vis higher-priced housing developments geared to college students (DuPree, 2020).

In the era of the Global Pandemic, the UF Gator Jewish Student Center (GJSC), located near Seminary Lane on 5th Avenue, has played a part in strengthening UF's ties with Black neighborhoods by helping to distribute governmentally funded face masks, in a collaboration with the African American community churches and civic organizations. The cloth masks were washable and were a great help to families in the Seminary Lane community and other Eastside African American communities.

UF GJSC leaders collaborated with African American church leaders. An agreement was reached between organizations to distribute protective face masks. African American churches sent members to the UF GJSC to pick up masks for transport to Black churches for broader, free distribution to adults as well as school children. On the day of the mask giveaway, African American church members directed long lines of traffic to African American church parking lots, as drivers rolled down their car windows to receive packages of masks. This was a team effort to distribute and to help maintain healthy habits by wearing a mask and keeping a social distance.

Now, as citizens and students walk down the street in Gainesville they wave and smile at each other and talk with their masks on. The communication has supported better understanding of each other's culture. African American and Jewish religious leaders made Gainesville a better and healthier place for all residents.

The UF African American Studies Program presented a proposal for educational opportunities where UF students communicated and earn class credit with various church and community organizations. Gainesville City Commissioners formed a partnership with UF to discuss housing problems related to gentrification. They also worked together to ameliorate inadequate housing conditions in Black neighborhoods. Thus, a long-term African American community housing need has been identified and acknowledged.

Religious Engagement Outcomes

Increased use of African American Holiness Pentecostal resources has influenced the evolution of academic research and community engagement during the last four decades. Reference sources have been available online and in print to enhance the study of the Pentecostal movement, which has been the fastest growing religious group (Banks, 1993).

The overall purpose of the Pentecostal study has been to gather and deposit documents in recognized academic locations available to the general public, information seekers and scholars. There have been several important milestones in the process of establishing access to archival materials. In 1990, a collection was deposited at the New York's Schomburg Center for Research in Black Culture. Then, in 1997, over 70 unknown Black religious periodicals were housed and microfilmed at the University of Wisconsin, Historical Society. In addition, a digital collection was opened in 2011 at the University of Southern California, Los Angeles. The two largest collections were placed in repositories in Washington, D.C.: Smithsonian Institution Anacostia Museum in 2006 and in the Manuscript Division of The Library of Congress, in 2020.

Change has taken place in the study and research of Pentecostalism today with a network of religious, academic, and public libraries, opening their doors with distance learning (ask the librarian, finding aids, online searching, zoom meetings) for info seekers and scholars as they have collaborated to include Black Pentecostals in religious history.

UF's African American Studies program continues to heed history's call to forge a bond with East Gainesville, as local residents have sought solutions to community housing needs. Through its support, UF has shown "Black Lives Matter" to UF students and faculty, a sense of dignity and pride encourages best practices for the greater good of learning and sharing Black History with all communities of the world.

Chapter 6, Section 3 Study Questions

1. What are your views on the University of Florida's engagement with religious institutions in the Gainesville community?
2. What role, if any, should religious institutions have at the University of Florida?
3. How important is it for you (if you have a religious affiliation) for the University of Florida to support your faith?

References for Chapter 6, Section 3

Alexander, E.Y. (2011). *Black fire reader: A documentary resources on African American Pentecostalism*. Wipf and Stock Publishers.

AFM on Azusa Street (1907). [Photograph] Wikimedia Commons website. https://commons.wikimedia.org/wiki/File:AFM_on_azusa_street.jpg

Banks, A. M. (1993, August). Black churches get little due, book says statistics show "Explosive" growth. *Religious News Service*.

Carnegie Foundation for the Advancement of Teaching Elective Community Engagement Classification [PDF file]. https://cdn.csu.edu.au/__data/assets/pdf_file/0010/3193327/carnegie-classification-framework.pdf

Chism, J. (2019). *Saints in the struggle: Church of God in Christ activists in the Memphis Civil Rights Movement, 1954-1968.* Lexington Books.

Davis, J.A. (1989, September 9). A holy quest when a librarian couldn't find information about Black Pentecostals in history books, she decided to write her own. *Sun Sentinel.*

DuPree, S.S. (1987). Documenting religious activity in non-religious and religious depositories with emphasis on Black Pentecostalism. *Society for Pentecostal Studies: Annual Meeting Papers.*

DuPree, S.S. (1989). A *biographical dictionary of African American Holiness-Pentecostals 1880-1990.* MAR Press.

DuPree, S.S. (1990). Documenting religious activity in nonreligious repositories. *Collection Building,* 10 (3/4), 30-36. https://doi.org/10.1108/eb023280

DuPree, S.S. (2020, July 8). Historian supports Seminary Lane staying true to its history. *Gainesville Sun.*

Essegbey, J. (2020, February 20). African American studies at the University of Florida celebrates 50 years. *African American Studies Program Booklet.*

Faulkner, J. W. & Smith, R.D. (2017). "It is written" in *Minutes of the Church of God in Christ held at Memphis Tennessee 1919-1932.* Flywheel Ministries Press.

Harn Museum of Art. (n.d.). *Eric Segal. University of Florida.* Retrieved March 24, 2021, from: http://harn.ufl.edu/linkedfiles/biography-ericsegal.pdf

Mason, C. H. (n.d). [Photograph, detail] Church of God in Christ website. http://www.cogic.org/foundersweek/promote/cg-2016-founders-1920x1080/

Ortiz, P. (2019) *From Segregation to Black Lives Matter: A symposium and celebration of the opening of the Joel Buchanan Archive of African American Oral History at the University of Florida.* The Samuel Proctor Oral History Program at the University of Florida. https://mediasite.video.ufl.edu/Mediasite/Catalog/catalogs/segregation-to-black-lives-matter-symposium

Seymour, W. J. (1910s). [Photograph] Wikimedia Commons website. https://commons.wikimedia.org/wiki/File:William_J._Seymour_(cropped).jpg

Sherrod, M.N., Jr. & DuPree, S.S. (2006). Researching African American Pentecostalism: The Church of God in Christ and the Azusa Street Revival [April 27, 2:00pm Conference Session]. *Azusa Street Revival Centennial*, Los Angeles Convention Center, California.

Stewart, A.C., Smith, R.D. & DuPree. S.S. (2017) A compendium: Bishop C.H. Mason, Sr. Founder of the Church of God in Christ. *Scholars Fellowship Academic Forum: Auxiliaries in Ministry (AIM)*. Charlotte Convention Center, North Carolina. CreateSpace.

Tinker, C. (2020, February 20). Panel urges UF to connect more to community, *Gainesville Sun*.

Chapter 7: Reflections on the African American Studies Program by Harry B. Shaw

Abstract: This chapter is a reflection on the development of African American Studies at UF by Dr. Harry B. Shaw, the first African American Associate Dean of the College of Liberal Arts and Sciences (formerly University College) on two levels: (1) professional and (2) personal. The chapter includes observations by Dr. Shaw about his direct involvement in the development of the African American Studies Program at the University of Florida. Dr. Shaw arrived at UF in 1973 as a faculty member in the Department of English and was engaged in the historical development of the Program, even after his retirement as Emeritus Professor in 2004.

Reflections on the African American Studies Program

My reflections on the history of the African American Studies Program at the University of Florida are both professional and personal and consist of chronicling and examining my observations of and direct involvement in the Program and its development from its beginning in 1970 through its 50th Anniversary in 2020. This examination considers the overall effects of a number of factors that include the Program's historical context, administrative and academic setting, and leadership through its trials, opportunities, accomplishments, and shortcomings.

More specifically, my views and judgements reflect my observations of the academic development of the African American Studies Program at the University of Florida in 1969 and the hiring of Dr. Ronald C. Foreman as the first Director of the African American Studies Program in 1970; the national, local, and University of Florida sociopolitical context of the early stages of the Program; along with my own professional connections with the University of Florida as a faculty member in the English Department and as an administrator in the University College and the College of Liberal Arts and Sciences. In addition, I will address the failure of the Program to attain departmental status during the

30 years of Dr. Foreman's leadership of African American Studies. I will also offer commentary on the strengths and weaknesses of the African American Studies Program; observations and reflections of the attitudes of the Black community toward the African American Studies Program and the University of Florida; and reflections on my professional life at the University of Florida, including lessons for today's advocates of African American Studies.

While the history of the African American Studies Program at the University of Florida may not be readily known even to those within the institution, reflection on its inception and development sheds important light on the histories and cultures of the University of Florida, the local community of Gainesville and surrounding area, the state of Florida, and the nation. The African American Studies Program was established in 1969. The first director was Dr. Ronald Foreman, and the Program enrolled its first students in 1970. It is also noteworthy that during the next year, 1971, when there were only three Black professors, one Black administrator, and 387 Black students at the University of Florida, the African American Studies Program awarded its first certificate. Key figures in the establishment of the African American Studies Program at UF included administrators Dr. Manning J. Dauer, Chairman, Social Sciences Division; Dr. Harry H. Sisler, Dean, College of Arts and Sciences; and Dr. Harold Stahmer, Associate Dean, College of Arts and Sciences. The faculty who assisted in the earliest development of the Program included Dr. Hunt Davis, Jr., (History); Dr. Seldon Henry, (History), Dr. Steve Conroy, (Social Sciences), Dr. James Morrison (Political Science); and Dr. Augustus M. Burns (Social Sciences, History). A number of students played important roles in the Program's beginning, including Samuel Taylor (the President of Black Student Union in 1970 and the First Black Student Government President in 1972); David Horne, a Doctoral candidate in History; and Emerson Thompson and Larry Jordon, undergraduate students (UF Liberal Arts and Sciences, 2020). Going beyond these essential facts, however, to reflect on the impetus and the circumstances that gave rise to the Program is equally telling because doing so allows these facts to be seen in proper perspective.

Like so many Black people at this time, emerging from the turbulent decade of the 1960s, I took personally every chapter, every page, and every sentence of the long history of brutality being played out across the nation against African Americans. I followed closely as this violence spurred an increase in organized Black resistance, particularly that beginning in 1960 with the lunch counter sit-ins in Greensboro, North Carolina. The 1960s were a continuous cycle of brutal racial repression followed by protest in the form of sit-ins, marches, and boycotts, or eruptions into violent riots in major cities, including New York, Newark, Chicago, Detroit, Cleveland, and Watts, Los Angeles. It is important to note that in too many instances, the authorities in the nation reacted to Black resistance against oppression by escalating violence against Blacks. The violence was perpetrated by a combination of racist vigilantes, organized mobs, police agencies, or—too often—even federal government entities, particularly the FBI.

The Civil Rights Movement and its rootedness in Black history and the violent response to it forms the historical backdrop to the demands by students for African American Studies departments in the 1960s. The decade was punctuated by a gruesome string of assassinated Black leaders, their sympathizers, and innocent Black citizens—some of the murders committed in prime-time, some in the middle of the night. In 1963 it was Medgar Evers, head of the Mississippi NAACP; four young Black girls, Addie Mae Collins, Cynthia Wesley, Carole Robertson, and Carol Denise McNair in the Birmingham 16th Street Baptist Church bombing; and John F. Kennedy, president of the United States. In 1964 it was three young civil rights workers, James Chaney, Andrew Goodman, and Michael Schwerner, in Philadelphia, Mississippi. In 1965 it was Malcolm X, leading figure in the Nation of Islam. In 1968 it was Dr. Martin Luther King, Jr. and Robert Kennedy, Attorney General of the United States. In 1969 it was Black Panthers Fred Hampton and Mark Clark in Chicago. While clearly the African American Studies Program at the University of Florida grew most immediately out of the unrest caused by the death of Dr. Martin Luther King in 1968, it also had its roots in the culmination of the turbulent, violent decade of the 1960s that prompted positive responses from the University of Florida and other institutions of higher education.

While this bloody and brave decade set the stage for the African American Studies Program at the University of Florida and ushered in a more ameliorative approach by some colleges and universities, the changes came with noticeable imperfections and with many schools reacting largely to the prod of federal court orders to desegregate. Still, institutions of higher education offered some of the nation's brightest rays of hope. In this setting of struggle—including walkouts and demands primarily by Black students for the African American Studies Program and the Institute of Black Culture—the Program began. The interactive dynamic that played out among violence, protest, and progress called to mind teachings of the great Frederick Douglass who said, "Power concedes nothing without a demand" and "If there is no struggle, there is no progress." Any progress made by African Americans at the University of Florida stemmed from a struggle against competing entities and often recalcitrant mindsets. From my vantage point of being in the Dean's Office, I was privileged to witness and be a part of the struggle.

Succinctly, that is the background—the setting—for the establishment of the African American Studies Program at the University of Florida, and my view of it. As I recall some of my own career experiences during the very early years of the African American Studies Program, I provide hints of what the general atmosphere was like locally on the ground.

It is worth mentioning that although I did not become part of the University of Florida African American Studies Program until 1973, three years after it began, I had some awareness of, connection to, and affinity with the Program since its inception. This insight was afforded by my prior colleagueship from 1968 to 1970 at Illinois State University with the Program's first director, Dr. Ronald Foreman. Together there we experienced some of the vicissitudes of African American professional life in higher education during the 1960s and 1970s. When he left Illinois State University in 1970 to become the Director of the African American Studies Program at the University of Florida, he kept me apprised of the early development of the Program.

As to the local atmosphere, it should first of all be remembered that in 1970 the University of Florida was one of those institutions under a federal court order to desegregate. Therefore, it seemed clear to me that simply because Black students were able to enroll at the University of Florida, to have an Institute of Black Culture, and to begin an African American Studies Program did not mean that suddenly and completely the whole University was converted like Paul on the road to Damascus. Rather, in my experience and observation, what moved things forward was a combination of progressive leadership at various levels of the University and the dogged determination of persons who were involved with the African American Studies Program per se, as well as those Black faculty members who were collectively involved in trying to safeguard the well-being and progress of Black faculty staff and students at the University of Florida. Notable in this effort were Dr. Jacqueline Hart, the Affirmative Action Coordinator, Dr. Roderick McDavis from the College of Education, Law Professor Michael Moorhead, Dr. Carlton Davis from the Institute of Food and Agricultural Sciences, Drs. Ronald and Grace Henderson from Sociology, and myself. We were some of a group who spent many hours during and after our workdays pooling our strategies to help keep things on a favorable trajectory. We had no choice but to be persistent. Although success was not always guaranteed, giving up was not an option.

The appreciation of the Black community for the efforts and products of the African American Studies Program was largely affected by their prior familiarity with and opportunities for exposure to elements of African American history and culture, often made available by the African American Studies Program. Speakers, artists, and classes were generally well received by Black gown but—not surprisingly—less well attended by Black town.

It should be kept in mind that, in those days, there really were not very many Black students on campus and only a handful of Black faculty. The University of Florida, under a federal court order to desegregate, faced two big problems: the need to hire more Black faculty members and the need to enroll more Black students. Building an African

American Studies Program without either of these critical masses would be especially difficult. As a newly appointed assistant Dean in University College, and as a friend of the Director of the Program, I felt a responsibility and looked for opportunities to help.

In the early 1970s there was no College of Liberal Arts and Sciences—it was created in 1978. Before then, there were the College of Arts and Sciences and the University College. University College was the lower division college which was primarily responsible for providing general education for the University of Florida. Arts and Sciences was an upper division college which provided courses leading to various majors. In 1978 the two colleges merged to form the present-day College of Liberal Arts and Sciences (CLAS). The new college moved into the newly constructed General Purpose A building (GPA), later named Turlington Hall.

It is unlikely that the following part of my reflections is recorded in any written history, but by way of providing context and atmosphere, I can reveal that my own situation in University College at first seemed tenuous at best. In 1973, during my interview process for the assistant deanship position in University College, the few Black faculty members who met with me told me that my immediate predecessor, a Black Assistant Dean, had been physically thrown out of his office by the college dean, Robert "Bob" Burton Brown. One of my new colleagues even estimated that I would last as little as two weeks in the job. The full story is very long, but the important thing is that I somehow exceeded this prediction by more than three decades in the college office, serving with four different deans.

It turns out that I was able to help the African American Studies Program in a fundamental way. Although my beginnings seemed tenuous based on the reputation of my very headstrong, irascible dean and his determination to live up to it, as far as I could tell, he treated me fairly. When I went to the first University College Assembly where I was introduced to department chairs and faculty, I was astonished to see only other one Black faculty member. In the following weeks,

I carefully but persistently expressed concern about the numbers of Black faculty. One day, the dean came into my office and told me that we needed to hire more Black faculty and that he was putting me in charge. Although I was surprised at this abrupt turn, I did not dare drop the ball.

I was able to convince Dean Brown and Vice President Robert Bryan to try a different approach to hiring Black faculty. Since pursuing Black superstar faculty had been largely unsuccessful because it seemed they were invariably more interested in elite universities like Harvard, Princeton, and Berkeley than they were in the University of Florida, I suggested pursuing promising Black ABDs—that is, doctoral candidates who had completed all but the dissertation.

Working with Dr. Jaquelyn Hart, Affirmative Action Coordinator, we set up what we called the Vita Bank. I sent out letters to Black ABDs across the country requesting vitas. Then I sent letters to all University of Florida departments informing them of the project and asking whether they had vacancies. Altogether in the first year of serious recruitment in 1974, primarily through this process, we hired 14 new Black faculty members in various departments.

One of the Black faculty recruits that I am most proud of is Dr. Mildred Hill-Lubin. In addition to sending her the usual letter, in 1974 I traveled to the University of Illinois to personally invite her to the University of Florida. I mention her not only because she became a lifelong dear friend and colleague in the English Department, but because she became such an important addition to the early African American Studies Program at the University of Florida.

The central administration was so pleased with our success that it turned the green light to red. As a result, very few Black faculty members were hired in 1975 and 1976. In 1977, the green light turned on again and the Vita Bank rolled into action, resulting in an unprecedented 20 Black faculty hires. Once again, the English Department, the African American Studies Program, and the University of Florida considered themselves very fortunate to have landed a star, Jim Haskins, among this group of recruits. Jim Haskins, as a scholar, writer, and professor, added immensely to the overall stock of the African American Studies Program in terms of prestige, attractiveness, and leadership.

Through logic that seemed short-sighted, the University turned the red light on again. Some of these hired Black faculty members remained at the University of Florida for years and the departments were made richer by their added professional resources. However, whenever University of Florida Black faculty left—either perishing for not publishing or excelling here and moving on to something bigger and better—some considered such loss a failure and criticized the system that had been called so successful. The unrealistic expectation was that once Black faculty had gotten into these hallowed halls, they would be content to stay here forever. The reality is that some Black faculty, like astute academics in general, used the University of Florida as a career steppingstone. I think the average time of employment for faculty in general at that time was about four years. Despite our efforts to proceed full speed ahead, the University of Florida continued to play "red light-green light" in hiring Black faculty for a number of years. But purely in terms of numbers and quality of Black faculty, the University of Florida was beginning to compare favorably to prestigious universities around the country.

One lesson here is that the successful recruiting and hiring of Black faculty has to be not only a concerted effort but a continual process. Another sobering lesson is that the University's central administration was much more easily pleased than we were.

Of course, many of us, remembering the early demands of Black students for Black Studies, were hoping that the increase in the number of Black faculty would positively impact the number of Black students on campus and vice versa. Therefore, simultaneously there was a similar effort to recruit and retain significant numbers of Black students whose presence would be of paramount importance to the prospects of a fledgling African American Studies Program and for whom the African American Studies Program was an attraction.

Because it was difficult and expensive to compete with more prestigious universities offering more attractive scholarships to recruit the top Black students, special efforts were made to locate average students. The bulk of Black students attending the University of Florida in the early years from 1969 through the 1970s were specially admitted. In fact, it was not until the year 1985 that the number of regularly admitted Black students was greater than the number of specially admitted Black students. But from these we had many high achievers, including student body presidents, dean's list honorees, and honor roll students, showing it is more important what one does with an opportunity than where one begins.

Enrolling specially admitted students meant also providing special programs to assure their retention and success. As Assistant Dean of University College, part of my responsibility was to supervise the directors of several minority programs. Two of these minority programs were federally funded: the Student Support Services Program, a special-admission minority program, and the Upward Bound Program, a minority high-school-to-college bridge program. I also wrote successful proposals for two additional minority programs funded by the University of Florida, the Student Enrichment Services Program (SESP) and the Academic Enrichment and Retention Services (AERS).

Moreover, Mr. John Boatwright, Director of Minority Admissions, and others continued to recruit and support regularly admitted Black students through a growing scholarship program, especially the National Achievement Scholarship Program.

The argument for continuing special efforts to attract and to retain Black students often met with opposition. For example, Vice President Robert Bryan called me into his office one day around 1979-80 and told me that schools in Florida had been integrated for 12 years. As a result, he pointed out, Black children and white children had been in school together and were exposed throughout to the same educational opportunities, therefore clearly there was no more need for any special programs for Black students at the University of Florida. Furthermore, he declared he intended to dismantle them all. Although that dismantling did not happen, the battle to preserve the programs against mindsets misguided by such logic and misinformation set the tone for the ongoing struggle for improving—and at times even defending the very existence of—programs to assist Black students (Lempel, 2018). In this atmosphere, the University's Black community had to find ways to work with its champions and circumvent its detractors to move forward.

Before 1990, the term "minority" was virtually synonymous with Black or African American. With the arrival of President John Lombardi and his provost, Andrew Sorensen, the—perhaps well-meaning—emphasis on an egalitarian approach to all minorities presented another challenge. Dr. Lombardi served as president of the University of Florida from 1990 to 1999. "Parity among minorities" was the motto of their approach to diversity efforts.

The good news is that minority student enrollment increased significantly. The bad news is that—ironically—Black enrollment first abruptly leveled off and then actually declined during this time.

The reasons were obvious to some of us. In the state of Florida, the academic profiles of admissible Hispanic students were only slightly below that of whites and the academic profiles of admissible Asian students was slightly above that of whites, but the academic profiles of African American students were considerably below the others for historic reasons. Once pitted against the children of wealthy Cuban refugees and the highly selected, talented Asian students, Black students—though capable of doing well—found increasing difficulty competing for scholarships or even being admitted. The lesson here is that friendly fire can obviously be just as harmful as enemy fire.

In 1999, there was a changing of the guard. Dr. Lombardi left the

University of Florida and Jeb Bush became governor of Florida. Governor Bush promoted a "race-blind" approach sanctimoniously called "One Florida" striking down Affirmative Action in the Sunshine State (Tucker, 2016). After seven years of Jeb Bush, Black student enrollment did not keep pace with overall growth of other minorities. While in 1999 Black students comprised 14.4% of the student body, their numbers and percentages of the student body began and continued to decline significantly (University of Florida Common Data Set 2006-2007). More recent figures show that percentages of other minorities continued to rise, but African Americans' enrollment percentages declined even further to below 10 to 5.97 percent of the student body in 2017, and African Americans have become the only minority group at the University of Florida that enrolled less than its percentage in the general population (Data USA: University of Florida, 2017).

The African American community applauds the University of Florida for valuing diversity and it continues to encourage and support a more equitable representation within the diversity. Since the need and the justification are just as great as they have ever been, hopefully with an abundance of goodwill and genuine desire for the best, the State of Florida and the University of Florida together will earnestly work to discover ways to achieve equitable enrollment of African American students. My observation is that if these efforts fail, it may lead to a bitterly ironic outcome that a diminishing number of Black students will benefit from the success of the African American Studies Program—which owes its very existence to the struggles and demands of African American students in the first place.

Although the solution to the problem of declining Black enrollment has yet to be addressed successfully, this major advancement of African American Studies toward departmental status has paralleled and grown out of the sustained efforts over many years by Dr. Foreman and all the Program directors who followed him to realize their visions of acquiring the key elements of adequate and suitable office space, enough autonomous faculty lines, and a viable interdisciplinary core curriculum. One measurement of the progress made by the Program is to look at the conditions of these elements early on and through the years.

When I came to the University in 1973, the one-room office for African American Studies was located on the 4th floor of Little Hall, and it was by no means a penthouse. Throughout the time that Dr. Foreman and I were at the University of Florida, our offices were usually in the same buildings or in close proximity. We moved from Little Hall to Turlington Hall, back to Little Hall again, and then to Walker Hall. We were moving forward and—for the most part—upward. Figure 7.1 shows some of the first African American faculty members at UF including Dr. Foreman, Dr. Mildred Hill-Lubin, Dr. Richard Barksdale, and myself.

Figure 7.1: 7.1 Newly hired faculty members in the African American Studies Program in the early 1970s (left to right): Dr. Ron Foreman, Director of AASP, Dr. Mildred Hill-Lubin, English, and Dr. Harry Shaw, Assistant Dean of the University College, with Visiting Professor Dr. Richard Barksdale of the University of Illinois. (Photo: H.B. Shaw)

Dr. Ronald C. Foreman, Jr. received his Ph.D. in Mass Communications from the University of Illinois. He taught at Shaw University, Knoxville College, Tuskegee Institute, and Illinois State University before joining the University of Florida in 1970 as the Director of the Afro-American Studies Program and faculty member in the English Department. For 30 years he directed Afro-American Studies, teaching the Program's core courses as well as a variety of literature courses in the English Department.

Among other duties, he served for many years as faculty advisor for the Black Graduate Student Organization and as a member of the Board of Directors of the Florida Folklife Association. In 1970, along with Dr. Carlton G. Davis of the Institute of Food and Agricultural Sciences and Dr. Elwyn Adams of the Music Department, Dr. Foreman was one of the first three tenure-track African American faculty members hired at the University of Florida. He and other faculty and students were instrumental in laying the groundwork for many of the policies and programs that today foster diversity and promote humane enlightenment at the University.

One of Dr. Foreman's immediate concerns and another measure of moving forward was the curriculum of the African American Studies Program. The curriculum in those early years consisted of one or two introductory courses in African American Studies and an upper division or senior seminar-level course. These were taught by Dr. Foreman. As I remember, one or two other courses might be taught by faculty members in the History Department. The goal of the Program was to have students complete enough credit hours to earn a certificate in African American Studies. Indeed, awarding certificates was supposed to be a way for the Program to justify itself.

There were immediately several challenges to achieving this goal. First of all, the limited number of courses that counted for African American Studies made them easy to overlook among the wide array of course offerings campus-wide. Additionally, at that time, especially among the general student body, the lack of familiarity with and interest in a non-traditional subject like African American Studies combined with the very small number of African American students on campus meant that there were relatively few certificates awarded.

Clearly being able to offer core courses of the African American Studies Program that also provided credit toward fulfilling the general education requirement would help build interest in the Program's introductory level courses. However, without a core junior and senior faculty to meet students' needs by providing courses that fulfill general education and certificate requirements, the certificate program enrollment continued to be low as students worked to meet their other graduation and major requirements.

In 1974, as Assistant Dean in University College, which was the college that provided the university's general education, to complement my efforts to increase the numbers of African American faculty and students, I saw another way to help the African American Studies Program while pursuing my own interests. I created the first African American literature course in the University College English Department. I was able to have the course offered for general education credit, helping to boost the number of students who earned certificates in the African American Studies Program.

It is accurate to say that Dr. Foreman could be conveniently relied upon to be businesslike and diplomatic when making the case for the needs of the Program, as indicated by his early vision and hopes for enlargement of the Program's library acquisitions and curriculum with a budget sufficient for expanding its core teaching staff to at least six faculty positions.

While Dr. Foreman had the requisite vision to assemble all the necessary parts of the Program to lead a department, during his tenure, he was never able to see the University leaders at various levels sufficiently aligned to accomplish the transition or even move meaningfully toward a minor or major. Mindsets either at the vice president's level or the president's level too often did not see the African American

Studies Program as central to the mission of the University of Florida. Furthermore, other competing programs also vied for valuable and scarce resources, which had to be husbanded carefully under the watchful eye of the Board of Regents of the State of Florida. I also reflect on the hard fact that the State of Florida during this time was still a Deep South state. Occasionally, I was reminded of this whenever I encountered visual vestiges of the once-pervasive system of racial discrimination. At that time, I could still see the rare residual "Colored" and "White" signs on bathroom doors at filling stations and—more alarmingly—even at the University of Florida's Shands Hospital. At that time also, very often Dr. Foreman was concerned with fighting for adequate funding to operate the Program, seeking funds for faculty lines, events, speakers, secretarial support, equipment, supplies, etc. In this context, I am reminded of John Milton's cogent line, "They also serve who only stand and wait."

In this context, when one wonders about why Dr. Foreman was not successful in achieving departmental status during his 30 years as the director of the African American Studies Program, one should remember that success is sometimes just holding on and not losing ground. While African American Studies programs at some universities achieved departmental status early on, some have never achieved it, even at prestigious schools. At some universities, support for Black or African American Studies programs has been discontinued, or they have become subsets within other academic units such as history departments. At universities across the country African American Studies programs waxed and waned; some flourished and some declined, depending on leadership and on the political/economic environment. The factors that dictated lack of success for Dr. Foreman to achieve departmental status for the African American Studies Program remained operant until very recently, when, under the leadership of Dr. Sharon Austin, the stars and various levels of administration were aligned favorably for the upward transition to begin.

The African American Studies Program directors who followed Dr. Foreman brought credentials and experience from around the country and echoed and extended his vision. Upon Dr. Foreman's retirement in 2000, Dr. Darryl M. Scott with a Ph.D. in History from Stanford University served as director of the African American Studies Program until 2003. He emphasized the need to attract a diverse faculty with broad interests in the social sciences and the humanities in order to develop a strong major and a well-rounded graduate program.

From 2003 to 2004, Dr. Marilyn M. Thomas-Houston with a Ph.D. in Cultural Anthropology from New York University served as the next director of the African American Studies Program and continued the theme of developing a strong African American Studies Program, stressing the interdisciplinary and holistic foundation of studying the Black experience. Her main goals were to build an undergraduate program that conferred both a Bachelor's degree and a graduate certificate, establish a strong research component that included internationalization, develop strong community relations through a service-learning component and community outreach initiative, and hire dynamic and productive faculty and administrative staff. She stressed the importance of acquiring outside funding to develop various resources, such as graduate assistantships and post-doctoral fellowships, faculty exchange programs with HBCUs, study-abroad programs that trace the African American Diaspora, and community history projects and exhibitions. Dr. Thomas-Houston's imaginative approach supported her goals and enriched the African American Studies Program with innovations like the annual Ronald C. Foreman Lecture Series, which features lectures by Black Studies scholars, and the Harry B. Shaw Undergraduate Travel Grant, which sponsors selected undergraduate students to attend and present their research papers at professional conferences.

When I retired from the University of Florida in 2004, Dr. Terry Mills replaced me as Associate Dean for Minority Affairs in the College of Liberal Arts and Sciences. From 2004 to 2006, Dr. Mills, with a Ph.D. in Sociology from the University of Southern California, served also as the Interim Director of the African American Studies Program. A major accomplishment of his was transitioning the curriculum from consisting largely of "special topics" courses to revising and receiving approval by the University Curriculum Committee for five courses that became general education courses and/or Gordon Rule courses and fulfilled the State of Florida's writing requirement. The impetus gained from getting these courses approved in turn set the groundwork for his second major accomplishment of the development of an 18-credit minor in African American Studies that was approved by the Curriculum Committee.

From 2006 to 2010, Dr. Faye Harrison with a Ph.D. in Anthropology from Stanford University served as director of the African American Studies Program and continued to strengthen the Program's minor and to lay the groundwork for the Program's major by adding to the number of courses eligible for general education and Gordon Rule credit and significantly growing the number of students taking African American Studies Program courses and receiving minors.

From 2010 to 2011, Dr. Stephanie Evans with a Ph.D. in African American Studies from the University of Massachusetts, Amherst, served as director of the African American Studies Program and continued to add to the number of students enrolling in African American Studies Program courses, maintaining the momentum of the Program's minor and continuing en route toward the major.

From 2011 to 2019, Dr. Sharon Austin with a Ph.D. in Political Science from the University of Tennessee served as director of the African American Studies Program. She continued the progress of the Program's directors before her, and under her helm in 2013, the Program began offering the major and awarded the first BA degrees in 2014. Under her leadership, the Program enjoyed popularity, becoming one of the fastest growing majors at the University of Florida. Most notably, with the aligned support and cooperation of Dr. David Richardson, Dean of the College of Liberal Arts and Sciences, Dr. Joseph Glover, Provost of the University of Florida, and Dr. Kent Fuchs, President of the University of Florida, she was able to lead the final successful effort to achieve approval to develop the long-sought departmental status for African American Studies.

To facilitate this effort, the African American Studies Steering Committee was established late in 2017 to review the status and make recommendations about the future of the African American Studies Program. The Committee consisted of Dr. Jacob U. Gordon, Professor Emeritus, University of Kansas; Dr. Bonnie Moradi, University of Florida Psychology Department; Ms. Stephanie Birch, African American Studies Librarian, University of Florida Library; Dr. Vincent Adejuma, Lecturer, African American Studies Program; and Dr. Mary Watt, Associate Dean, College of Liberal Arts and Sciences. A final report of the Committee included a strong recommendation for a departmental structure, a new director, faculty, resources, and a strategic plan. On April 23, 2018, African American Studies Program stakeholders (faculty, affiliates, the Advisory Committee, and Associate Dean Watt) overwhelmingly voted to approve the African American Studies Steering Committee Final Report and Recommendations (UF Digital Collections, Institutional Repository).

In the fall of 2019, the dean of the college, Dean Richardson, accepted the Steering Committee's Final Report and appointed Dr. James Essegbey as Interim Director of the African American Studies Program, pending a national search for a permanent director. Dr. Essegbey, with a Ph.D. in Linguistics from Leiden University in the Netherlands, has served from 2019 to 2020 as interim director of the Program. The dean also promised four new faculty tenure-track positions. Subsequently, Dr. David Canton, who was the Director of the Africana Studies Program at Connecticut College, was selected as the new Director of the African American Studies Program, effective August 2020. He is expected to lead the Program toward a departmental status.

While the approach of African American Studies will continue to be interdisciplinary, a recognized major advantage to the departmental status is greater autonomy to hire full-time tenured and tenure-track faculty in African American Studies without the reliance on faculty from joint appointments in other departments. Goals for the coming department include having a graduate program that offers Master's and doctoral degrees in African American Studies as well as a Graduate Certificate in Race and Ethnicity. Fittingly, the African American

Studies Program in 2019 moved its offices to adequate and suitable space in Turlington Hall.

Recently, I toured the new offices of the African American Studies Program on the first floor of Turlington Hall and can say truly that looking back at office space is one clear measure of the Program's progress. Dr. Foreman would be pleased with the new offices. He would also be pleased to see the fulfillment of his vision of Program's needs, including enlargement of the Program's core teaching faculty, expanded library acquisitions, and broadened curriculum, supported by non-academic career staff.

Fortunately, today African American Studies does not have to be overly concerned with meeting quotas for granting students certificates; the Program is pursuing higher goals. When I look back to where the Program was and see how far it has progressed, I can very much appreciate the tireless talented leadership of the African American Studies Program—including contributions of the aforementioned past directors. Additionally, as applies more specifically to the present trajectory toward departmental status, these efforts could not have been successful without the vision, cooperation, and partnering of Dean Richardson, Provost Glover, and President Fuchs.

As the Program moves forward, there should never be the question about what one can do with a major in African American Studies. Literally the sky is the limit. Dr. Mae Jameson, the NASA astronaut, earned an African American Studies major from Stanford University and former First Lady Michelle Obama holds a minor in African American Studies from Princeton University. In fact, the dynamic, multicultural, multidisciplinary curriculum of African American Studies is the epitome of a liberal education—inclusive of topics often avoided by other curricula, yet vitally relevant in explaining and shaping the world around us.

Speaking of majors, according to the most recent former Program Director, Dr. Sharon Austin, the University of Florida's African American Studies Program has among the largest number of majors in the country, considerably more than most African American Studies programs or departments at peer universities. This accomplishment speaks highly of the effectiveness and dedication of the directors and the faculty of the African American Studies Program, especially in light of the aforementioned serious enrollment challenges for African American students.

As the Program transitions into a department, it will reasonably anticipate hiring more faculty and recruiting and retaining more Black students at the University of Florida. By doing so, the new department will be fulfilling the stated mission of the University of Florida and thereby helping the University to legitimately put into effect its top tier classification. For all students and faculty at the University of Florida, for all Americans, and indeed for all the world, the kind of unveiling and sharing of the African American experience done by African American Studies scholars and teachers is altogether essential to any true and unredacted version and understanding of the American experience. For this reason, my great expectation for the African American Studies at the University of Florida is that it will indeed look back and move forward.

The light is green now, and the future should be bright.

Chapter 7 Study Questions

1. What are some of the critical issues raised by the author about the status of Black Education at UF?
2. How do you compare the author's reflections in this Chapter to any other one Black literary writer in African American Literature?
3. To what extent are the author's experiences similar to those experienced by Black Faculty and Administrators at other Historically White Colleges and Universities (HWCUs)?

References

African American Studies Steering Committee. (2018, April 24). *Final Report & Recommendations*. University of Florida. Retrieved March 29, 2021, from https://ufdc.ufl.edu/IR00010296/00001

Data USA. (2017). *University of Florida: Enrollment by Race & Ethnicity.* Retrieved March 29, 2021 from https://datausa.io/profile/university/university-of-florida#enrollment

Lempel. L. R., (2018). The Long Struggle for Quality Education for African Americans in East Florida. *Journal of Florida Studies*, 1(7), 16-25. Retrieved from http://www.journaloffloridastudies.org/files/vol0107/LEMPEL_Integration.pdf

Tucker, N. (2016, January 7). He got his way. Then he got a mess. *The Washington Post.* Retrieved March 29, 2021 from https://www.washingtonpost.com/sf/national/2016/01/07/decidersbush/

University of Florida: College Liberal Arts and Sciences. (2020). *African American Studies History.* Retrieved March 29, 2021 from https://afam.clas.ufl/history

University of Florida. (2007, April). Common Data Set 2006-2007, *Enrollment and Persistence: Enrollment by Racial/Ethnic Category.* [University data report]. Retrieved from https://ir.aa.ufl.edu/media/iraaufledu/common-data-set/cds2006-07.pdf

Chapter 8: The Life and Times of Stephan P. Mickle (1944-2021): First UF African American Graduate and the College of Law Connection by Jacob U'Mofe Gordon

Abstract: The life and times of the first African American Senior District Judge of the United States District Court for the Northern District of Florida is presented in this chapter by Professor Emeritus Jacob U'Mofe Gordon, University of Kansas. Judge Stephan P. Mickle was the first African American to receive an undergraduate degree from the University of Florida (1965). He subsequently earned two UF degrees: a Master of Education 1966 and a Juris Doctor in Law in 1970. Judge Mickle received the University of Florida's Distinguished Alumni Award in 1999. His wife, Evelyn Marie Moore Mickle, was the first African American to receive a Bachelor of Science in Nursing from the UF's College of Nursing in 1967. These reflections conclude with remembrances from his colleagues, law clerks, faculty, and dean of the Levin College of Law at a special ceremony honoring Judge Mickle's decades of service in the pursuit of equal justice.

Stephan P. Mickle was born on June 18, 1944 in New York City. He is one of four children by his parents, the late Mr. Andrew R. Mickle, from South Carolina, and his wife, Mrs. Catherine Berry Mickle. They both graduated from Bethune-Cookman College (now Bethune-Cookman University) in 1955 and 1957, respectively. They became successful educators in the Alachua County Public Schools. Perhaps Mr. Mickle's major contribution to the City of Gainesville in Alachua County was his service as Director of Aquatics, where he taught swimming to generations of children in Gainesville. Stephan's three siblings were Andrew (deceased), Darryl L. and Jeffrey A.

As educators, Stephan's parents imbued the values of education, hard work, and fairness in their children. These values led them to success, notwithstanding racial barriers against African Americans, which were especially marked at that time. Andrew was a geologist;

Darryl became a veterinarian in Atlanta; Jeffery is an educator in Ocala, Florida; and Stephan became the first African American graduate from the University of Florida and the first African American to practice law in Alachua County, Florida (Crabbe, 2008, April 4).

In 1965, at a critical junction in the American Civil Rights Movement, Stephan P. Mickle received a Bachelor of Arts in Political Science from the University of Florida, becoming the first Black student to graduate from the University. He received a Master of Education from the University of Florida in 1966. In addition, he received his Juris Doctor (J.D.) from the Frederic G. Levin College of Law at the University of Florida in 1970. In doing so, Mr. Mickle became the second Black student to graduate from the University of Florida's Levin College of Law; the first graduate was Mr. W. George Allen (1936-2019) in 1962 (Dobson, 2019). A civil rights activist and lawyer, W. George Allen was born in Sanford, Florida to Lessie Mae Williams and Fletcher Allen. According to his autobiography, Allen grew up with his mother and stepfather, Bruce Brown, in segregated communities in Florida (Allen, 2010). He graduated from Crooms High School, going on to graduate from Florida A&M University, one of the Historically Black Colleges and Universities (HBCUs), in 1958. Prior to his graduation, Mr. Allen worked for the U.S. Army Intelligence, where he was the only African American. Although he was accepted to Harvard School of Law, he chose instead to become the first Black student at the University of Florida Levin College of Law. He had a successful legal career and public service in Broward County before his passing in 2019 (Tinker, 2019, November 19). In October 2012, the Levin College of Law and its Center for the Study of Race and Race Relations, the University of Florida Association of Black Alumni, and the University of Florida Alumni Association held a tribute for Allen, marking the 50th Anniversary of his graduation (Figure 8.1). Yet in interviews through the years, Allen recalled the discrimination he endured while studying in Gainesville, Florida (Dobson, 2019, November 8).

Stephan P. Mickle was an attorney in the Office of Legal Services at the Equal Employment Opportunity Commission in Washington,

Figure 8.1: With wife Evelyn holding the Bible, Stephan P. Mickle is sworn in as the first African American U.S. District Court Judge in the Northern District of Florida. (Alumni CLAS Notes. Spring 1999)

D.C. in 1970 and had a private practice in Fort Lauderdale, Florida. In 1971, Mickle became an adjunct professor at the University of Florida College of Law, a position he held for 38 years. He was also a special assistant public defender for the Eighth Judicial Circuit in 1974. He was a judge on the Alachua County Court from 1970 to 1984 and was a circuit judge of the Eighth Judicial Circuit from 1984 to 1992. In 1993, he began serving as the first Black federal judge in the First District Court of Appeal.

President Bill Clinton nominated Judge Mickle to the United States District Court for the Northern District of Florida on January 27, 1998, to the seat vacated by Maurice M. Paul. Judge Mickle was confirmed by the U.S Senate on May 14, 1998. He took the oath of office from Chief Judge Joseph Hatchett of the U.S. Court of Appeals on August 28, 1998 (Figure 8.2). He served as Chief Judge from 2009 to 2011.

Figure 8.2: Judge Mickle honors Attorney George Allen (JD 1962), the first African American to graduate from the Law School at UF. (Gainesville Sun. 10.17.2012).

Judge Stephan P. Mickle's career was marked by many "firsts" as reported by several sources, including Wikipedia (2020):

- First African American to serve as a federal judge in the United States District Court for the Northern District of Florida, May 22, 1998 – June 22, 2011.
- First African American to receive the University of Florida's Distinguished Alumni Award in 1999.
- First African American to serve as Adjunct Law Professor at the University of Florida for 38 years.
- First African American to be honored by the Levin College of Law at the University of Florida with an unveiled portrait, which now hangs at the Advocacy Center of the College of Law.

On October 23, 2020, the Levin College of Law at the University of Florida—in the midst of the COVID-19 pandemic—organized a virtual "Celebration of Life and Career of Judge Mickle." The occasion was the unveiling of the Portrait of Judge Mickle (Figure 8.3). Many signatories were present at this special event, which was presided over by the Dean of the College, Professor Laura A. Rosenbury.

Figure 8.3: In October of 2020 the Law School unveiled a portrait of Judge Mickle which will hang in the Martin H. Levin Advocacy Center. (UF Levin College of Law. 2020)

Mrs. Evelyn Moore Mickle, the wife of Judge Mickle, was in attendance. Ms. Evelyn Marie Moore Mickle was born in 1947 to Reverend Frazier and Gretchen Whittington Moore and is a native of Suwannee County, Live Oak, Florida; she was the 11th child of 15 children. Her parents were farmers; her father was a pastor and school bus driver and her mother was a wife and homemaker. Evelyn and Stephan Mickle are the parents of two daughters and two sons, and the grandparents of five grandchildren.

Evelyn Moore Mickle was the first African American student admitted into the College of Nursing at the University of Florida and the first

African American student to graduate with a Bachelor of Science in Nursing (BSN) from the College of Nursing in 1967. Mrs. Mickle's experiences as a pioneering African American female student were harrowing to say the least; she endured a tremendous amount of racism. Mrs. Mickle shared her experiences as a student at a 2009 public program by the Samuel Proctor Oral History Program, *Florida Black History: Where We Stand in the Age of Barack Obama*: https://www.youtube.com/watch?v=mkeBwBeKY7A&t=2667s

A licensed registered nurse with the Florida State Board of Nursing, Mrs. Mickle's career experiences include a wide range of areas in health care: psychiatry, pediatrics, internal medicine, juvenile detention, day care, hospital and clinic supervision, school nursing, community health nursing, etc. A commemorative brick was laid in her honor as the first African American graduate in Nursing from the College of Nursing at the University of Florida. The brick was placed at the North East corner of the University Auditorium. Mrs. Mickle currently serves in the Gainesville community as Mt. Carmel Women's Ministry Leader (Interview. 2020, January. Samuel Proctor Oral History Program).

Reflections

As indicated earlier, Professor Laura A. Rosenbury, Dean of the Levin College of Law at the University of Florida, presided over the ceremony to unveil the portrait of Judge Stephan P. Mickle. Several colleagues, former law clerks, law students and friends of the Mickle family came to share their reflections about Judge Mickle. Here are a few select edited reflections. We begin with Dean Rosenbury's remarks:

Dean Laura Rosenbury: It is my honor and privilege to welcome you to this virtual celebration of the life and career of Judge Stephan Mickle. We have an outstanding group of guests who will be joining us today, and I am so happy that Judge Mickle and his family are also able to be here with us to enjoy it all. As a matter of housekeeping, since this is a Zoom presentation, please remain on mute for the duration of the program to limit interruptions. We also recommend selecting the speaker view on the upper righthand corner of your screen for the best viewing option. 2020 has undoubtably been a year like no other. Everything about the way we live and work together has had to change and adapt to the logistics of a new normal. When I reflect on these past months, I have to admit, they've been very difficult, but I know my difficulty—our difficulty—is nothing compared to what life must have been like for Judge Stephan Mickle when he first arrived at the University of Florida in 1962. Although he ended up becoming Judge Mickle years later, Stephan Mickle first had to do what many of us have never before experienced in our lives—being the first. The first to forge ahead when no one else looked like him on the University of Florida campus; the first to persist, despite the challenges and obstacles that Stephan Mickle faced as a young Black man at the University of Florida. In 1965 Stephan Mickle became the first African American to earn an undergraduate degree at the University of Florida. He then earned a Master's degree in education in 1966. And in 1970, Stephen Mickle became the University of Florida's second African American Law School graduate. He began his legal career here in Alachua County, and he continued to be the first at each step of the way. During the next hour, we are going to hear from several people who will share stories about their relationship with Judge Mickle and his impact on their lives, an impact that has extended to so many of our lives, our careers, and our community. We will begin our program with some context about Judge Mickle's legacy at the University of Florida, context that will be provided by Marna Weston from Oak Hall Academy and UF's Samuel Proctor Oral History Program. Marna, the floor is yours.

Marna Weston, *faculty member at Oak Hall Academy and UF's Samuel Proctor Oral History Program.*

Marna Weston: Thank you very much, Dean Rosenbury, for your incredibly gracious introduction and for appropriately framing the occasion for today. Distinguished barristers, Judges Turner, Hinkle, and Walker, Chairman Cunningham, our moot court president, Ms. Love, the Mickle family, ladies, and gentlemen, a beautiful sunrise welcomed us this morning and led us each to this midday service, and in our own individual ways we all celebrated it. For myself I praise God. I praise God for waking me up this morning, praise God for this beautiful ceremony where the University of Florida recognizes African American achievement and excellence. I praise God for the individuals and the family that we celebrate with this unveiling today. I was invited to provide context for these festivities. *Context* is an interesting word. I hope over the course of these brief moments that I'm able to provide some context to such a great life. Now you know I was raised a church-going boy. I was son of Baptist ministers, the child of children of the movement and part of the movement—the strategy that was used was to build courage for the obstacles people would face with the freedom song, a mixture of common religious hymns and secular music. As the elders would put it, to deliver the lesson, we need at least one piece of song. [Singing] "I woke up this morning with my mind, my mind it was stayed on freedom! Oh, woke up this morning with my mind, my mind it was stayed on freedom. Oh, woke up this morning with my mind, my mind it was stayed on freedom! Halle-lu, Halle-lu, Halle lu-jah!" I woke up this morning with the honor of talking about Judge Mickle, but to honor the man, we must honor all of the cloth in the tapestry that made him. We're gonna hear today of humble beginnings. We will hear today of being welcomed and not welcome. We already have some from our Dean. We will hear of family and of love, and there are undoubtedly stories of professional achievement from this honored list of distinguished guests, and we hunger for them on this day as we honor Judge Mickle. Eleven years ago, when Dr. Machen tapped Florida Bridgewater-Alford, Dr. Glover, and our brother in all things historic, Dr. Paul Ortiz, the first African Americans at UF, and when the Black Alumni Association took the occasion of a home football game to gather our Black alumni, I was able to speak with W. George Allen, Dr. Reuben Brigety, Little Jake, and most importantly Judge Mickle and Mrs. Mickle. From that meeting with Mrs. Mickle, our first African American graduate from the nursing school, I first learned of how the University of Florida of that era was really not the University of Florida of the era that we enjoy today. The institution did not celebrate diversity. The institution did not acknowledge the graduation of Black students or invite them to join the Alumni Association as—of course—

we do now. Mrs. Mickle shared with me a narrative of exclusion and painful feeling, but she also shared a life with the man that we recognize and honor today. And of course, by way of doing so, we also honor her. The Dean has already indicated how Judge Mickle was the second African American Law School graduate and the first African American undergraduate. He was nominated by President Clinton, and from that Judge Mickle became the first African American chief judge of the Northern District of Florida. Now today, those who follow me will have more interesting anecdotes on that. So, I'm going to allow them to speak to that series of firsts that happens statewide, nationally. I'm going to leave some water in the well for them. From my humble place I'm here and providing context. I'd like to draw your attention for just a moment to the what-ifs. What if Constance Baker Mobley and Charles Hamilton Houston had not been there to advocate that Black students attend law schools in their own states? It was the custom before the 1960s, for the Board of Control in Florida to offer to pay the most qualified Black student advocates to go to schools in other states. What if there had been no Constance Baker Mobley or Charles Hamilton Houston? What if Virgil Hawkins had not given up his rights to attend the University of Florida? After the struggle of struggles, one that probably warrants, you know, a historic marker from down in Okahumpka to the University of Florida. But if he had not done what he did—What if there had not been a George Starke Jr. or a W. George Allen to proceed a Stephan Mickle, who would come here, just to struggle, which he and his wife, both did? How we remember our firsts is equally important to what could have been. And I want to thank you, Mr. Hawkins for all that you did that made Stephan Mickle and Mrs. Mickle possible. Today, we're celebrating Judge Mickle while he's here with us, as we should. Let's remember that Mr. Hawkins received his degrees after he was gone. But what if the UF Law School did not have a Stephan Mickle as a student? What if there had never been a President Clinton to nominate him? I mean, if you think about it, to place it in context, outside of President Bush, not knowing how much a loaf of bread and a gallon of milk costs or Ross Perot having all those charts... That leadership that we are celebrating today might have been lost. Elections have consequences. Instead, a marvelous tapestry will be unveiled today, and we will celebrate a meticulous, professional, and immaculate career in service that was built. And this community has been served exceptionally by Judge Mickle as an attorney, as a jurist at every level. And now, more than ever, the finest legal degree granting institution in America at the flagship institution, in the State, can say thank you. Judge Mickle, we love you, we respect you, and now a permanent symbol of that affection is being offered, and it is important to have a permanent symbol, because the absence of that symbol could say so much more. Its presence assures an understanding of the value that you and your family hold and the love that you hold in all of our hearts. Judge Mickle, Mrs. Mickle, your daughter Stephanie, the entire Mickle family. We thank you so much for your sacrifices and your struggles. And I'm reminded of the words of another song that resonates from Judge Mickle's career, it's a song that my Dad really enjoyed; "If I could help somebody." [Singing] "If I can help somebody, as I travel along, if I can heal somebody, with a word or a song. If I can show somebody he is traveling wrong, then my living shall not be in vain." Thank you, Judge Mickle for having a life we're celebrating, one not in vain. One of service and purpose to the people, not only of our state but to the entire nation. Thank you.

The Honorable Larry Turner *was Judge Mickle's classmate and longtime friend from the class of 1970. Larry is also the founding partner of Turner, O'Connor, and Kozlowski.*

Larry Turner: Thank you Dean. I appreciate this opportunity. I especially appreciate the opportunity to speak about my friend Stephan Mickle, who I have known since law school. In fact, we met in law school. I was a year up ahead of stuff until I got married and had to work for a year, until my wife completed her undergraduate degree. In the meantime, Stephan entered the law school and we graduated together. We were, at that time, friendly, but we had not become friends. That is, we didn't spend much time together. However, towards the end of law school, we began doing that. We were part of the study group for the Florida Bar Exam. Florida Bar Examination in those days was essay predominantly. It was a three-day exam, and we had to go as I recall to Miami to take it. Stephan and I shared—we wrote down together, we shared hotel room—and we studied, and we studied, and we studied. At those study sessions is when I first got impressed with Stephan for who he really was and what he was really like on a couple levels. First, Stephen was always the best prepared of all of us. He came in prepared. He had reviewed the information, he understood the information, and he taught us the information. I credit Stephan with getting me through the bar exam. So, Stephan, thank you for helping me pass the bar exam so that I could have a career as a lawyer, a short time as a Judge, and then as a lawyer again. The vernacular of the day was he "carried me" through the bar exam. And frankly, without his help, not sure I would have made it. We found out—I found out years later, he found out more quickly—from one of our study partners, McFerrin Smith also a judge later on, that the three of us had scored in the top 10% of the class, the people who took the bar exam that year. So, I thank you for that as well. You made me look good. Stephan, after graduating in 1970, came to Gainesville in 1971 having worked for the Equal Employment Opportunity Commission for a while. And Stephan, in his own quiet and powerful way, was always a barrier breaker. And the first barrier I was aware of him breaking outside of being the second Black graduate of the law school and so forth, was when he came to Gainesville to be a member of our local Bar. The local Bar Association in those days met at the Gainesville Golf and Country Club, and of course the Gainesville Golf and Country Club was a segregated, all-white institution and simply did not permit people of color—African American or otherwise—to be there unless they were in the service industry of some sort. Well, some of us, myself included, younger lawyers, resented that, we didn't think that was a good policy to have. So, when Stephan came to Gainesville, we now said, "What are you going to do? Where are you going to meet now? Are you going to tell him he can't join our Bar Association, or he can join, but he can't come to our meeting or lunches?" It created a dilemma. So, they took it to the Board of Directors of the country club, many of whom were members of our Bar Association. And the Board of Directors said, "Well, gee, I tell you what, we'll let him come, he can come into the building and he doesn't have to come in the back door. He can come in the front door. However, he must go directly into the dining room, have his luncheon, and leave by the front door. He's not to go anywhere else in the building." So it was that kind of in-your-face ugly stuff, even then among professionals and semi-literate people. I was told I have three to five minutes. I've got a timer go in here and I've been over four already, so I'll keep cut this short. One of Stephan's lasting legacies is that he and a few more of us, the Young Turks, we called ourselves, saw that people did not have the ability to hire lawyers, except in the criminal justice system, of course, where there was a public defenders' system. And, as a result, often failed in any kind of legal process they were involved in because they didn't have representation and of course they didn't know how to navigate the system of law. So, we got together a group of volunteer lawyers, again, the Young Turks plus Claire Gehan—who is another legend in her own right, the first woman to graduate from the University of Florida College of Law—and Claire and the rest of us got together and we formed a volunteer group of lawyers who would... We got someone to donate a space that we could use one night a week as a storefront where we could meet with prospective clients, and we would take turns meeting with prospective clients there. And then we take them back to our office eventually and represent them pro bono. Stephan was one of the first people to step forward for that he was one of the bulwarks of that. He was always making breaking down barriers and kicking in doors, metaphorically. That storefront today is Three Rivers legal services. It's got services in 17 counties, has offices in Jacksonville, Lake City, and Gainesville, and employs over 50 lawyers. I'm sorry, 24 lawyers, total staff of 50—one of his legacies that many people don't know about. But for Stephan Mickle, Three Rivers Legal Services would not exist today. There is more! There is much more I could tell you, but I see my time is up. So, let me close with this. We know the proverb, all of us, "behind every great man, there's a great woman." Evelyn, I see you there. Evelyn has been, and continues to be, that woman for Stephan, and she, in her own right is a great person, as many of you know. She has always been with him, behind him, next to him. And frankly, oftentimes leading him. So, my dear friends, Stephan and Evelyn please accept these comments with my respect, my admiration, and my love, to both of you. Thank you.

Judge Robert L. Hinkle, the Senior Judge of the United States District Court for the Northern District of Florida.

Judge Hinkle: Good afternoon, Dean, and other guests. Perhaps you'll forgive me if I start with a personal note to Stephan and Evelyn. It's good to connect, even over the computer screen, with COVID shutting down court events and travel. It's been too long. Mary Lou and I send our best. When I was asked to be involved in this program, I was very honored, and of course immediately said yes. I figured we have a good man, and a good family and a good school—bound to be a good event. It's always good to connect with the University of Florida. University communities are special. They always engender loyalty, but none more than the University of Florida. Gators are a proud lot. And if you're double Gator—well, that's really special. Judge Mickle has always been proud of this University, and the University has always been proud of him, and rightly so. We had a historian explain some of that, and that's proper that an explanation come from historian, because to most people in attendance, the idea of being the first African American in school is a matter of history. For most in attendance, by the time they entered school, there was already at least some integration, so stories about being the first were historical. But for Judge Mickle, and Larry, and me and a couple of others, we went through it. We started at segregated schools, and by the time we got out of school, there was at least some integration. The one thing I would say about that is I've come to understand that this was a lot harder than most of us realized at the time. Certainly, a lot harder than we whites realized at the time, but I think harder than most African Americans realized at the time. And much harder than people realize, now. It took a special kind of person. I doubt if Judge Mickle ever told very many people that, "Yeah, this is really hard," and anybody let on, because it does take that special kind of person and the kind of person that was able to do this probably didn't go around saying, "well, by the way, this is really hard." We all owe a debt of gratitude to those who did this, it needed to be done, it needed a special kind of person to do it. And I had a couple of quick notes about Judge Mickle. As a judge, he ran a good courtroom, just the right atmosphere, just the right decorum in the courtroom, always got very high marks for how he ran the court room. And then I tell you one story about us as his colleagues. We were at judges' meeting one time. As judges, we sometimes get together and talk about how we're doing our job, and you can share notes and so forth, and a new judge asked a question about sentencing. Judge Mickle didn't speak up a lot of meetings, but if he spoke, he had something to say. And he took that question they responded to it on the merits. But then he said, "And you're gonna to have to live with every one of those sentences." Sentencing is the hardest thing we do. And I think that statement captured his approach as a judge. He knew it was important and he communicated that very well. Criminal cases wind up with motions. Years later, the law changes. There's been a First Step Act, now we're dealing with a lot of Compassionate Release questions, and so I would sometimes, since Judge Mickle has been retired, get motions directed to cases that he handled the sentencing. And when I pick up one of his cases, I always know that the sentence that he imposed was no accident, that he took it seriously and that this was his considered judgment. That I think is a story about how he approached his career as a judge. So, Judge Mickle, I end by saying congratulations on today's event and portrait, even more on your outstanding career, and thank you for doing what you've done.

Midori Lowry, *Judge Mickle's former law clerk, is currently serving as an assistant Public Defender for the Eighth Judicial Circuit.*

Midori Lowry: So good afternoon, everybody. My name is Midori Lowry and I am a 1994 graduate of the University of Florida College of Law and I'm speaking here today because I had the immense honor and privilege to be Judge Mickle's law clerk for 16 years. If you want to know some things about Judge Mickle, some great things, I can tell you. And it's not just about his legal mind, his demeanor on the bench, or his commitment to his work, but also what he was like as a person, a very noble person. And what stood out very prominently is Judge Mickle has a great love for his family. He's been married for over 50 years to Mrs. Evelyn Mickle, who you've heard in her own right is great, the first Black graduate of the nursing school in 1967, at the height of the Civil Rights Movement. And Mrs. Mickle was the one who picked the artist, Carl Hess, to paint Judge Mickle's portrait, and you'll get a chance to see she has great taste, because that is a beautiful portrait. Judge Mickle has three children and a nephew who he raised, and Judge Mickle is a very devoted son to his mother and father who were also prominent members of the community. He lived in the same neighborhood with them, the same neighborhood that he grew up in an East Gainesville. One of the rules for our office for me and the other law clerks was to get Judge Mickle the message immediately whenever family members called. Judge Mickle was a very busy man, extremely diligent in his work, but his family took priority. And I can remember at times, his daughter Stephanie would call, or his son Pierre, or his other daughter, Amy, and Judge Mickle would answer the phone, and I could hear him say "Hi, Pumpkin," or "Hi, Amy" or "Hi, Pierre." The love in his voice was very genuine, very true, very caring and it was just wonderful to see that, and he brought that same spirit to his work. He cared very much about making the right decisions and getting through to people about really what matters most. And I'll let you know in Federal court, there's usually a gap about 60 days between taking a plea and the date of sentencing, and when taking a plea, it's customary to ask defendants basic questions about their family, like how many children do you have. Judge Mickle would sometimes make it a point to ask the defendant the names and ages of their children, sometimes even how to spell their names, and I hope you can imagine how sobering that was to stand before Judge Mickle who looks very imposing, and being reminded that children—your children—are important to him, and they should be important to you. Now Judge Mickle had very high standards. He ran a very tight schedule in court, and he expected everything to run smoothly, and it was amazing because he never yelled. He never banged this gavel. You could just tell what was expected. And when you look at the portrait, I think the artist captured the essence of that in the way Judge Mickle is holding that book in his portrait. We had a case once were a lawyer actually fainted in court, once pre-trial conference when Judge Mickle was discussing the schedule. He did recover and tried the case the following month, but you could tell when you're standing in front of Judge Mickle that there was no nonsense and there was a sense of his greatness there. Let me tell you something else. It's kind of fun working with Judge Mickle. Judge Mickle had an all-female staff, with the exception of one term law clerk, our beloved Ronald Layton. But other than Ron all the other law clerks and courtroom deputies, Cheyenne Starke and Carolyn Graham, were female. And we all got along. And that's what happens when people care about each other and about doing the right thing. And I credit that to the tone Judge Mickle set in the office, and also to Rebecca Butler who was Judge Mickle's judicial assistant in State court and throughout his tenure on federal court and almost throughout his entire career. There was a real family atmosphere in the chambers. Judge Mickle would invite us to his house for Christmas, or he would have us over he said to express his appreciation. I remember one year in particular, when his neighbor, Mrs. Morgan, came over and played the piano, and we all sang Christmas carols, and it was just wonderful. Judge Mickle always had an open-door policy in his office, literally, his door was always open. And we could go into his office and talk with him and ask him questions. Sometimes I'd walk by and I'd ask Judge Mickle what he was doing and he would say, "Dori, I'm contemplating the form of the good." The form of the good—that's from Plato. The form of the good is what allows us to see and understand justice, truth, equality, and beauty, and it is said to exist outside space and time, and is eternal, perfect, and changeless. And I took that as Judge Mickle telling me that he was praying, because he was very devout and he prayed a lot. One of the things that I learned from Judge Mickle is a Bible saying. It's "don't light a candle and put it under a bush." And it means that goodness that is done in this world should be acknowledged, celebrated, emulated, because no matter how hard things get, how dark things are, the light will always shine. So, I think it's very fitting that Judge Mickle's portrait is here at this law school, his alma mater, where people will see it, and I hope they're inspired by his life. Thank you.

Chief Judge Mark Walker *from the United States District Court for the Northern District of Florida.*

Chief Judge Mark Walker: Thank you, Dean. I'd like to correct the record from the get-go, based on the technical difficulties. I'd like to clarify, I did not get my undergraduate engineering degree from FSU, it was purely an accident that I wasn't able to unmute the microphone. As many of you know I succeeded Judge Mickle when he took senior status. That means I'm sort of like the quarterback who followed Tim Tebow at UF. It's a difficult thing to follow a legend. And I'm humbled every day, recognizing that I followed a legend like Judge Mickle. In 1956, about 10 years before Judge Mickle got his master's from UF, the United States Supreme Court wrote, "there can be no equal justice, where the kind of trial a man gets depends on the amount of money he has." For 50 years, first as a lawyer and then as the judge, Judge Mickle has done his very best to ensure equal justice under law and his efforts have benefited generations of Floridians. Proverbs teaches us that a good man leaves an inheritance to his children's children and there is no doubt Judge Mickle is a good man. His children and his grandchildren are blessed to have been raised by a man who instilled in them a passion for justice. Because of the example Judge Mickle set for them. They understand, as Justice Marshall once said, "where you see wrong or inequality or injustice, you must speak out." For those who clerked for Judge Mickle, appeared before him as lawyers, or served with him as judges, we are all beneficiaries of his wisdom and his great example. And it is only right and proper that we honor him today. But here's my hope, and I know we're here to talk about Judge Mickle, but in terms of his legacy, I hope that after today every law student that walks by Judge Mickle's portrait, pauses, and takes the time to reflect upon his life, and I hope after they do that, that they'll commit themselves to follow his example to do their very best to ensure equal justice under law. As lawyers and judges, we can never do more, and we should never strive to do less. Congratulations Judge Mickle, I can think of no judge more deserving of this honor and I'm grateful for the opportunity to speak this afternoon. All the best. Thank you.

Elizabeth Rowe, *the Irving Cypen Professor and a distinguished teaching scholar here at the Levin College of Law.*

Elizabeth Rowe: Thank you, Dean. In thinking about what I would say today, I realize that we have the span of several generations here to celebrate Judge Mickle, and that how each of us processes, the significance of this event will vary. We got here in 2020: a year that will definitely be in the history books for all kinds of reasons, and a year when most of our current law students are people who were born in the late [19]90s. Generation Z is already in law school. So, having that in mind, and thinking about what Martin Luther King said, that "we are not makers of history, but we are made by history," I'd like to frame this occasion with a little bit of history and also to consider how as individuals, especially since we're here to recognize and honor an incredible individual, each person shapes others both directly and indirectly. So, as you've heard, it was 1965 when Judge Mickle graduated from the University of Florida. This was the same year of the passage of the Voting Rights Act. In the same year in which Malcolm X was assassinated. A year later in 1966 he received his master's from UF. And then the following year, another great, his dear wife Evelyn Mickle, was also the first in graduating from the College of Nursing. But that year was also the year that Thurgood Marshall was appointed to the US Supreme Court. The following year, 1968, Martin Luther King was assassinated, and Senator Robert Kennedy was assassinated. Two years later, continued, and we mark the occasion of Judge Mickle graduating from the UF law school. That was the year 1970 when the Black Law Students Association was established and named after George Allen, the first Black person who graduated from the UF law school. It was also the year that the UF faculty became integrated and seven Black law professors were hired. In 1972, Judge Mickle started teaching as an adjunct professor at the law school. And this is a position that he held continuously, until very recently, when he retired. And all of this, a lifetime's worth, was all happening before I was even born. And if we fast forward to today, as just one example, and I'm sure there are so many others, I see how the circle of my life so many years later in my career has reflected Judge Mickle's. I too graduated with a bachelor's and a master's from UF in the early [19]90s and received the law degree. I've also had the privilege of being a member of this distinguished UF law faculty, including with five other Black tenured faculty colleagues, as we prepare hundreds of students each year to become lawyers. I met Judge Mickle when I was an undergrad at UF. I served as an intern in his chambers, and it was that experience and his guidance that convinced me to apply to law school. Over the years, he would continue to be an influential presence in the biggest moments of my life. I called him within minutes of receiving my acceptance from Harvard Law School. He officiated my wedding. He and Mrs. Mickle attended my law school graduation, and he was also one of the first people I called when I was considering leaving private practice to become a professor. As I have gotten older and evolved in my career, in my life, I have come to gain even greater appreciation for Judge Mickle. Even more than who he is as a person, what he symbolizes, and his many firsts, and the many doors he has opened has had lasting impact on each of us both directly and indirectly, and it continues to multiply. So many of us stand on Judge Mickle's shoulders. We can only aspire to have the strength of character and determination that he displayed all these years, as we encounter our own challenges in life. It's difficult to put into words, what it will feel like for so many of us who walk on this campus each day to see a portrait of a person who represents so many firsts, and who embodies for all of us, the ideals of excellence and integrity, grace and courage, compassion, and strength. This itself is yet another first, which I hope will continue to remind and inspire this great law school community to even greater heights. I thank Dean Rosenbury, our trustees, our faculty, Mike Farley, the Mickle family, and especially Judge Mickle, for yet another historic occasion.

April Ziegler Walker, 1997 *graduate of UF Law, who now practices with Upchurch Watson, White, and Max.*

April Ziegler Walker: Thank you, and good afternoon to everybody. First let me say that sitting through Midori's comments brought back a lot of memories, memories that I had already begun to think of as I began preparing for today. And I found myself a bit overcome with some emotions as I thought back that indeed chambers was very much like family. Judge Mickle indeed treated us like family. And I'm so appreciative of that, and I thank you Dori for those words. I thank you all for the opportunity to share in the celebration. I have to say, I think

I may have been somewhat of a wisecrack during my years. I clerked with Judge Mickle from 1998 into 2000 and I'm watching his screen. And I think my goal will be to garner what I think is a smile or laugh behind his mask. So, let me share what I prepared, which will hopefully keep me from shedding tears, in the next three minutes. I thought back that I had the distinct honor of being Judge Mickle's very first law clerk hired in [19]98, which was so exciting for me. I had started my private practice. I was in my first year of law school and when the door opened to interview with Judge Mickle and clerk for him, man, I raced through that door, because what law school student doesn't want to work for a federal judge. Frankly, the value of that clerkship would be lost on me until some years later. So, let me just say that because I was the first hire, I was also consequently the first to be pulled out of chambers. Judge Mickle put me out and gave my title to Dori, and all in good jest. It was great. I can think of one thing Judge Mickle used to say, and I think he may have had something on the wall. He used to say, "poor planning on the part of an attorney doesn't create an emergency on my part." Something to that effect. And I have to tell you, because I had already started practicing, I used to rush in. There were days that I would be reading through an emergency motion. And I'd be like, "Judge, we got to decide this. We got to get to this!" And Judge, being Judge, knew that just because an attorney says it's an emergency doesn't mean it's really an emergency. So, I did learn to govern myself by that as a lawyer. Years later, I'm glad I learned that lesson first as a clerk. But earnestly, I remember Judge Mickle as always being mild-mannered, steady, and deliberate. He always carried himself with dignity and self-respect, which we expect of a judge. But remarkably, I have to say in those two years I saw him treat everyone with respect and dignity. Everyone. During those years, we worked in Gainesville, but we were also responsible for the Panama City Docket. And so that's two courthouses of employees, security guards, staff, US Marshals, federal probation officers, waitresses, and lawyers, litigants—every single person Judge Mickle treated with dignity and respect. I never heard him say a harsh word. He was never arrogant, nor was he ever brusque or abrupt, and I have to say that is something else. He treated people well. I practice litigation for a lot of years I returned to the law firm I left, eventually to be a partner there and I love litigation. I decided, some years later to devote my legal work to conflict resolution and alternative dispute resolution, which I do now. And I must say, I think it's because I understand the impact we have when we treat each other well, and as lawyers, whether we're in court or not, how we are guardians and of this process, whether it's in court, whether it's in mediation, people look to us in ways that we don't realize as representatives of our profession, and I'm just so thankful that Judge Mickle had given me that early example of treating people well and conducting myself and ways of dignity and grace. So, Judge Mickle, I would say you are a trailblazer, but frankly, you've blazed many trails. You've impacted so many people, lawyers, and non-lawyers alike, in so many positive ways, and so I humbly say thank you for everything that you did for me, thank you for everything you've done for the profession, for your family and of course to Rebecca and Midori. God bless you all. Thank you Judge.

Nick Zissimopulos, *a 2002 graduate of UF Law, and now managing partner of Glassman and Zissimopulos here in Gainesville.*

Nick Zissimopulos: Thank you, Dean Rosenbury, Judge Mickle, and Mrs. Mickle, hello and thank you for this great honor to be able to say a few words today. I do need to correct the record. I was not a clerk. I think if anyone goes back and looks up my grade point average you would quickly see that I was probably not eligible for that. So, I don't want anyone to be confused with that, but for lawyers like me, we learned first about Judge Mickle from the stories, people like my trial practice instructor, Larry Turner. And from the stories what we learned was that Judge Mickle was a legend. And that's the way he was talked about whether it was his groundbreaking work as a student, or his brilliant legal career, or his work as a judge, at every different level in the state and them into the federal court. But when you get the chance to meet Judge Mickle, what we learned, and what I learned, is that in addition to those stories being completely 100% true—that he was a legend—I also learned that that he was a legend who was full of grace, and full of humanity, and full of kindness. That together is what made him such a special and unique man. I had opportunities to practice in front of judgmental as a criminal defense lawyer, and I can tell you that the words that April just spoke with the words that are on my paper here. The dignity that he showed folks. The lawyers in the room he would compliment and those compliments meant a lot at the end of the trial. The court staff, the US Marshals. And one of the things that I remember most having tried a handful of trials in front of Judge Mickle is that as you know in the courts when the judge would go in and out all the parties and all the lawyers and everyone would stand up as the judge came in and out, and we would stand up as the jury came in and out. And the judge would always remain seated, while the jury came in and out. But when the jury went back to deliberate, Judge Mickle would stand up and he would make a point of telling the jury that he was standing up for them as a sign of respect. I just remember that moment, and he would do that every trial, and it was something that stood out and it was an example of his humanity. After getting to know him as a lawyer practicing in front of Judge Mickle, I then had the opportunity to kind of get to know him as a teacher. And he has been an example to me of how to be a teacher in the law. He was instrumental in starting the trial advocacy program here at the University of Florida. It was wonderful because not only did it give him an opportunity to teach students, but it also gave lawyers in the community an opportunity to come in and be part of that. And every week three, or four, or five lawyers in the community would come and be guest judges. And I have fond memories of being a very young new fresh lawyer, coming into those meetings where we sit around with Judge Mickle and the other lawyers and his assistants, and we would talk about the class and what we were going to work on. And there were always refreshments. My memory is that there were carrots and cookies. I remember some carrots being leftover at the end. Always felt like it was a test, where you're going to take the good snack or not-so-good snack. I think all the cookies eaten but the carrots are sometimes left behind. But just that we in those meetings when we sat around and Judge Mickle would sit there, and he would ask us all, "How are you doing, how's the practice going, you know, how are your law partners?" He just he cared about us, and to have this legend show that sort of humanity was something. I have fond memories of watching him teach and watching him interact with students. And then when he retired, it was perhaps one of the greatest honors of my life, that I was able to continue on and help teach that class for some semesters what the class remained. And every single semester that I had an opportunity to teach the trial advocacy class, I made sure that I spoke his name because I wanted to make sure the students knew why that class existed and knew the legend that had created that class. And I think it is truly wonderful that there will now be this portrait so that his memory and his accomplishments will be known by the students that are there now and forever into the future. I thank you Judge Mickle for again, letting me be part of this, and I wish you all the best. Thank you all.

Anitra Raiford *is a 2012 graduate of UF Law who now practices with Shook, Hardy, and Bacon in Tampa.*

Anitra Raiford: Good afternoon, Gator family. It is a pleasure to be here today to honor one of my real-life heroes. Like most people with some success in their life, I could not be where I am without the help of others, many of whom are speaking on this call today. I stand on the shoulders of giants. But the biggest giant whose shoulders I stand on is without a doubt the Honorable Stephan P. Mickle. Since I am a graduate of the University of Florida and the University of Florida Levin College of Law, like Judge Mickle, I know that I owe my higher education to Judge Mickle's willingness to blaze a path for so many people, including myself. I was lucky that the gifted education from Judge Mickle did not end there. And this is because he hired me to serve as a judicial law clerk for him. I'm very grateful that he selected me as the last law clerk hire for the 2012 and 2013 term because my experience working for him changed my life for the better. Working in his chambers was like attending a masterclass each day. I find myself modeling my career after his. For example, I find myself always being mindful and my cases that my clients' money, liberty, and reputation is at stake, like Judge Mickle was always aware of in his cases when he presided over matters. Therefore, as an attorney, I always take my cases very seriously and I try my best to be a zealous advocate. I find myself serving the Bar Community in the UF Law community like Judge Mickle, who gave his time wisdom and resources to these communities, including by teaching classes at the law school like we just heard. I also find myself being able to remain steadfast toward my goals, even if I hit a little bump in the road. I say this because Judge Mickle taught me then that everything may not go my way in my career, but at the end of the day, things will work out if I have faith, work hard, and maintain my integrity. Today, if I face a hard time in my career, I remember this lesson. I remember what he overcame, and I know that because of Judge Mickle that I can overcome any hardship too. Judge Mickle, thank you for all that you have given to me, and congratulations on this honor.

Ebony Love *is a current UF Law student. Ebony serves as the President of the Florida Moot Court Team and as a Law School Ambassador. Ebony was previously president of the W. George Allen chapter of the Black Law Students Association here at UF Law, and she now serves as the Southern Regional Chair of the National Black Law Students Association. Please join me in welcoming Ebony.*

Ebony Love: Greetings, everyone. My name is Ebony Love and I've been asked to speak today about Judge Mickle's legacy and what it means to me as a current student who live in the trail that he is blazed. But before I do that I want to talk about when I first met the Mickle family. Because of the Mickle family, I am a double Gator. In 2016 I was proud to serve in the Black Student Union as the Secretary of the Black History Month committee. In 2016 I learned about the story of Evelyn Mickle. It was then that I learned that Evelyn Mickle was the first Black student to graduate from UF's nursing program. It was also then when I realized that Evelyn Mickle was never afforded her pinning ceremony when she was a student here at the University of Florida, simply because of the color of her skin. In 2016 we rectified that by giving her pinning ceremony and giving her flowers while she was still here, and today we rectify that as well, with this unveiling of the portrait that we'll see in a few minutes. Before I came to law school I worked at the National Center for Civil and Human Rights. The museum has a saying called "Live the Legacy." And the saying refers to Martin Luther King Jr. and the legacy that he left behind. When I think about Judge Mickle being a trailblazer, it's because he lives his legacy. Because of Judge Mickle's legacy at University of Florida being the one of the first Black students to graduate from the undergraduate program, and the first to graduate from the law school, I could become a double Gator, earning my history degree, and then also earning my law degree. His work in the Gainesville community is unparalleled because he is a charter member of the Atlanta chapter of Alpha Phi Alpha fraternity incorporated, which is the same fraternity that Martin Luther King Jr. belonged to. In my personal capacity, I've seen Judge Mickle at events, both on and off campus, always having a kind word and always willing to speak with anyone who has a question for him. One of my most profound memories of Judge Mickle is when he swore in former professor and now Judge Meshon Rawls. I looked around the packed courtroom, and I remember being overwhelmed with emotions because I could feel Judge Mickle passing the baton off to the next generation. Judge Mickle stood tall and regal in his robes, while Judge Rawls stood to his side in her salmon pink suit, which was a nod to her sorority. His voice came out soft but firm and the entire room held their breath as Judge Mickle administered the oath. Judge Mickle has taught us countless times how to leave and live your legacy. I could talk about his unwavering support to the W. George Allen chapter of the Black Law Students Association. But I don't have to because it's been permanently recorded by the Center of the Study of Race and Race Relations, and it also lives on in the memories that countless Black students from the University of Florida have had with Judge Mickle. I could talk about his dedication to the Gainesville community, but I don't have to because the proof is seen through the current Alpha Phi Alpha fraternity alumni chapter here in Gainesville. I could talk about his lasting impact as a trailblazer on students like myself, but the proof will come on when we live in his legacy and we make a lasting and positive impact on the legal field. We will be excellent attorneys, we will be brave advocates, and one day we will be judges. Before I close, I was inspired by some of the previous speakers who came before us.

Last year I did serve as a President of the W. George Allen chapter of the Black Law Students Association in its 50th year. During that year, we had a t-shirt, and I'm just going to read off what the t-shirt actually said, because I think that it is kind of sums up Judge Mickle's legacy. On the front of the shirt, there were sayings that were associated with alumni and professors who have impacted Black law students here at the University of Florida. The shirt reads: "breakthrough like Hawkins, trailblaze like Starke, empower like Land, innovate like Nunn, build like Cash-Jackson, educate like Jacobs, challenge like Holiday, advocate like Rawls, mentor like Williams-Harris, leave a legacy like Allen, and inspire like Mickle." Thank you Judge Mickle for inspiring the next generation of change-makers.

James Cunningham Jr., a 1978 graduate of UF Law and this year's Chair of the Law Center Association Board of Trustees.

James Cunningham Jr: Thank you, Dean Rosenbury. Let me begin by taking you to a time and a mentality. The likes of African Americans were one time told that everything we did we had to do it impeccably, because our responsibility was to uplift the race. That's a huge responsibility for anyone. But the fact that this responsibility was put on the shoulders of Judge Mickle and carried so well by his wife with him, as demonstrated by all the comments that have been made today, shows that there could not have been two better people to behave impeccably and to uplift the race. All of you assembled here now are here to say to Judge Mickle: "Well done." Take this bouquet of flowers. Enjoy them. We're here to say thank you, Judge Mickle. What you did mattered. It was important. And because of a time in which we live, we are missing the opportunity to be able to hug Judge Mickle. And, in every sense of the word, to be able to touch history. I grew up down in Ocala. And I referred earlier to uplifting the race. Judge Mickle and his wife were known to African Americans and Blacks in Ocala and held up as examples to little Black boys and Black girls there. The portrait that will be hung up today will continue holding him up as encouragement, as an example, to not just Black boys and Black girls but to everybody who comes through the University of Florida Levin

College of Law. When one of his earlier law clerks talked about how she stands on his shoulders, let's be clear about something. All of us stand on the shoulders of Stephan Mickle, because of the impeccable manner in which he has conducted himself. So, thank you very much, Dean. Thank you very much Judge Mickle and also to your family for all of the support they have given you. Dean Rosenbury, it is my honor to represent the 10 members of the 2021 Law Central Association Executive Committee and gifting to the College of Law his beautiful oil painting of our colleague, our friend, LLC, emeritus member Judge Stephan Mickle. Judge Mickle was indeed a trailblazer and a role model for all of us, and it is our hope that this portrait will be hung in the law college's most visible and prominent space. And, so, if you will do us the honor now Dean Rosenbury of unveiling the portrait of Judge Mickle. [Applause]

Stephanie Mickle, *daughter of Judge Mickle, is a 2004 UF Law School graduate.*

Stephanie Mickle: I think Joe Genco may have had something to say about technology not working for the younger folks. So, thank you for bearing with me. To Dean Rosenbury, Chairman Cunningham, and members of the Law Center Association Executive Committee, Scott Hawkins, Greg Weiss, Courtney Graham, Judge Barksdale, Rebecca Brock, Derek Bruce, Brian Bergun, Lee Gun, Joe Thakur, Carter Anderson, and Mike Farley, and all who played a part today. We want to express our deep gratitude to you for making this day possible. Thank you very much. Our Dad has asked me to tell you how proud he is to be a graduate of the University of Florida and the University of Florida Levin College of Law. He wants you to know that he met our Mom, his beautiful wife, Evelyn, of 52 years during his first year of law school, and they lived in Married Student Housing and Corey Village right down the hill from the school. He wants you to know how proud he is at this portrait is being gifted and dedicated and how proud he is of this portrait will hang here, at the University of Florida Levin College of Law in the Martin Levin Trial Advocacy Center, which focuses on the education and training of trial advocacy, moot court trial team, the development of courtroom effectiveness skills, which, as many of you know, he loved teaching. And he has asked me to tell you how proud he is that his oldest daughter is a graduate of the University of Florida Levin College of Law as well. To each of the persons who share reflections, Judge Larry Turner, Judge Hinkle, Judge Walker, Anitra, April, Dori, Elizabeth, Nick, and Ebony. Wow, it is such a joy to hear your memories and reflections as friends, classmates, law partners, colleagues on the bench, clerks, students, and mentees. Thank you. To President Fuchs, Provost Glover, members of the Board of Trustees, the University of Florida Association of Black Alumni, and the entire Gator Nation. Thank you. To our dear family and friends who have been there throughout the years of various stages of our Dad's career. Thank you. You've been in our Dad's corner and that means the world. To Carl Hess, the artist who painted this wonderful portrait, thank you so much for capturing our Dad's joy of teaching law and trial advocacy to hundreds of law students for 45 years since the inception of the CLEO program in 1971 at the University of Florida, in this beautiful rendering. And to each of you who are logged on from all across the country. Thank you for being here, virtually, to celebrate with us. We understand that there were more than 300 RSVPs here today. It is our delight to accept this portrait dedication, on behalf of Judge Mickle and the Mickle family. It has been interesting to reflect on the impact of our Dad's integration of the University of Florida in 1962 and his legal career during this most unusual year of 2020. What we are experiencing right now in our country is unprecedented. We are simultaneously in the middle of a global pandemic, a national election, a Supreme Court nomination, and confronting centuries of racial injustice and inequality. Change is happening now faster than ever before. Black Lives Matter protests are taking place across the globe and our country is redefining what equality looks like. The University of Florida has the opportunity to be on the right side of history. This moment in time will without a doubt impact many generations to come. This is just one reason that the law school's decision to dedicate this portrait of our Dad in the Martin Levin Trial Advocacy Center is even more meaningful. When people enter courthouses, classrooms, and law schools and see people who look like them, it shows them that the sky is the limit for what they can achieve in their careers. We have heard countless lawyers and litigants say that they knew if our if they had a case in front of our Dad, that he would treat the parties fairly without fail. They might not like the sentence or the verdict, but at least they had confidence that they would receive fair and impartial justice in his courtroom. And we are so pleased and delighted that our father's legacy through this portrait will continue to be a part of moving this University forward. The Mickle family intends to continue that legacy. It is our family's intention to endow a gift that would support the University of Florida's law school's recent scholarship for graduates of historically Black Colleges and Universities seeking to enter the legal profession, BALSA, and the University of Florida Center for the Study of Race and Race Relations. Thank you again, Dr. Rosenbury, the Law Center Executive Committee, and the Law School itself for this beautiful portrait.

Judge Stephan P. Mickle passed away on January 26, 2021 at his home in Gainesville. He was 76 years old.

Chapter 8 Study Questions

1. Briefly discuss in 250-500 words some of the major issues presented in this Chapter.
2. What are some of your reactions to the struggles that Judge Mickle went through from being the first African American undergraduate at UF to gaining national prominence as the first African American to be appointed as a Federal Judge in Northern Florida?
3. How would you characterize Judge Mickle and his wife, Evelyn Moore, as role models to all those who believe in Equal Justice for All?

References

Allen, W.G. (2010). *Where the Bus Stops*. Self-published autobiography.
An Oral History with Evelyn Moore Mickle [Interview]. (2020,
 January). *Samuel Proctor Oral History Program*.
Crabbe. (2008, April 4).
Dobson. (2019, November 8).

Federal Judicial Center. (n.d.). Retrieved October 15, 2020, from https://www.fjc.gov/

Samuel Proctor Oral History Program [Public Program]. (2009). *Florida Black History: Where We Stand in the Age of Barack Obama*. Retrieved from https://www.youtube.com/watch?v=mkeBwBeKY7A&t=2667s

Tinker. (2019, November 19).

Chapter 9: Summary and Conclusions by Jacob U'Mofe Gordon and Paul Ortiz

The 50th Anniversary commemoration of the African American Studies Program at the University of Florida was a momentous and cultural milestone in the history of our institution. The first part of the commemoration featured a day-long public program titled: "Looking Back and Moving Forward: African American Studies at the University of Florida Turns 50, The Ronald C. Foreman Symposium at the University of Florida." The following day, students, faculty, and members of the broader community gathered to honor the program's founders as well as to dedicate a historical marker in honor of the 50th Anniversary. These events brought an impressive number of African and African Studies stakeholders to the campus. They reflected on the past; celebrated the present, and articulated strategic plans for the future of African American Studies at the University of Florida. The interactions among the participants and observers in attendance at the two days of events on Thursday, February 20, and Friday, February 21, 2020, were collaborative, insightful, inspiring, and optimistic.

The events were also marked by academic panels and musical entertainments provided by *Pazeni Saudi*, the University of Florida African Choir, Ms. Lesa M. Phillips, University of Florida Guest Services Specialist, and Choral Music presented by the 1000 Voices of Florida, led by Ms. Joy Banks, President, and her daughter, Ms. Ra'Chelle Banks of Gainesville, Florida.

The historical marker was placed and unveiled at the heart of the campus, Turlington Plaza, outside the newly renovated home of the African American Studies Program. At the unveiling of the historical marker, the Dean of the College of Liberal Arts and Sciences, Dr. David E. Richardson, reaffirmed the commitment of the College to provide resources, including the hiring of four tenure-track faculty, for the advancement of the Program toward departmental status. He noted, "I urge all of you to support our shared aspirations for the future.

I will need you also contribute to the University's aspiration for African American Studies to become one of the very best departments in the country. I predict that the department will become nationally recognized for its already robust undergraduate programs, expansive scholarly excellence, and its people and their contributions to the world of knowledge and indeed a liberal education." The Dean's final remarks expressed great optimism when he added, "African American Studies will take its rightful place in the vision of the University and its students." Dr. W. Kent Fuchs, President of the University of Florida observed:

> The marker we are about to unveil...is more than simply metal and paint. It represents the willpower, vision, and commitment of the many women and men who built the African American Studies Program, and who continue to make it vital to UF. With today's unveiling, we celebrate the Program's founders for their commitment to equity and inclusion—in an era when it was not always welcomed. We celebrate the individuals who overcame many challenges to sustain and grow this Program over the past five decades. And we celebrate the academic leaders, faculty, staff, and students who are raising the visibility of the African American experience ... and indeed are making the African American experience more and more a part of the University of Florida experience. I am very pleased, today, that during Black History Month, we will officially, through our newest historical marker, recognize the African American Studies Program as one of the defining elements of the University of Florida ... and of being Florida Gators yesterday, today, and tomorrow.

The members of the Committee on the Historical Marker were introduced by Dr. James Essegbey, Interim Director of African American Studies Program at the University of Florida, who recognized Dr. Mary A. Watt, Associate Dean, College of Liberal Arts and Sciences; Mr. Joseph M. Kays, Director of Research Communication; Dr. Nina C. Stoyan-Rosenzweig, Assistant Vice President for Communications; Mrs. Florida A. Bridgewater-Alford, Associate Director of Learning,

Development & Integration; Dr. Carl Van Ness, Curator of Manuscripts & Archives Department, UF Library, Special & Area Studies Collections; and Dr. Sharon Wright Austin, former Director of the African American Studies Program.

In commemorating the 50th Anniversary, the Honorable Lauren Poe, Mayor of the City of Gainesville, declared February 21, 2020 as an African American Studies Day. The Mayor urged all citizens of the City of Gainesville to join in the celebration of this historic event. The Honorable Commissioner David Arreola of the 3rd District in the City of Gainesville read and presented the Proclamation.

City of Gainesville, Florida
Office of Mayor Lauren Poe

PROCLAMATION

WHEREAS, the African American Studies Program was established as an academic unit in the College of Liberal Arts & Sciences at the University of Florida in 1969; and

WHEREAS, the Black Student Union was central to the establishment of the African American Studies Program at the University of Florida; and

WHEREAS, the African American Studies Program was established in the best interest of the University of Florida, the City of Gainesville, and the State of Florida; and

WHEREAS, the African American Studies Program developed the Bachelor of Arts degree in African American Studies in 2013; and

WHEREAS, thousands of students successfully completed courses in African American Studies during the past 50 years at the University of Florida; and

WHEREAS, the African American Studies faculty and students have made significant contributions to knowledge and the advancement of African American Studies in the American Academy and the global community; and

WHEREAS, the African American Studies Program at the University of Florida celebrates its 50th Anniversary in 2019.

NOW, THEREFORE, I, Lauren Poe, by the authority vested in me as Mayor of the City of Gainesville, do hereby proclaim February 21, 2020 as

AFRICAN AMERICAN STUDIES DAY

in the City of Gainesville and invite all our citizens to join me in participating in all activities related to African American Studies Day.

IN WITNESS WHEREOF, I have hereunto set my hand and caused to be affixed the official seal of the City of Gainesville, Florida, this 21st day of February, A.D., 2020.

In addition to the aforementioned activities, the 50th Anniversary Committee recognized six pioneers and stakeholders in struggle for the development of African American Studies Program at the University of Florida. Students, past and present, prominent members of the Black Alumni Association and the Alachua Community Leaders were in attendance for the ceremony to recognize the Honorees: Dr. Ronald C. Foreman, the first Director of the African American Studies Program; Mrs. Lakay Banks, Dr. Roy I. Mitchell (UF's first Black Administrator), Dr. Harry B. Shaw, Judge Stephan P. Mickle, Judge Emerson R. Thompson (who helped establish AASP as an undergraduate), and Dr. David L. Horne. The celebration took place on Friday, February 21, 2020 in the Florida Auditorium at the University of Florida. The following are photos of some of the **Honorees** (Figures 9.1 and 9.2).

Figure 9.1: Mrs. LaKay Banks, a Gainesville resident, provided encouragement and support to several of the early African American students at UF, including George Allen, first African American graduate of the UF Law School. (AASP Booklet. 2019)

Figure 9.2: Dr. Harry B. Shaw, one of the first African American faculty members and former Associate Dean of CLAS. (AASP Booklet. 2019)

Moving Forward

This commemorative volume of the celebration of 50 years of African American Studies at the University of Florida has attempted to chronicle Black struggles for equal access to higher education and efforts to roll back systemic racism at an institution located in the former Confederate South. While we have shared many stories about the origins and growth of the African American Studies Program at UF, there are many more stories that need to be gathered, preserved, and promoted—and we hope that this volume will encourage students and scholars to continue to write senior theses, dissertations, and books on African American Studies.

The book has also been written in the spirit of optimism, with the belief that "there's a light at the end of the tunnel." It does not, however, provide answers to many of the questions frequently asked by students of African American Studies. These research questions include the following: Why did African American Studies Program fail to achieve a departmental status in 50 years? What factors were responsible for this failure? Was institutional racism a factor? Did the leadership of the Program fail to understand the significance of a departmental status in a major research university such as the University of Florida? Where did the fault lie? The Program leadership or the University leadership? Also, what role did national and international events play in the development of African American Studies at UF? These include the Third World Movement, the Anti-Apartheid Movement, the Vietnam War, and other crisis moments in world history.

Our optimism is greatly buttressed by the spirit and study habits of recent cohorts of African American Studies students at UF, including the graduating class of 2021. The newest generation of African American Studies students are carrying on the activist and intellectual traditions of their predecessors whose dogged pursuit of justice established the program in the first place. There are many examples to draw from. In the summer of 2020, scores of African American Studies majors participated in the city-wide petition campaign that resulted in the renaming of a local elementary school in honor of Carolyn Beatrice Parker, an African American female scientist who originally hailed from Gainesville. Prior to this change, the elementary school was named in honor of J.J. Finley, a Confederate general who fought to preserve the institution of slavery in the South during the Civil War. Additionally, two summers prior to the renaming, African American Studies students joined in an alliance with Hispanic and Latinx students to demand robust new buildings to house the Institute of Black Culture as well as the Institute for Hispanic-Latino Cultures (La Casita). This multiracial alliance was mobilized again in the wake of the police killing of George Floyd on May 25, 2020, in Minneapolis. African American students led a broad coalition of Latinx, Asian, Jewish, and other groups in a renewed Black Lives Matter democracy movement which rapidly became a global phenomenon for equal justice.

As we move forward and notwithstanding any potential obstacles, the prospects for an improved African American Studies academic enterprise at the University of Florida are more promising than ever. To begin with: a new Director, Dr. David A. Canton has been appointed, following a successful national search; the College has provided a budget for hiring four tenure-track faculty members, the new Director has been charged with the responsibility of working towards departmental status. In response to this charge, he has articulated his vision, not only for departmental status but to develop the M.A. and Ph.D. degree programs in African American Studies at the University of Florida. It is expected that in so doing the University of Florida will attain an equal footing with its peer institutions. As the famous American singer-songwriter Sam Cooke predicted in one of his seminal songs, "A Change is Gonna Come." The real change at the University of Florida has been a long time coming, but it is on its way!

Chapter 9 Study Questions

1. In light of this book how would you characterize the Black experience at the University of Florida and in the City of Gainesville, Florida? (250-500 words)

2. What do you find in common amount the Honorees at the 50th Anniversary of the African American Studies at the University of Florida? (250-500 words)
3. What is the significance of African American Studies Historical Marker on the campus of the University of Florida? (250-500 words)

Appendix: List of Publications by African American Studies Program Faculty at UF

Books and Book Chapters

Celeste, M. (2016). In a Room without Windows: Seeing Haiti beyond the Earthquake. In N.T. Clitandre, C. Michel, M. Racine-Toussaint, & F. Bellande-Robertson (Eds.). Remembrance: Loss, hope, recovery after the earthquake in Haiti = Re-mémoire: Chagrin, souvenir, espoir après le séisme en Haïti. UCSB Center for Black Studies Research.

Celeste, M. (2017). Race, Gender, and Citizenship in the African Diaspora: travelling Blackness. Routledge/Taylor & Francis Group.

Chafe, W. H., Gavins, R., & Korstad, R. R., **Ortiz, P.** (2014). Remembering Jim Crow: African Americans tell about life in the segregated South (Paperback edition.). The New Press, in association with Lyndhurst Books of the Center for Documentary Studies of Duke University.

Conwill, W.L. (2015). De-colonizing Multicultural Counseling and Psychology: Addressing Race Through Intersectionality. In R. D. Goodman & P. Gorski (Eds.). De-Colonizing "Multicultural" Counseling through social justice. Springer. https://doi.org/10.1007/978-1-4939-1283-4_9

Evans, S. Y. (2007). Black women in the ivory tower, 1850-1954: an intellectual history. University Press of Florida.

Evans, S. Y. (2009). African Americans and community engagement in higher education: community service, service-learning, and community-based research. SUNY Press.

Evans, S. Y., Domingue, A. D., & Mitchell, T. D. (2019). Black women and social justice education: legacies and lessons. State University of New York Press.

Foreman, R. (1984). First citizens and other Florida folks: essays on Florida folklife. Bureau of Florida Folklife Programs, Division of Archives, History, and Records Management.

Geggus, D. P. (2001). The impact of the Haitian Revolution in the Atlantic world. University of South Carolina.

Geggus, D. P. (2002). Haitian Revolutionary Studies. Indiana University Press.

Geggus, D. P. (2014). The Haitian Revolution: a documentary history. Hackett Publishing Company, Inc.

Graham, N. J. (2017). Begin with a Failed Body: Poems. Athens: University of Georgia Press.

Harrison, F. V. (1991). Decolonizing anthropology: moving further toward an anthropology for liberation. Association of Black Anthropologists.

Harrison, F. V. (2005). Resisting racism and xenophobia: global perspectives on race, gender, and human rights. AltaMira Press.

Harrison, I. E. & Harrison, F. V. (1999). African-American pioneers in anthropology. University of Illinois Press.

Hebblethwaite, B., & Bartley, J. (2012). Vodou songs in Haitian Creole and English = Chante Vodou and kreyòl ayisyen ak angle. Temple University Press.

Henson, B. (2019). Low Frequencies in the Diaspora: The Black Subaltern Intellectual and Hip-Hop Cultures in The Handbook of Diasporas, Media, and Culture. In K. Mitchell, R. Jones, & J.L. Fluri (Eds.). Handbook on critical geographies of migration. Edward Elgar Publishing Limited.

Hilliard-Nunn, P. (1998). Representing African American Women in Hollywood Movies: An African-Conscious Analysis. In J. Hamlet (Ed.). Afrocentric Visions: Studies in Culture and Communication. SAGE Publications, Inc.

Hilliard-Nunn, P. (2019). Black Female Agency in Haile Gerima's Bush Mama and Sankofa. In M. Reid (Ed.). African American cinema through Black lives consciousness. Wayne State University Press.

Johnson-Simon, D. (2004). Culture keepers-Florida: oral history of the African American museum experience. Printed by the author.

Kendi, I. X. (2012). The Black campus movement: Black students and the racial reconstitution of higher education, 1965-1972 (1st ed.). Palgrave Macmillan. https://doi.org/10.1057/9781137016508

Kendi, I. X. (2016). Stamped from the beginning: the definitive history of racist ideas in America. Nation Books.
Kendi, I. X. (2019). How to be an antiracist. One World.
King, D. W. (1998). Deep talk: reading African-American literary names. University Press of Virginia.
King, D. W. (2000). Body Politics and the Fictional Double. Indiana University Press.
King, D. W. (2008). African Americans and the culture of pain. University of Virginia Press.
Nixon, A. V. (2015). Resisting paradise: tourism, diaspora, and sexuality in Caribbean culture. University Press of Mississippi. https://doi.org/10.14325/mississippi/9781628462180.001.0001
Nunn, K. (1999). Rosewood. In R. L. Brooks (Ed.). When Sorry Isn't Enough: The Controversy Over Apologies and Reparations for Human Injustice. NYU Press.
Ortiz, P. (2005). Emancipation betrayed: the hidden history of Black organizing and white violence in Florida from Reconstruction to the bloody election of 1920. University of California Press.
Ortiz, P. (2018). An African American and Latinx History of the United States. Beacon Press.
Pearlman, L. (2019). Democracy's capital: Black political power in Washington, D.C., 1960s-1970s. The University of North Carolina Press.
Preston, A. N. (2019). A Seat at the Table. In S.Y. Evans, A.D. Domingue, & T.D. Mitchell (Eds.). Black women and social justice education: legacies and lessons. State University of New York Press.
Preston, A. N. (2015). Mary Mcleod Bethune in Florida: bringing social justice to the sunshine state. History Press.
Reid, M. (1997). PostNegritude visual and literary culture. State University of New York Press.
Reid, M. (2019). African American cinema through Black lives consciousness. Wayne State University Press.
Rosenberg, L. (2007). Nationalism and the formation of Caribbean literature (1st ed.). Palgrave Macmillan.
Russell-Brown, K. (2004). Underground codes: race, crime, and related fires. New York University Press.

Russell-Brown, K. (2009). The color of crime (2nd ed.). New York University Press.

Russell-Brown, K., & Davis, A. J. (2016). Criminal law. SAGE.

Saunders, T. (2016). Toward a Hemispheric Analysis of Black Lesbian Feminist Activism and Hip Hop Feminism: Artist Perspectives from Cuba and Brazil. In E.P. Johnson (Ed.). No tea, no shade: new writings in Black queer studies. Duke University Press.

Saunders, T. L. (2015). Cuban Underground Hip Hop: Black Thoughts, Black Revolution, Black Modernity (First edition.). University of Texas Press.

Schuller, M., Schuller, M., & **Thomas-Houston, M. M.** (2006). Homing devices: the poor as targets of public housing policy and practice. Lexington Books.

Scott, D. M. (1997). Contempt & pity: social policy and the image of the damaged Black psyche, 1880-1996. University of North Carolina Press. https://doi.org/10.5149/uncp/9780807846353

Sensbach, J. F. (1998). A separate Canaan: the making of an Afro-Moravian world in North Carolina, 1763-1840. Published for the Omohundro Institute of Early American History and Culture, Williamsburg, Virginia, by the University of North Carolina Press.

Sensbach, J. F. (2005). Rebecca's revival: creating Black Christianity in the Atlantic world. Cambridge, Mass.: Harvard University Press.

Shange, N. (2010). For colored girls who have considered suicide, when the rainbow is enuf: a choreopoem (1st Scribner trade pbk. ed.). Scribner.

Shaw, H. B. (1980). Gwendolyn Books. Boston: Twayne Publishers.

Shaw, H. B. (1986). "Perceptions of Men in the Early Works of Gwendolyn Brooks," in Black Poets Between Worlds: 1940-1980. Knoxville, TN: University Press of Tennessee.

Shaw, H. B. (1987). "Maud Martha: The War with Beauty," in A Life Distilled: Critical Essays on Gwendolyn Brooks. Champaign-Urbana, IL: The University of Illinois Press.

Shaw, H. B. (1990). Perspectives of Black Popular Culture. Bowling Green, Ohio: Bowling Green State University Popular Press.

Simmons, G.Z. (2006). African American Islam as an Expression of Converts' Religious Faith and Nationalist Dreams and Ambitions.

In K. van Kieuwkerk (Ed.). Women embracing Islam: gender and conversion in the West (1st ed.). University of Texas Press.

Simmons, G.Z. (2010). From Little Memphis Girl to Mississippi Amazon. In F.S. Holsaert (Ed.). Hands on the freedom plow: personal accounts by women in SNCC. University of Illinois Press.

Thomas-Houston, M. M. (2005). "Stony the road" to change: Black Mississippians and the culture of social relations. Cambridge University Press.

Villegas, M. R., Kandi, K. & Labrador, R. N. (2014). Empire of funk: hip hop and representation in Filipina/o America. Cognella Academic Publishing.

Wright Austin, S. D. (2006). The transformation of plantation politics: Black politics, concentrated poverty, and social capital in the Mississippi Delta. State University of New York Press.

Wright Austin, S. D. (2018). The Caribbeanization of Black Politics: race, group consciousness, and political participation in America. State University of New York Press.

Articles and Other Media

Acosta, M. M., Foster, M., & **Houchen, D. F.** (2018). "Why Seek the Living Among the Dead?" African American Pedagogical Excellence: Exemplar Practice for Teacher Education. Journal of Teacher Education, (4), 341. https://doi.org/10.1177%2F0022487118761881

Adejumo, V. E. & Arvelo, Callean. (n.d.). Impacts of Cultural Hegemony (Hegemonic Masculinity) On Black Queer Masculinity: Perspectives in Resistance and Social Justice. Submitted to Journal of Black Studies.

Adejumo, V. E. (n.d.). Defense of Dreams or Continued Nightmares? In Black Power in Florida. Eds. Guzman, W. and Densu, K. Submitted to University of Florida Press.

Alteri, S., Birch, S., & Huet, H. (2018). Racism, Representation, and Resistance in Children's Literature, 1800-2015 (Exhibition). George A. Smathers Libraries. http://exhibits.uflib.ufl.edu/RacismRepresentation/

Banton, N. E. (2009). Nipple Matters: A Black Feminist Analysis of the

Politics of Infant Feeding among African American Mothers (Doctoral Dissertation). Georgia State University.

Bateman, L. B., **O'Neal, L. J.**, Smith, T., Li, Y., Wynn, T. A., Dai, C., & Fouad, M. N. (2017). Policy, System and Environmental Correlates of Fruit and Vegetable Consumption in a Low-Income African American Population in the Southeast. Ethnicity and Disease, 27, 355-362. https://doi.org/10.18865/ed.27.S1.355

Birch, S., Kester, B., & Reboussin, D. (2019). Teaching African and African American Experiences: A teacher resource guide (Online Resource). http://guides.uflib.ufl.edu/afam_k-12

Busey, C. (2017). Más que Esclavos: A BlackCrit examination of the treatment of Afro-Latins in U.S. high school world history textbooks. Journal of Latinos and Education.

Catey, A. S. (2011). The constitution of subjects in the long revolution: race, the police power, and the everyday shaping of the ensemble state (Doctoral Dissertation). University of Florida.

Celeste, M. (2018). "What Now? The Wailing Black Woman, Grief, and Difference," Black Camera: An International Film Journal, (9)2, 110-131. https://doi.org/10.2979/blackcamera.9.2.08

Celeste, M., Vargas-Betancourt, M., Vargas, N., Hernandez, J. Addie, Y. Mosley, D. Hebblethwaite, B., Ortiz., Saunders, T., Henson, B. (2018). Intersections on Global Blackness and Latinx Identity. Intersections: Research into Teaching Grant. Funded by the Andrew W. Mellon Foundation, through the UF Center for Humanities & the Public Sphere. Award amount: $30,000.

Conwill, W. L. (2010). Domestic violence among the Black poor: Intersectionality and social justice. International Journal for the Advancement of Counselling, 32(1), 31-45. https://doi.org/10.1007/s10447-009-9087-z

Crump, B. L. and **Hunter, I. L.** (n.d.) A Critical Analysis of the Trayvon Martin Case and the Stand Your Ground Laws. National Bar Association, Trial Lawyers Section.

Davidson, J. M. (2012). Encountering the Ex-Slave Reparations Movement from the Grave: The National Industrial Council and National Liberty Party, 1901-1907. Journal of African American History, 97(1-2), 13-38. https://doi.org/10.5323/

jafriamerhist.97.1-2.0013

Davidson, J. M. (2014). Deconstructing the Myth of the "Hand Charm": Mundane Clothing Fasteners and Their Curious Transformations into Supernatural Objects. Historical Archaeology, 48(4), 18-60. https://doi.org/10.1007/BF03376927

Davidson, J. M. (2015). "A Cluster of Sacred Symbols": Interpreting an Act of Animal Sacrifice at Kingsley Plantation, Fort George Island, Florida (1814–39). International Journal of Historical Archaeology, 19(1), 76. https://doi.org/10.1007/s10761-014-0282-1

Felima, C. A. (2009). Haiti's Disproportionate Casualties after Environmental Disasters: Analyzing Human Vulnerabilities and the Impacts of Natural Hazards. Journal of Haitian Studies, 15(1/2), 6-28.

Felima, C. A. (2017). Disaster Narratives of Flood Experiences in Cap-Haitien, Haiti: An Anthropological Study (Doctoral Dissertation). University of Florida.

Harn Museum of Art. (2018). History, Labor, Life: The Prints of Jacob Lawrence (Exhibition). Curated by Storm Jansevan Rensburg, SCAD Museum of Art, with support from the Jacob and Gwendolyn Lawrence Foundation. Curated by **Carol McCusker**.

Harn Museum of Art. (2018). I, Too, Am America: Civil Rights Photographs by Steve Schapiro (Exhibition).

Harn Museum of Art. (2018). Resilient Visions: Haitian Art (Exhibition)

Hart, E. E. (2018). Black Radicalism Reconceptualized: Struggle and Resistance in the Ohio Valley. Ohio Valley History, 18, 92-96.

Henson, B. (2019). Black invisibility: reframing diasporic visual cultures and racial codes in Bahia. African and Black Diaspora: An International Journal.

Henson, B. (2019). "Look! A Black Ethnographer!": Fanon, Performance, and Critical Ethnography. Cultural Studies ↔ Critical Methodologies.

Herman, H.S. (1994). A Tribute to an Invincible Civil Rights Pioneer. Crisis, 101(6), 22-24.

Hilliard-Nunn, P. (2008). In the Shadow of Plantations (Film). Produced by the Alachua County Communications Office. https://www.youtube.com/watch?v=AMjWEjQy7yI

Houchen, D. F., Smith, M. (2019). Beauty, joy, and wellbeing: Rethinking Black southern women's agricultural labor. Activist History Review.

Houchen, D. F., Walker, D., **Turoctte, F.**, & **Birch, S.** (2018). Black Educators: Florida's Secret Social Justice Advocates, 1920-1960 (Exhibition). George A. Smathers Libraries. http://exhibits.uflib.ufl.edu/FloridaBlackEducators/

Houchen, D. F. (n.d.). An "Organized body of intelligent agents," Black teacher activism during de jure segregation: A historical case study of the Florida State Teachers Association. (In Press) Journal Negro Education.

Liversidge, J. & **Turcotte, F.** (2019). Bo Diddley: An American Original (Exhibition). George A. Smathers Libraries.

Moore Taylor, C. (2010). Free in Thought, Fettered in Action: Enslaved Adolescent Females in the Slave South (Doctoral Dissertation). University of Florida.

Nunn, K. (1993). Rights Held Hostage: Race, Ideology, and the Peremptory Challenge. Harvard Civil Rights Civil Liberties Law Review, 64(63). Reprinted in Reader on Race, Civil Rights, and American Law (Davis, Johnson, & Martinez, eds., 2001).

Nunn, K. (1997). Law as a Eurocentric Enterprise. Law and Inequality, 15(323). Reprinted in Critical Race Theory: The Cutting Edge (Delgado & Stefancic, eds., 2d ed. 2000).

Pearlman, L. (2014). More Than a March: The Poor People's Campaign in the District of Columbia. Washington History, 26(2), 24-41.

Pimentel, C. N., & **Busey, C.** (2018). Hollywood Films as Social Studies Curriculum: Advancing a Critical Media Literacy Approach to Analyzing Black Male Representation. Critical Education, 9(4), 1-17.

Preston, A. (2014). Mary McLeod Bethune Trail (Online Resource). In partnership with the Mary McLeod Council House & Lucy Craft Laney Black History Museum. http://www.nps.gov/mamc/historyculture/upload/Bethune-Trail.pdf

Saunders, T. (2016). Towards a Transnational Hip Hop Feminist Liberatory Praxis: A View from the Americas. Social Identities: Journal for the Study of Race, Nation and Culture, 22(2), 178-194.

https://doi.org/10.1080/13504630.2015.1125592

Saunders, T. (2019). Afro-Feminismos en Cuba: Perspectivas de la Habana (Film). https://www.facebook.com/watch/?v=357818304849911

Schorb, J., Birch, S., Pearlman, L., Vrana, H., Russell-Brown, K., & Dale, E. (2018). Intersections on Mass Incarceration. Intersections: Research into Teaching Grant. Funded by the Andrew W. Mellon Foundation, through the UF Center for Humanities & the Public Sphere. Award amount: $30,000.

Simmons, G. Z. (2002). Racism Today in Higher Education. University of Florida Journal of Law & Public Policy, 1, 29-44

Stevenson, R. (2018). Jumping Overboard: Examining Suicide, Resistance, and West African Cosmologies During the Middle Passage (Doctoral Dissertation). Michigan State University.

Steverson, D. (2015). Zora Neale Hurston's Racial Politics in Jonah's Gourd Vine. Explicator (73)3, 226-228. https://doi.org/10.1080/00144940.2015.1065223

Steverson, D. (2017). Madness, Melancholia, and Suicide in Sue Monk Kidd's The Secret Life of Bees. South Carolina Review, (50)1, 108-123.

Steverson, D. (2020). "Don't nobody wanna be locked up": The Black Disabled Veteran in Toni Morrison's Sula and August Wilson's Fences. College Language Association Journal (forthcoming).

Vargas, N. (2018). Ideological Whitening: Does Skin Color Shape Colorblind Ideology Adherence for Latina/os? Ethnic and Racial Studies, 41(14), 2407-2425.

Vargas, N. & Stainback, K. (2016). Documenting Contested Racial Identities among Self-Identified Latina/os, Asians, Blacks, and Whites. American Behavioral Scientist, 60(4), 442-464. https://doi.org/10.1177/0002764215613396

Villegas, M. (2017). Nation in the Universe: The Cosmic Vision of Afro-Filipino Futurism. Amerasia Journal 43(2), 2-24. https://doi.org/10.17953/aj.43.2.25-46

Weech-Maldonado R., Hall A., Bryant T., **Jenkins K. A.**, Elliott M. N. (2012). The relationship between perceived discrimination and patient experiences with health care. Medical Care. 50(9 Suppl 2), 62-8. https://doi.org/10.1097/MLR.0b013e31825fb235

www.ingramcontent.com/pod-product-compliance
Lightning Source LLC
Chambersburg PA
CBHW041641300725
30361CB00007B/81